# THE COMPLETE TRAIL HORSE

# Also by Dan Aadland

*Treading Lightly with Pack Animals:*
*A Guide to Low-Impact Travel in the Backcountry*

*Horseback Adventures*

*Women and Warriors of the Plains:*
*The Pioneer Photography of Julia E. Tuell*

*Sketches from the Ranch: A Montana Memoir*

# THE COMPLETE TRAIL HORSE

*Selecting, Training, and Enjoying Your Horse
in the Backcountry*

DAN AADLAND

**The Lyons Press**
Guilford, Connecticut
An imprint of The Globe Pequot Press

The Lyons Press is an imprint of The Globe Pequot Press.

10 9 8 7 6 5 4 3 2 1

Printed in the United States of America

ISBN 1-59228-251-2

Library of Congress Cataloging-in-Publication data is available on file.

To Mona, Rockytop, Marauder, Mary, Angel, Ace, Red,
Penny, Big Red, Misty, Sugar, Major, Rodeo, Monty,
Little Mack, Redstar, Doll, Pride, and Skywalker:
partners, all, on the trail.

# CONTENTS

**Part I —** **Selecting the Trail Horse** 3
    1. Champions in Another World 5
    2. Just the Right Horse 11
    3. Horse Breeds for the Trail 41
    4. The Gaited Breeds 53

**Part II —** **A Horsemanship Primer**
    **—A Survival Review** 71
    5. Reviewing the Basics 73

**Part III —** **Training for the Trail—**
    **An Overview** 91
    6. Approaching the Task 93
    7. Starting a Young Horse Under Saddle 111
    8. The Neck Rein 129
    9. Training on the Trail 137
    10. Advanced Trail Training 169

**Part IV —** **Hitting the Trail: Ethics,**
    **Equipment, and Techniques** 179
    11. A Room in Our House 181
    12. Equipment for the Trail 187
    13. Techniques for the Trail 217
    14. Competition on the Trail 225

Part V — Packing In                          231
    15. The Ultralight Approach              233
    16. A Packing Primer                     247
    17. On the Trail with Pack Animals       259

Part VI — A Wilderness Camp                  265
    18. Filling the Niche                    267

Epilogue                                     279

Appendix: A Suggested Gear List
            for Pack Trips                   281

Bibliography                                 285

About the Author                            287

Index                                        289

# Acknowledgments

I must thank more teachers than I can ever name for whatever knowledge of horses that has found its way onto these pages. There were the ranchers of my boyhood, horsemen on whose words I hung, men and women who *used* their horses, who relied on them daily, whose bonds with them were strong. Elmer, my late father-in-law, the gentle cowboy trainer, was prominent among these. Helpful nationally known figures—both personally accessible, and tolerant of my occasional challenges—were trainer/clinician David Lichman and Dr. Deb Bennett, whose writings and correspondence, particularly regarding conformation, have been invaluable.

Closer to the ranch, I appreciate the support of the men and women of Beartooth Back Country Horsemen, and of our arena staff; the excellent trainer Travis Young, whose eclectic approach has much to do with his success; and helper-at-large Whitney DeVilbiss. Most of all, for this book and for all my efforts on the printed page, I thank Emily, my number one editor—my partner on all the trails through life.

**A Note on the Text:** Hampered by "his/her" and "he/she," and eschewing the current use of "their" and "they" as singular, I have used primarily the singular male in reference to horses, my advocacy of mares notwithstanding. I've also followed the example of the women so vital in the formation of Back Country Horsemen of America in assigning the term "horseman" to all humans who have mastered the art.

# THE COMPLETE TRAIL HORSE

# PART I

## SELECTING THE
## TRAIL HORSE

# 1

## Champions in Another World

*And God took a handful of southerly wind,*
*blew his breath over it and created the horse.*
—Bedouin legend*

Although many years have passed, and many trails since then have
melted together in my memory, I can still feel the sharp wind that
greeted us when we crested that ridge. At 9,600 feet of elevation even
a July breeze has bite. I was walking, not riding, leading Major, Sugar
walking behind him, his lead rope slipknotted to the horn of Major's
saddle. All three of us were winded from a very steep climb in air stingy
of oxygen, a climb made necessary by the most embarrassing of reasons:
I had lost the trail. On a mountainside of spruce and pine and pretty
clearings, a wilderness mountainside that was once an avenue to a gold
mine, an old, grown-over bulldozer road acted as trail part of the way
up. But it forked once, then again, and was made even more puzzling by
several horse and game trails, none used by human travelers this year,
veering from it here and there. Then it all petered out.

Several times I had stopped and pulled out the map and compass.
Yes, I was just where I was supposed to be. Sighting south down the
Slough Creek valley and into Yellowstone Park, then comparing angles

---

*For this and several of the epigraphs used I am indebted to Steven D. Price's *The Quotable Horse Lover*
(New York: The Lyons Press, 1999).

to several prominent peaks, proved that. But where was the trail? We were above the timberline in terrain relatively open. There was only one way to settle this, and that was to go straight up the mountain to the top of the ridge. If all were well, according to the contours on the map I would be able to peer over and see far below me a little gem named Horseshoe Lake.

It was soon too steep to ride. The two young horses never questioned, never complained, scrambling with me on turf turned now to alpine tundra, spongy green footing sprinkled with slick rocks and truck-sized granite boulders. On the knife ridge, in a place between boulders just large enough to squeeze the three of us, balanced between a steep slope behind us and a sheer cliff in front of us, I leaned into the wind and saw the lake far below. Yes, we were precisely where we were supposed to be. Not that our problems were solved. We needed to descend the slope, angling this time north around the mountain. Eventually we were sure to strike the trail.

It did, indeed, work that way. But in this year of late snows, no one had used the trail so far this summer. (During the drive to the trailhead in Yellowstone Park, we had waited for a snowplow on top of Beartooth Pass, this in mid-July.) The trail angled along the steep mountainside and disappeared into a bank of snow that rendered it invisible for several hundred yards. I could see the trail emerge from the snowbank on the far side, wondered just what would be involved in getting there, and worried about two possible scenarios. Was the snow so deep the horses would flounder in it, helpless? (The bank appeared to be at least several feet deep.) Or, worse, would this old, compacted mountain snow be icy and slippery? The idea of the three of us losing footing and going into an uncontrolled slide down the mountain was too terrible to contemplate.

Luckily, neither nightmare proved true. I pressed Major gently into the bank. His hooves sank 6 inches into the compacted snow and no farther, just right, deep enough to give him footing but not deep enough for tough going. We eased across the snowfield, down the steep trail (now turned again into a deserted dozer road), and farther down to the blue-green alpine lake. In a grove of stunted, alpine fir, all three of us a bit shaken, we paused briefly. I ate a sandwich. Major and Sugar cropped a little of the sparse grass.

And up there by that lake, accompanied by two young horses on whom my life absolutely depended, the recent words of a friend from farther east, from the world of gaited show horses, came back to me. He was discussing a mare he had for sale. "She won't make it in the show ring," he said, "but she'd make someone a dandy trail horse." In other words, the mare in question could not hit just the right "lick" to impress a judge and win a ribbon, but she was perfectly capable of the things Major and Sugar had just been through. How preposterous! Without knowing it, my friend was insulting a world of which he knew nothing, a world intensely demanding, a world with no room for rejects or second best.

Never mind my friend's particular perspective in the world of Tennessee Walking Horses. I've heard the same line from all sorts of equestrian specialists. "He won't make a roping horse, but . . . " "She's not dressage caliber, but . . . " "He's not quick enough to make a reining horse, but . . . " "She's not tall enough for jumping, but . . . " And each time after the "but," the same piece of misinformation, that the horse will surely make a fine one for the trail.

I've become quite aggressive in my answers to this line. "What makes you think your reject from reining (or dressage or show or jumping) can live up to my requirements for a trail horse? For that matter, what makes you think that champions in your event could live up to my requirements for a trail horse?" On this solo jaunt of several days on the trail, Major, carrying a heavy man, and Sugar, carrying a pack, had: ascended from 5,500 feet elevation to 9,600, then gone back down, back up, and back down again; progressed through a string of loose, free-running horses and mules without panic; met both moose and elk on the trail with some fear, yes, but without losing composure; crossed countless streams of various sizes; crossed many bridges; been ridden and led off-trail; progressed with surefooted security on trail so rocky it had been blasted out of the mountainside with dynamite; negotiated deadfall in the forest off-trail and on parts of the trail not cleared; and, grazed hobbled and stood quietly tied to a highline.

There is much more. Sugar, as packhorse, accepted the bumps and bangs of pack boxes hitting trees when he veered too close, tolerated the breeching under his tail, led with loose lead rope behind Major.

And Major, carrying me, accepted ponying another horse without worry about the lead rope occasionally creeping up under *his* tail, giving Sugar a little pull when necessary to remind him to stay close. Three days of rocky trails created no soreness of foot, no physical maladies beyond becoming tired.

The complete trail horse is the ultimate equine generalist. He is, in every respect, what mankind from ancient times until today has sought as the "saddle horse," horseback transportation that is tough, enduring, and comfortable. In this sense, many arena champions are not saddle horses. They have too often been bred and trained to excel at one specialized activity, and they may not possess the range of physical and mental attributes needed to cope with the challenges Major and Sugar met on this particular trip.

It's certainly true that many trail riders don't habitually tackle this level of challenge and perhaps will never tackle it. Trail riding, in one form or another, is America's fastest growing equine activity. The term is a loose one, encompassing brief rides on groomed trails through urban parks, as well as massive, organized affairs headquartering in giant

*The wide-open country of the West is challenging for trail horses.*

recreational vehicle parks with miles of trails radiating out from the central location, the rides involving hundreds of equestrians. Out west the term "trail riding" falls somewhat short of accuracy, because in open country, riding is often off-trail through a variety of terrain. Such vast, open stretches of the American West create problems of another sort for horses. Given their favorite sort of country—the great open, with visibility for many miles in every direction—horses have strong, primitive instincts to take off and run with a herd.

Riders involved in less challenging types of trail riding have every right to ask if the complete trail horse, as we'll come to know it in this book, is really necessary. A solo trip through wilderness from Yellowstone Park through the rugged Beartooth/Absaroka Wilderness Area is hardly in the cards for many, after all. "Can't any horse capable of walking quietly up the trail, following the tail of the horse in front of it, suffice for much of the trail riding I'm likely to do?" one might ask.

Yes, it can. But if you sail, and your horizons are normally limited to the cove or the bay, isn't it nice to have a boat seaworthy enough to handle the sudden squall? If the speed limit on the highway is 65 miles per hour, are you content with a car that will go no faster? Probably such a car would be limited in other ways as well, in acceleration when passing, for instance. Simply because your back is strong, should you be satisfied with a horse that trots so roughly it jars your spine at every step? Simply because you do not anticipate anything spooky, emergencies of any sort, surprises of any kind, is it safe to ride a horse that cannot handle them if they arise? Is the horse that you could not ride safely back to the trailhead, alone, to get help for an injured companion a good choice for trail riding?

Few of us would enter into dressage or jumping or cutting without insisting on a horse that had a chance to be competitive. If our pleasure is centered on quality time in the saddle, the scent of pine in the breeze, the anticipation of the scene around the next bend, perhaps we should seek just the right horse for the task. We should not fall into the trap described by an outfitter friend who has witnessed hundreds of riders taking to the trail in the Bob Marshall Wilderness in Montana. "They show up at the trailhead with a $30,000 pickup, a $25,000 trailer, a $2,500 saddle, and a horse they bought through the sale ring for $500. Then they wonder why they aren't having any fun."

Not that it's mostly a matter of cost, because some of the best trail horses have inexpensive origins. My friend was describing the same misplaced priorities we've discussed, the same attitude that *any* horse will do for the trail. Well, it won't.

In that wilderness negotiated by Major and Sugar and me, in the late afternoon of this long summer day, on top of the second mountain pass where the little-used trail was marked only by rock cairns, we stopped to rest and look to the east. Across a big valley, perhaps 5 miles away through air crystal clear at this elevation, was a massive solitary mountain peak, a rock fortress that rose from the ground around it like the turret on a giant's castle. At its base, surrounding the peak, was the velvet of dense pine. The late sun was beginning to subtly change the color of the entire scene, edging it toward yellow. I wondered just how many humans had seen this, had seen it the way I was seeing it now. And I reached down and patted Major and reached out and gave Sugar a knuckle rub on his sweaty forehead.

For this, for getting me to this spot at this time to see this beautiful sight, these two horses would not get a trophy or ribbon. But by every possible measure, they were champions.

# 2

## Just the Right Horse

*I wish your horses swift and sure of foot.*
—Shakespeare, *Macbeth*

The complete trail horse is a synthesis of breeding, training, and conditioning, an ideal for which to strive. But no one owning a horse sound and safe enough to walk down a groomed trail should forgo trail riding, and we want to make that clear from the start. Many of us at one time or another, if asked what is the best horse for a given activity, have answered, "Well, the horse I happen to have." That's perfectly fine. No horseman with an inclination to hit the trail should refrain completely because his or her horse falls short in some of the areas we'll describe; that is, within the limits of safety.

But those of us for whom horses are an essential part of the good life will likely own many. For the most part, we outlive them, and many of us are like collectors of classic cars. Owning just one is unthinkable. Furthermore, complete trail horses are both born and made. The horse you already own can probably be improved for the trail, made safer, looser in the walk, more accustomed to spooks on the trail. While many horses may never become one of our trail champions, few horses are completely unsuitable for trail.

But there *are* unsuitable horses, and we might just as well deal with these from the beginning. Some of the following disqualifiers are correctable; some are not. Some are also subjective, but they spring from a lifetime of horsemanship in the backcountry, of learning as much as I can from both old-timers whose lives and work depended on partnership with horses, as well as from modern teachers.

## The "Hyper" Horse

When we say "hyper" we do not mean "spirited." Many of us (I am one of them) love spirited horses, horses with big motors and no quit. Unfortunately, many competitive activities lend themselves to focused, go-for-broke athletes. The racehorse, the Saddlebred show horse, the barrel horse, may profit from huge stores of pent-up adrenalin which, when released, help them win. If bred specifically for that event, the nervousness may be genetic, may be impossible to soothe. If it is the result of training, rehabilitation for the trail may be possible.

Horses we classify as hyper cannot stand still, work themselves into a sweat doing nothing, may run away if given the slightest opportunity, and probably spook more easily than those with relaxed dispositions. Riding them is like flying a jet plane: there is very little margin for error. Imagine trying to help an injured companion with such a horse, leading a packhorse with one, surviving a terrible lightning storm while mounted on one. A laid-back attitude is not necessarily a trail requirement (some of my best ones have not matched this description), but we do want a horse that won't dance us off the side of a ledge trail.

## The Antisocial Horse

Yes, they exist, horses that are habitually nasty to others, that kick, bite, and always seem spoiling for a fight. Since for many trail riding is a very social activity, the horse that is dangerous to others creates an obvious problem that may, or may not, be correctable by training.

## Horses That Can't (or Won't) Walk

Very few competitive arena events require a good, bold, rapid walk, so an unfortunate byproduct of arena competition has been de-emphasis of this gait. After years of breeding with this lack of emphasis, the horse world is choked with horses that walk slower than humans and must break into a rough trot in order to progress faster. But the walk is our very most important trail gait. Usually, three feet are on the ground at any one time during the walk, so it is surefooted. All feet hit the ground at different times, so the walk is normally smooth for the rider. If a horse must trot in order to maintain the speed of a good, brisk human walk—say around four miles per hour—it is not my idea of a trail horse.

Maybe this judgment is a bit harsh, and I'll admit it is subjective. If you like going extremely slowly on the trail, enjoying a leisurely pace, the slow-walking horse may be just fine for you. If posting to the trot suits you, or if you're a lucky individual who owns a horse that trots relatively smoothly, proceeding down the trail in this gait may be just fine. But there are a couple of caveats. The trot is not a surefooted gait for a rough trail, because it is a two-beat suspension gait. In other words, the left front and right rear feet hit the ground simultaneously. Then there is a moment of suspension (no feet on the ground) followed by impact of the right front and left rear. Defensive football players are taught to take quick, short, choppy steps, their coaches exhorting them to avoid leaving their feet, because turning or adjusting is impossible during suspension. The trot is similarly limiting on extremely rough trails.

Horses with poor walks can often be improved by simply emphasizing the gait, working with the horse to stretch out and relax, urging for more speed but not allowing it to cross that threshold into the trot. But only so much can be done for certain horses, those whose genes have been selected for everything else, the walk left very much behind. In my experience, you will find many poor walkers among heavily muscled, short-legged, wide-chested horses, those bred for quick-twitch muscles in this era when horse trailers are available for transportation to the arena. Quick acceleration and ability to turn on a dime are their forte, not covering long distances smoothly.

## Stallions

Here I can be accused of hypocrisy, because my young stallion Pride is a cross between a Mercedes-Benz and a Hummer on the trail, and I ride him to the mountains whenever I can. Surefooted and smooth-gaited, Pride's fluid muscles under my body feel like a massage, while the lodgepole pines on the side of the trail whip by like the slats in a picket fence. But there are some limitations. Pride would be barred from most organized trail rides because most prohibit stallions. I think the prohibition is wise.

A stallion is a stallion is a stallion. The person who forgets that is doomed to an eventual (and possibly painful) reminder. Never mind all the stallion owners who claim their animals are "just like geldings." Given the right (or, rather, wrong) scenario, the stallion will again become a stallion. Yes, like Pride, many stallions have been trained to act like gentlemen under saddle even when a mare in heat passes by. But how about that lunch stop, when your horses are tied waiting, and that same mare, poorly tied by its owner, breaks free and goes visiting? How about the gelding that is caught between them, that now represents a threat to the stallion, an intrusion into his territory? Do you want to be responsible for the consequences?

Thus I ride Pride to the mountains alone, or with a few close friends who know me and my horses, know Pride, know that they must, like me, remember that he is a stallion. It is not ethical for me to inflict even the slightest anxiety or extra risk on trail riders beyond those few friends, so in all other situations I ride a gelding or a mare.

*The author limits trail rides on his stallion to those with a few good friends who understand the precautions necessary with even gentle, well-trained stallions.*

## Unsoundness

It goes without saying that any unsoundness causing pain to a horse is a disqualifier. If a horse "favors" a leg or foot or shoulder, limps on it, something is wrong, something is causing pain or stiffness, and riding the animal will increase that discomfort. Temporary unsoundness, an injury that will heal, is one thing. But a permanent condition or one likely to return on the trail can't be tolerated.

In today's horses, unsoundness is often the result of breeding trends that emphasize one or two particular abilities or attributes (specialization again) at the expense of the large picture. Fine bones often go with small feet and delicate heads, perhaps desirable in the show ring. But what happens when you breed for fine bones, tiny feet, and massive muscle structure? You get the all-too-common horse, sometimes called "Western" in build today, weighing 1,200 pounds but with size 00 feet. And what eventually happens to such horses after their earlier triumphs in the ring, perhaps as halter horses? They break down.

Our cowboy farrier put it best, when discussing the "big horse, little feet" syndrome. "When I get called to work on horses like that, I know the job isn't going to last very long. Once they're ten or twelve years old, those horses just aren't around anymore."

Potential unsoundness is a more serious worry on the trail than it is in many other sorts of horse uses, simply because help is often far away. Even in relatively urban settings, the trail horse may be miles from the nearest horse trailer or veterinarian when a problem occurs. The arena horse, by contrast, can often be pulled from competition into a stall, for quick medical attention.

Since it is always more enjoyable to discuss the positive, let's turn to building our perfect trail horse, to the attributes toward which I gravitate when looking for equine partners like Sugar and Major. Again, all of us love and enjoy horses that may not be perfectly suited for the task at hand. The ideal described here does not suggest that all others are unsuitable, nor should it be taken as criticism of a certain breed or type.

That said, in building our hypothetical "perfect" trail horse, we indeed are looking for a type that has *not* been emphasized in recent years by many of the current breed registries. We are looking for mankind's oldest equine partner, a horse bred to carry a rider long distances in security and comfort. My father-in-law Elmer Johnson, born in 1903, cowboyed on such horses most of his life. He would pronounce the words *saddle horse* with a particular emphasis, an admiration, a brightening in his eyes that recalled miles and miles across big, open Montana on a very special sort of animal.

## Gelding or Mare?

We can start with the converse of the "disqualifiers" just discussed. Our ideal will normally be a gelding or mare, not a stallion. Of the two, which? It is continually curious to me that so many riders quickly assert that they want a gelding, not a mare. Geldings, so they say, deprived of one of life's greatest distractions, are more even-tempered, are less likely to quarrel with other horses, and are thus more reliable in temperament. Because of reproductive cycling, they go on to say, mares are more variable in attitude, nastier with other horses, and too disruptive during heat (estrus).

I will not claim there is nothing to this, but I must say these conclusions do not match my experience. In looking back over countless pack trips into the mountains, humans and horses living in a tight, family unit, I can remember very few excursions when mares were not part of the string. When I look back on problems, I can identify just as many caused by geldings as by mares. When it comes to dominating other horses, both mares and geldings of the past come to mind. Major (grown now to advanced middle age) can be extremely rough on other horses, while being the ultimate pussycat with humans.

Yes, some mares have greater than normal attitude swings during their 21-day cycles, but there are geldings that get grouchy for one reason or another as well. The mare owner who is convinced something must be done to modify cyclical behavior can confer with his or her veterinarian. Mares can be held off their cycles by hormone treatment, and they can even be spayed. I would not jump to conclude either is necessary, however. Such treatment may dampen some of the built-in advantages mares have as saddle horses.

Yes, I mean *advantages*. Many riders feel mares have more drive than geldings, less quit when the going gets tough. Many feel mares are smarter (or seem to be), learn more quickly, and try harder. Do some self-examination. When you see a horse behave in a way that does not please you, if it is a mare, do you attribute it to that fact? If it's a gelding, do you attribute it to something else? Is some latent male chauvinism involved, some macho factor, some preference for things male? (I've seen this attitude in *both* male and female horsemen.)

Don't overlook your dream horse because it happens to be female. That happens too often. The advantages of mares more than make up for the disadvantages, and the mare has another crowning superiority compared to the gelding: when you decide she's the ultimate horse, you have a chance to reproduce her in hopes of getting another. If she's really that good, she is the correct animal to breed. (If I ride geldings more than mares it is because I breed horses and cannot resist raising colts out of the very best mares.) Do *not,* however, take the opposite path of relegating the inferior mare to broodmare status. The flawed mare does not deserve broodmare status, just as the flawed male does not deserve to be a breeding stallion.

## Does Size Matter?

Not much, unless we are talking about extremes. Height in horses is normally measured at the withers, in hands (4 inches each) followed by a dot and a second number, which indicates the number of inches (not tenths) beyond the number of hands. Thus 15.2 means 15 hands (60 inches) plus two inches, or a total of 62 inches at the withers. (I take time to discuss this point because I'm increasingly seeing hands expressed incorrectly, as in "15.5," which apparently is intended to mean fifteen and a half hands, but in fact would add up to 16.1 hands.)

In the early twentieth century, the US Army Remount Service did extensive tests on saddle horses of various size to determine an ideal height. One discovery was that, although the average large horse could carry a bit more weight than the average small horse, its advantage lessened as size increased. As horses got to 16 hands and beyond, they lost efficiency. Thus the 16-hand, 1,200-pound horse, could carry slightly more, but not proportionately more, than the 15-hand, 1,000-pound horse.

Extremely tall horses, those standing 17 hands (68 inches at the withers), are quite rare among most saddle-horse breeds (though quite common among warmbloods). They may be appropriate for Olympic jumping or dressage, but if riding one on the trail you'd soon tire of climbing on and off and of ducking under branches. A tall person on a horse of this height will, on a trail cleared to Forest Service specifications, spend much time bent at the waist!

More important, what is to be gained by a horse so large? Will it carry you better? Faster? With more endurance? Probably not. And, it may well lose something in a certain sort of athletic ability, that of keeping its feet securely underneath itself on a rough trail. Yes, such a horse will step over logs on the trail with a bit more ease, and that can be handy. Overall, if you own one of these giants, don't stay off the trail, but I would not recommend choosing a horse of this size even if you *are* tall and heavy.

I did ride a wonderful horse named Marauder for several years as my primary ranch and trail mount. He was an honest 16.2, or a bit better, barefoot. Short of back and easygoing in temperament, Marauder did everything asked of him, though he was not as "catty" on cows as smaller horses I've used. On winter mornings during calving season, hampered by long underwear and cold-weather boots, limbs stiff from cold, I'd find myself searching for a stump, a corral fence, anything to use as a mounting block, and I'm six feet one. If Marauder carried my weight (well over 200 pounds) more easily than the much smaller Little Mack, a faithful buddy with whom I've crossed many mountain passes, I could never detect it.

On the other end of the spectrum, there is no clear-cut line as to when a horse is too small to handle the trails while carrying a person of average size. Traditionally, horses smaller than 14.2 are classified as ponies, but that doesn't mean they are incapable of carrying a full-sized person. The tough little Icelandic ponies live in uncompromising territory and not only carry large men over rough country, but do it at high speed, thanks to their *tölt*, a smooth, four-beat gait. (We'll be addressing "gaited" horses, those having an alternative to the trot, at length.) Welsh ponies and the smaller Shetlands are known for tough feet and hearty constitutions.

Weight, not just height, enters here. A Quarter Horse 14.3 in height may well weigh the same as or more than a Saddlebred of 15.2. During its testing, the Army Remount Service determined it was best to limit total weight carried to one-fourth the weight of the animal. Since cavalrymen carried a heavy rifle, water, and other equipment, the army restricted the size of the men themselves to 175 pounds. It is said that the average cavalryman weighed around 130. As we mentioned earlier, the Remount Service found that efficiency tended to wane as horses became extremely large. It's probably safe to say that a 600-pound Welsh pony can safely carry a larger percentage of its weight than a 16.2, 1200-pound Thoroughbred.

At first glance, the 25 percent limit may seem quite liberal. After all, that amounts to 250 pounds for a 1,000-pound horse. But add your weight to a Western saddle (if that is what you use) perhaps supplemented by a breastcollar, bridle and halter, saddlebags, water, extra gear, and the weight limit can be reached surprisingly quickly. Exceeding it somewhat may not be a problem on shorter rides with a fit horse, but the total must be watched closely. (Later in this book we'll deal with the major problem I associate with the saddle-pack systems available for packing your camping gear along with you on your saddle horse: The weight can quickly mushroom.)

Aesthetics also enter in. The tall rider does not like the feeling that his or her feet dangle below the horse's barrel, which may hurt not only appearance, but also the ability to give cues with the feet. That said, do not overlook the smaller horse. My wife's grandfather, who cowboyed in Montana during the 1880s, often buying bands of horses from the Crow tribe to train during the winter and sell for profit, preferred smaller horses even though he was a heavy man. His simple explanation was that they were tougher.

## Age

We only include mention of the horse's age for the trail to remind the reader of an old principle: the younger the rider (in years of experience with horses), the older the horse should be. Training (and we'll discuss this later, at length) is primarily instilling desirable habits, while not allowing undesirable ones to become instilled. Endless repetition of the *right thing* while forbidding the *wrong thing* makes a saddle horse. The training of a young horse, even if superbly done, is shallow, lacking these years of repetition. An inexperienced rider is too likely to let things slide, to unknowingly allow small infractions. Small infractions too easily become big ones. Then you have a horse that will not ride out from the barn, that will not stand still to be mounted, that will do things his way because he now has a choice.

If your experience is limited, it's best to start with a good older horse, seven, ten, or even fifteen years old. Don't overlook that teenager. Remember, endurance horses don't even reach their peak until ten or so, and many are still winning when pushing twenty. The well-treated trail horse of sound conformation should be long-lived.

The flip side is that reliable older horses are often hard to find and tough to purchase, because their owners hang onto them. And, of course, worse than an unruly youngster is the older horse that has developed bad habits, the horse being unloaded because its current owner cannot handle it.

The most rigorous trail challenges should not be undertaken by immature animals, because of the likelihood of injury to the animal. Most horses are not physically mature until five to seven years of age, and geldings, especially, continue to grow during those years.

*An old, experienced mare, a fine choice for a young rider.*

## Conformation for the Trail

This is a big one, so we'll first throw out a disclaimer. Only so much can be explained by conformation. Successful breeders and trainers all have stories of horses that were built wrong for a particular task, but succeeded while their superbly-constructed stallmates failed. Sometimes a horse not ideally built to run still wins the race. A horse lacking the normally accepted conformational traits for jumping sometimes excels, when every empirical judgment predicts otherwise.

Older readers might remember a 1950s western named *Tumbleweed*. The main character, played by Audie Murphy, must make a treacherous desert crossing and asks friends for a horse with which to do so. They tell him he can have their very best. However, what is left in the corral for him is an ugly white creature, swaybacked and big-headed. Feeling as if he's the butt of a potentially deadly joke, the cowboy nonetheless must make the trip, so he mounts "Tumbleweed" and sets out. On the trip he encounters horrible obstacles, but the horse handles them all, even finding and digging a pothole for water when the cowboy is overcome by thirst. Only gradually does it dawn on the man that his friends weren't letting him down after all. Tumbleweed really was their very best horse—he just did not look like it!

We'll leave it to modern science to eventually sort out why animals (and humans) sometimes perform physically in ways their physiques would not imply. Meanwhile, the conformation of the horse standing in front of us is the most tangible predictor. Let's start from the ground up, remembering that this subject is huge—proper matter for entire books—and that we'll be tackling only a brief introduction.

"No foot, no horse," goes the old saying, along with the ditty: "For the want of a nail the shoe was lost. For the want of a shoe the horse was lost. For the want of a horse the rider was lost. For want of a rider the battle was lost. For want of the battle the kingdom was lost . . . " Our culture, for at least a couple of millennia, has recognized the importance of horses' feet. But how often to you hear breeders brag about the feet on their horses, the ample size compared to the horse's weight, and the thickness of the hoof wall (essential for ruggedness and shoe-holding ability)? More breeders *should* be proud of these things, and more should emphasize them in their breeding programs.

We earlier mentioned the "big horse–little foot" syndrome. It arose because large feet were associated with draft horses, with mixed breeding, with "cold blood." Refinement of the animal meant trimmer feet, and that was okay to a point. But in the good old American tradition of "if a little is good, more will be better," the feet were literally bred out from underneath certain lines among several breeds. How was this possible? Well, you will hear this refrain frequently from me, but it was possible because of good roads and horse trailers. The soundness horses need to cover many miles under saddle was not essential, because the horse only performed in short bursts on arena sand. Or, the animal was judged in halter class only, and, if successful, not asked for further accomplishments.

We want good feet of ample size on the trail horse. The thickness of the hoof wall is particularly important. Farriers are among the best predictors of soundness here. They quickly recognize the sort of feet

*The points of a horse, illustrated on the author's senior stallion The Pride Piper.*

they're repeatedly called to re-shoe, what sort seem prone to lameness, to brittleness, cracks, and other maladies.

Above that hoof should be pasterns of moderate length, with angles of around 45 degrees. The angle of the pastern should blend naturally with that of the foot. The pasterns are the shock absorbers of the horse's limbs, sparing the horse (and you) from jarring when the foot hits the ground. Too long, and too angled, however, could mean weakness over the long haul. Too steep, and your bad back will feel the concussion every time a hoof contacts the trail.

The bone between the hoof and the knee (or hock on the rear legs) is called the cannon. Here, again, many modern horses fall far short of their wild ancestors, the hand of man having refined them to the point of weakness. Dr. Deb Bennett, the renowned expert on skeletal structure in horses, tells us the circumference of the front cannon bones, measured just below the knee, should be no less than 7 inches for each 1,000 pounds of weight. Measuring this is easy and very appropriate for trail horse prospects. Dr. Bennett goes on to say that it's probably a myth that Arabian horses have denser bone. The secret of Arabian toughness, she says, is that the breed has held size and weight in check, matching bone mass.

Here again we see the soundness disadvantage of many extremely large horses, for few meet the 7 inch per 1,000-pound requirement. Conscious of this, owners of large warmblood stallions often advertise cannon bone circumference right along with pedigrees. Do draft horses have enough bone by this standard? Hardly ever. My own beautiful and very athletic Belgian gelding Lefty weighs, in svelte condition, perhaps 1,800 pounds. His appearance would suggest generous bone, but his cannon bone measures only 9½ inches. The "rule" would require 12⅗ inches! Why can draft horses survive with less? They hold up because they are not asked to do what saddle horses do: to run, jump, race, cut cattle, or carry a rider over rough terrain. They operate at a walk or trot, their bones adequate to hold up under their immense strength when pulling in harness.

All horses in existence today are the results of mankind's attempts at designing the perfect animal through selective breeding. Certainly nearly all are prettier to our eyes than the primitive animals

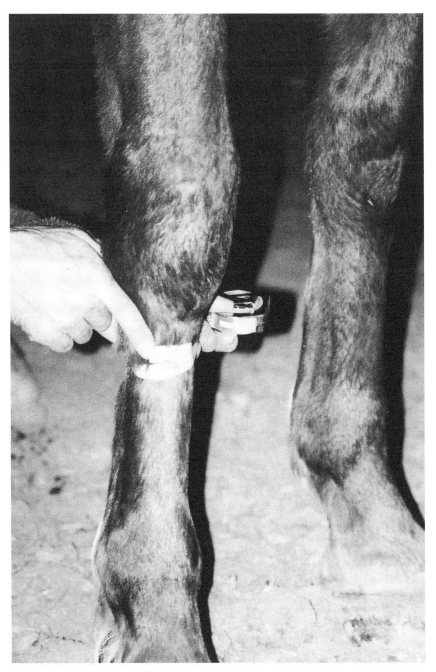

*Measuring a horse's bone—this colt, at 2½ years of age and 900 pounds has 8 inches of bone.*

reconstructed from bones by paleontologists (though perhaps less rugged). But the "design" of horses is always a compromise. The massive muscling of the bulldog-style Quarter Horse would weigh down an endurance horse over the long haul. Conversely, a rail-thin, 800-pound Arab endurance animal would come up short trying to stop a big steer at the end of a lariat rope.

The issue of muscle structure is further complicated. We are told that muscle cells come in both "quick-twitch" and "slow-twitch" variety. All muscles supply power by contraction. Quick-twitch muscles contract rapidly. They are the muscles of the football lineman or linebacker, the weight lifter, and horses bred to sprint race. Slow-twitch muscles are the muscles of endurance. All horses have both, but the bulldog type mentioned above is endowed with a preponderance of quick-twitch cells, while his endurance cousin is supplied with a generous percentage of slow-twitch cells.

Where should the trail horse fall? Both types mentioned above can take you down the trail, but our "complete" trail horse, it seems to me, should fall somewhere between the two extremes. The bulldog type will have poor endurance, because fueling those magnificent muscles takes immense quantities of oxygen and nourishment. Few horses with extreme muscling walk rapidly, and they often have rough gaits. On the other end, the endurance Arab will take you to hell and back, but you'd better be built just like him: lean and tough. He's made to trot, and his disposition may not be compatible with leading a pack string up a ledge trail.

Many years ago I experienced ten weeks of some of the most inventive mental and physical challenge (or should I say torture?) devised by man: OCS (officer boot camp) in the United States Marine Corps. In my platoon was a good-natured physical specimen, chiseled, it seemed, out of pure rock. A weight lifter and body builder standing six-three, with muscles on his eyelids, this Marine put most of the rest of us to shame—or so it appeared.

But over the weeks, challenged to run, survive forced marches over hill, dale, and swamp carrying packs and rifles, performing on obstacle courses, then, through it all, trying to stay awake during academic classes, our overmuscled friend did no better than anyone else and had more problems than some. If I noticed a particular body type among the men who excelled, the key word was "moderate." The very most capable Marines had moderate muscling, were lean and hard, and were usually medium-sized in height and weight. They resembled Greek statues, not Mike Tyson, in physical appearance.

Horses are not humans, but there is much to be learned from these human examples. Many mistake massive muscling for overall physical ability, and even for stamina. But look at the true working horses of the world, those that still carry military equipment in Afghanistan, for instance, and you see something more closely resembling the lean endurance champion. We certainly hope to never stress a trail horse even close to such limits of endurance (or, for that matter, at the level of challenge met by Marine officer candidates), but we can certainly learn something about muscling by looking at equine and human survivors. It's simply this: muscles are like big V-8s in automobiles. They furnish power, but they require fuel. Additionally, they are extremely heavy.

Weight can be an enemy of the trail horse. For a horse called upon to carry a rider, saddle, and gear, superfluous muscle of the sort suited for sprinting or for lateral movement becomes a burden, not an asset. The burden is even more pronounced when combined with bone structure too slight to carry it properly. Witness some overmuscled halter class horses weighing well over 1,000 pounds as yearlings, but lacking proper bone, skeletal development, and foot size to carry their bulk. My impression is that few such horses go on to accomplish much later in life, except perhaps to breed additional animals to win the same show classes. Many do not stay sound.

These are the reasons we want moderation in muscling for the complete trail horse. In human terms, think of Michelangelo's statue of David. Every muscle is fit and functional. The trail horse, as equine generalist, should be the equivalent of a decathlon champion, not the specialist. The trail horse should have a good rear end, his "motor," muscular, but not massive, for you'll soon see flecks of lather on massive rear ends when pulling that mountain pass.

Leaving advanced, scientific evaluations of conformation to Dr. Bennett and her colleagues, we'll have a look at a horse named Pride that I consider excellent for trail, save one detriment: the fact that he is

Laid-back shoulder

Hock angle  Short back

Height—15.2
Weight—1,000
Cannon bones—7¾"

*Conformation features considered desirable by the author as illustrated on Pride, son of The Pride Piper. Pride's build is slightly "uphill," though photo makes that difficult to see. Author would prefer this feature to be a bit more prominent.*

a stallion. No horse is perfect, but this one comes close enough to my ideal to be kept as a stallion and to be bred to mares selected with similar care. Again, horses built quite unlike Pride often do just fine on the trail, so we'll consider most of his conformational assets to be plusses, not necessarily requirements.

At age six (he might grow a little yet), Pride is 15.2 and weighs around 1,000 pounds. His front cannon bones measure 7¾ inches in circumference, ample for his weight with some room to grow. We've discussed feet and pasterns, so it is adequate to point out that Pride has feet with good, thick, hoof walls, and they are large enough for his weight. His pasterns angle nicely, but are not so low or long as to suggest any sort of weakness.

Let's jump to Pride's top line. We see that the withers are a smidge higher than the croup, so this horse is built "uphill," a characteristic nearly always suggesting smoother gaits than you'll find in the horse built "downhill," with croup higher than withers. (A downhill build is primarily suited for racing.) It would please me if Pride were built just a little bit more uphill. Strength is also indicated by the way the withers seem to rise from the middle of the back. The old timer's characterization was, "short back, long belly," a saying that also reflects preference for an angled shoulder and long hip.

Prominent withers are important for the trail horse in several ways. They serve to hold the saddle, to keep it from sliding forward on steep downhill grades and, in turn, they help prevent the sores likely to result if the cinch (girth) slides too far forward. Good withers help hold the saddle in place as you mount and allow a looser cinch, which is easier on the horse.

The effectiveness of high withers has been brought home to me many times while packing in the mountains. On a long trip down a drainage to the trailhead, after several enjoyable but physically tasking days in the wilderness, I've sometimes been lazy about getting off periodically to check the cinches on the packhorses. One such time, after 10 miles in a fast flat walk downgrade (packs always tend to slip more going downhill than uphill), caution got the best of me and I stopped to check things. I was horrified to see a full inch of daylight between the cinch on the front packhorse and the bottom of her chest. She was a high-withered mare, and the packs, perfectly equal in weight, had not slipped one whit, despite a cinch that was, for practical purposes, nonexistent. Good withers and a back shaped properly for the saddle had kept me out of trouble.

Good withers were also the conformational feature that made early-day cowboys able to rope off horses saddled with center-fire rigs, that is saddles with just one cinch hung approximately in the middle of the saddle, and with no breastcollar at all. Comparing photographs (such as those of L. A. Huffman) of Montana ranch life in the 1880s shows a very different sort of horse from those considered "Western" in build today. Most are narrower and higher-withered, really closer to the conformational ideal for the trail that we have been discussing. Breastcollars were unknown, and rear cinches were not common. Yet these cowboys roped full-sized steers, their saddles holding primarily because of the high-withered build of their horses. True, their animals would probably not have competed with today's broader, rounder, and more muscular West-

JUST THE RIGHT HORSE **29**

ern performance horses in arena events. But I suspect they excelled when gathering the cattle required an all-day circle, and they probably got the cowboy to that Saturday night dance, 25 miles away, in a comfortable canter, an easy trot, or a ground-eating single-foot.

Back to Pride: notice the extremely short back on this horse. A back is measured from the point of the withers to the top of the croup. This measurement, compared with total length of the horse's body (a photograph must be viewed directly from the side) tells the relative length of the animal's back. Pride's back is well under 50 percent of his total body length. Why a short back? It is stronger. Place a pine board between two chairs relatively close together, and you can probably stand on it. As you increase the distance between the two chairs, the board becomes progressively less able to hold your weight.

The trail horse is often called upon to carry more weight than the racehorse, three-day eventer, dressage performer, endurance competitor, or cutting horse. Particularly with overnight packing systems used by trail riders who camp out with their horses, but who do not take pack animals, weight builds up rapidly (sometimes too rapidly).

Notice that the overall appearance of Pride's top line looks as if it were made to accommodate a saddle. That is no accident. It *is* made to accommodate a saddle. Today there is much emphasis on the "natural" state of the horse as a herd animal of the plains. While this is appropriate in our quest to better understand horses, too often the human factor goes unmentioned. Horses are not like domesticated bison or elk, wild until very recently, then suddenly tamed by man. Even the mustang is a domestic animal, bred by Spanish horsemen (and others, since mustangs are a mixture), and only feral (reverted to the wild) for relatively few generations. Yes, their herd instinct is strong, but also strong is the hand of man in everything including the slope of their shoulder (sloping shoulders first became popular because they best accommodated the collar in harness) and, yes, the saddle-friendly shape of their backs. The great Greek horseman Xenophon championed a back shaped quite differently from the one I am advocating. Why? To the Greeks the horse was a war animal, and saddles had not yet been invented. A cavalryman going into battle bareback needed a broader, more comfortable back to cling to.

True, earlier people did not necessarily geld stallions and select only the best for breeding. But they certainly selected certain types for riding, others for food. Thus, an "evolution" far more rapid than natural selection took place.

Note that Pride's shoulder is quite "laid back," that is, angled back at around forty-five degrees. Most consider this a desirable trait, though what it actually accomplishes is a little less clear. I tend to associate a well-angled shoulder with freedom of movement up front, and with smooth gaits, but some of this is aesthetics as well. It just *looks* good to me, as does the way the base of Pride's neck sets into his shoulder. Notice, too, that his croup slopes down toward his tail, a characteristic of gaited breeds, and associated with ability to reach forward with the hind legs.

The hock angle on the hind legs gets considerable attention in studies of conformation. The standard recommendation is for a hind leg with a hind cannon bone that points, if extended from its rear by an imaginary line upward, to just intersect with the back of the animal's hindquarter. This is a good guideline, though not absolute. Many horses, particularly gaited animals, do very well with just a bit more crook to the hind leg. A horse whose imaginary line just misses the hindquarter (in the direction of what is called sickle hocks) may well be a good walker. Conversely, the horse with a straighter hind leg (postlegged) may well be a good jumper, but will probably be rough in gait. Extremes in either direction can lead to physical problems.

So far we've been paying attention to Pride from the side. Let's have a look from the front. Pride's chest is moderate in width. Note that the outline of his body between his front legs when viewed from low in front is that of an inverted V (or a pyramid, right side up, if you wish). This characteristic brings back a conversation from long ago.

Her name was Rosie, a fairly stocky bay, perhaps the first horse I could really consider my own. I'd worked summers on ranches since age fourteen. Normally, when there was a job to be done on horseback, I drew the horse no one else wanted to ride, the extra one kept around for the summer help. These were usually not dangerous, but they were often the stubborn, ill-mannered sort that required a constant, hard presence of your heels in their ribs to keep up with the crowd. They were always rough in gait, with a trot that felt as if your body was strad-dling a pair of pile drivers.

Rosie was a cut above, well trained, athletic, capable of running like the wind. She had her quirks—pulling back when tied, spooking at ir-rigation tarps—but I reached a state of rapport with her that I'd not yet felt, and I suspect Rosie had much to do with my subsequent life with horses. I commented to my future father-in-law Elmer once about the power in her wide chest. We were sitting on the bank of an irrigation ditch, our horses cropping grass, their chests at our eye level. "Yes, she's powerful all right, but I don't care for the wide, flat place between her front legs. For endurance we used to look for a chest that was a little narrower, with an upside-down V between the front legs." He held his hands out in front of him as he faced me, their edges toward me, the hands angling together at forty-five degrees to touch on top at the fin-gertips. "Like this."

The wisdom of old-timers (Elmer was born in 1903) sometimes means little when you are young and first hear it. But it sticks around. Many years later I read in *Equus* that endurance was normally associ-ated not with width in the chest but with depth from withers to ster-num. And years after that, I covered an endurance ride for a piece I was writing and looked at the chests of the competitive horses. You guessed it: every single one was narrow to moderate in width, with Elmer's in-verted V between its front legs. Now, I can't claim that this characteris-tic in itself makes for endurance, but it is apparently associated with things that do. And, while it's true that any sound horse in good physi-cal condition has enough endurance for what 90 percent of trail riders do, I'll still lean toward endurance, rather than sprint-racing ability, in choosing for the trail.

When judging width of not only the chest but of the animal's entire torso, another factor enters in, and we'll refer to it often in this book. That factor is rider comfort. It is no sin to think of one's comfort on a long ride, because, after all, don't most of us do this for pleasure? None of us have knees made to bend in two directions. The horse with the pork-barrel torso pressures our knees to bend both from front to back and sideways. Straddling the horse with a narrower build is pure joy by comparison.

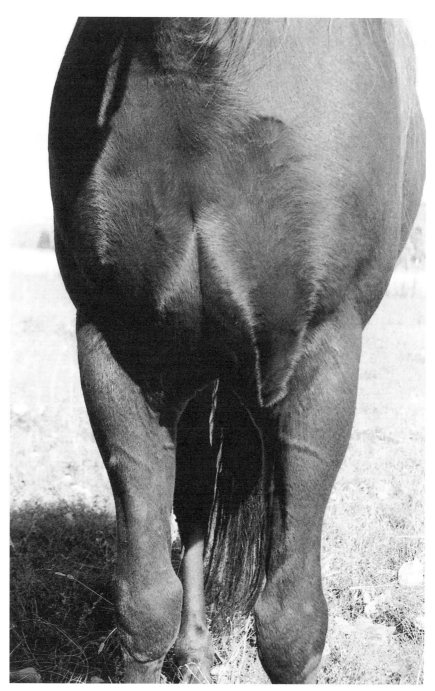

*Pride's chest is moderate in width showing Elmer's "inverted V."*

Finally, let's have a look at Pride's hindquarters. They are powerful, but not massive. The hocks are slightly in, the hind toes pointed slightly out. This is correct and normal and does not indicate a "cow-hocked" condition. (Volume III of Bennett's *Principles of Conformation Analysis* gives an excellent explanation of proper hind leg configuration.)

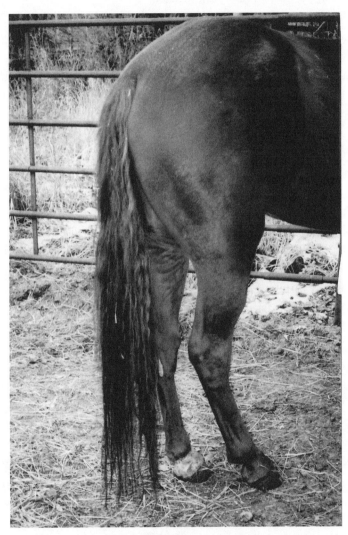

*Pride's hindquarters are powerful but not massive, the hocks slightly in, the toes pointed slightly out, correct and normal for a horse.*

## Disposition for the Trail Horse

This, too, is a big one, and unfortunately, even more difficult to study. Conformation, if an imperfect predictor of an animal's capabilities, at least has concrete parameters. For the trail horse, disposition is probably the more important of the two, but nearly impossible to quantify. Knowing this, breeders invariably advertise that their horses have nice dispositions. Who can prove them wrong?

Further, disposition is a subjective judgment. What's ideal for me may not be for you. I like horses of high courage with much "go." I'd far rather work on slowing one down than having to kick one up over the mountain. Perhaps instead of being a result of a type A personality, this stems from a lifetime of work genuinely requiring good horses, horses that perform in a no-nonsense fashion.

In addition to writing, breeding, and training horses, I operate a small cow-calf operation. As I write in February, our cows are calving left and right. Yesterday, I watched with binoculars as two cows calved in quick succession, the second taking time to lick hers off initially. (Mother cows remove afterbirth that way, but even more importantly, stimulate blood flow with their rough tongues, getting the calves up on their feet and nursing.) Fine so far. Then, something in her brain slipped a cog and she turned to her neighbor's calf and began mothering that one instead.

Now we had a situation. A wet calf was lying in the snow unattended. Unless properly "mothered" it would not live long. I drove out with a pickup and tried to handle the situation on foot, but to no avail. The cow would not even look at the right calf. The only thing to do was to snatch the newborn, take it to the corral, then get the cow in with the correct calf. That would likely resolve the matter. But getting her to the corral was a job for a horse, a good horse.

In a paddock nearby, sharp-shod, kept there for just such eventualities, was my gelding, Little Mack. There was no time for warm-up games, no time for anything but a twenty-second currying of the saddle area, cinching up, and quickly turning him in a 360-degree circle from the ground. (I *always* do that before mounting a spirited horse on a cold morning, easing any "hump" under the saddle.) Then I was aboard and through the gate and into the field. The cow, sticking like glue to the wrong calf, fought us at first. Little Mack stayed on her, ducking left, then right as needed, going just fast enough to turn her when she tried to break away on the treacherous, icy ground. In little more time than it takes to tell it, the errant cow was in the corral with the correct calf—confused for just a bit, but nursing it within an hour—and Little Mack was munching a reward of grain.

Those of us from a "using horse" tradition have learned to prize horses that love to work, horses with "heart," horses that need no more than a subtle nudge of leg or calf to kick up into the next gear. To us, calling a horse "laid back" may not be a compliment. But it's perfectly fine to lean the other way. The fact that some riders see this differently is amply shown by the very existence of Western pleasure classes in some breeds, show classes that reward an extremely slow walk and trot.

Mark Twain got along considerably better with boats than with horses. In Carson City, Nevada, he was conned into buying a "Genuine Mexican Plug." The horse, which he later learned had been recommended by the salesman's brother, promptly bucked him sky-high. So when Twain later traveled to Hawaii and needed to rent a horse to tour the island, he claims to have asked for "an excessively gentle horse. A lame one if they had such!"

What we all *can* agree on, is that the trail horse must not be an excessively spooky or flighty animal. I use the adverb "excessively," because to expect a horse to have no spooks, no tendency to flee, is to expect it to desert its very nature. Horses are creatures of flight. Under certain circumstances they will stand and fight, but primarily they flee, and in nature they do it unhesitatingly, in the time it takes to blink.

Much of horse training consists of teaching horses to overcome this tendency to run away when frightened. With most horses, *all* tendency to spook will never completely leave them, no matter how thorough the training program. That's why you won't hear me describe horses using terms such as "bombproof" or "foolproof," though I will own that some, such as city police horses, come extremely close. Good training will eliminate much of the spookiness and, perhaps more importantly, teach the horse the acceptable ways to spook while eliminating the unacceptable ones (such as attempting to turn and flee).

This said, horses vary considerably in this respect. Some are afraid of their own shadows and continue to be, even after much conditioning. Others are unflappable. For the trail we do want to avoid the horse that constantly looks for an excuse to jump out of his skin. Nearly all of this sort gradually improve, but there are a few that do not, and those will remain unreliable, and even dangerous, on the trail.

My least favorite equine disposition is that of the horse that seems laid back and easygoing, even lazy, but then, with no warning, blows its cork. My mental image of this sort includes clouds of dust, broken lead ropes and halters, splintered corral poles, and, if you are in the way, worse. I would much rather work with an animal that is nervous all the time than with one of those.

Of course, there is an entire laundry list of undesirable traits that may be due to disposition, that may be the results of mistakes in training, or that may be a mixture of the two. Some trainers go so far as to claim all such traits are really people problems, training mistakes that can be corrected. I disagree. If human beings can vary to the extent they do, it seems logical horses can as well. There may not truly be any "bad" or "evil" horses, but there are ones with whom I do not care to spend my time. Life is very short, and I would just as soon spend it with pleasant friends.

Furthermore, even if a trait has been induced or allowed by poor training, we still must observe that such poor training resulted in a given problem with this horse, while ten others, suffering the same errors, were more forgiving. A horse that goes over backwards with a rider has, in my mind, disqualified itself from use by humans. Yes, half the trainers on the block may claim they can correct this, and I've heard some pretty extreme and bizarre approaches to doing so. Perhaps this horse was allowed to get "light in front" by an incompetent rider or trainer. Perhaps a frightened rider exacerbated the situation by hauling back on the reins rather than forcing the horse forward. The next step was rearing, the next was the very most dangerous thing a horse can do: going over backwards, and likely injuring or even killing someone.

There are two points here. Yes, the horse was mishandled. Yes, also, this particular horse had a dispositional trait: it tended to handle pressure by going up in front. In any case, the animal is, in my opinion, not safely usable by humans, and the best thing you can do is stay completely away from it.

If you visit a breeding farm in search of trail horse stock and are warned to stay ten feet away from the fence of a breeding stallion, whom you observe laying back his ears and threatening you, turn around and go back to your car. Don't get me wrong: stallions must be allowed their territory, and only the very ignorant would crawl into a strange stallion's paddock or stall. However, there are many stallions whose basic nature toward humans is that of friendliness, and you have every reason to question why anyone would save an ill-tempered animal for the task of producing offspring.

It is always questionable to compare human traits with those of horses, but it is probably safe to consider disposition in horses to be the counterpart of personality in humans. Most psychologists consider personality to result from both heredity and environment. From what I've observed in horses, the same seems true of what we call disposition.

If I could choose the perfect upbringing, the ideal early environment for the potential trail horse, it would be structured as follows: The foal would have a dam that was friendly and at ease with humans, for the dam is the early trainer of the foal. The foal will spook if she spooks and run away if she runs away. This foal would be imprinted at birth by human beings who rubbed it, picked up its feet, spoke softly to it, and these actions would be repeated for the first few days of life. These humans would be kind, but intolerant of disrespect. They would not allow physical domination (kicking or biting) even if it began as playfulness. After a couple of days of imprinting and halter training, the foal in our ideal environment would be *left alone to learn to be a horse.*

That last sentence might surprise you, but the pampered foal, the one made into a pet, too easily becomes disrespectful of human beings. Many trainers feel the overly friendly colt can sometimes be more difficult to train than the horse never before handled. Discipline seems to hurt its feelings, perhaps, or impulsion cannot be taught gently, because the horse only knows to come toward the trainer for a treat or a pat.

*A future trail horse. What he becomes will rely upon disposition (both environment and heredity), training (both by other horses and by humans), and exposure to as wide a variety of stimuli as possible.*

As to the physical environment of the horse, we'll generalize: Open space is better than a stall, big pastures better than small paddocks, hills better than flat land. The foal that runs in the open and through obstacles such as streams and ditches, that is loaded and unloaded into trailers alongside its mother, that intermingles with deer and livestock, is halfway toward being a trail horse, long before a human ever steps onto its back.

# 3

## Horse Breeds for the Trail

Among the "light horse" breeds, there are no bad ones for the trail. We have deliberately stayed away from discussion of breeds to this point, for that reason and for several others. First of all, the traits of conformation and disposition advocated in the last chapter can be found in virtually all breeds. Second, many fine trail horses are "grade" (unregistered), identifiable as to breed only by hearsay and by their conformation and way of going (a judgment that can be inexact).

This is not to say, however, that all breeds produce an equal percentage of horses with the attributes we touted, such as a short back, uphill build, fast walk, high withers, moderate muscling, and so on. Quite the contrary. We must go back again to the prevailing uses of particular breeds and to the corresponding breeding emphasis. Often the emphasis has much to do with bringing home ribbons and trophies for the tack room walls. We all like to do that, but we have to ask whether the events in which these awards were won are remotely connected to our requirements for the complete trail horse. Some, such as halter competition in particular breeds, obviously have nothing to do with a horse's ability to traverse rough country. Others, such as three-day eventing, do emphasize extreme physical ability, and may be far more relevant.

We must also look at the genetic background, and at whether the most publicized use of animals within that breed is really the one in most widespread practice. For instance, most Tennessee Walking Horses are used by owners as smooth, ground-covering trail animals, for field trials (where horses must really cruise to keep up with the dogs), as gentle family horses, and so on. Yet the crown jewel of the Tennessee Walking Horse Breeder's and Exhibitor's Association is a show animal with appendages (awkward pads) on its feet, doing an extremely artificial, exaggerated show gait. Only a small percentage of Walking Horse owners are interested in that sort of "big lick" animal, however, and a high percentage hold it in disdain.

Similarly, I know many ranchers with rugged, using-type Quarter Horses, who have absolutely no interest in overfed halter types or "peanut rollers," (slow-walking, low-headed Western pleasure animals). They have work to do with their horses, and they pretty much know what sort of animal will get the job done.

So any discussion of breeds carries an added difficulty. The breed registries are so vast in many cases, that the gene pool within a given breed is huge. Simply saying that a horse is a Morgan or an Arab does not tell you as much as we could wish. Still another difficulty is the sheer number of registries that now prevail.

Many years ago *Western Horseman* magazine could publish its annual all-breed issue with little editorial confusion. There were around ten major registries, and the magazine could publish this issue with an article on each of them. Then registries proliferated, forcing the editors to settle for several articles on the breeds that have come in recent years to be considered the "Western" ones, with short notes on other popular registries in the back of the magazine. Now they have returned to eight or ten articles on the largest registries and a massive listing of others in an appendix.

Why so many registries? First, breed registries are good business. Charging for foal registration, transfer when an animal is sold, and other assorted services, generates considerable income. Second, politics tend to enter in and split existing registries. A "foundation" registry begins, vowing to return the breed to its original intent, the belief being that the original registry has strayed in its emphasis. Other registries begin because a particular cross (Morgan/Arab, Arab/Thoroughbred, Appaloosa/Tennessee Walking Horse) has been successful, and someone feels the type produced should be a distinct breed. Still other registries start because someone produces a remarkable grade stallion, too good in its breeder's opinion to be gelded, and a breed is literally built around that one animal.

The existence of hundreds of breed registries is confusing to say the least. All have their pitches. Many claim to be formalizations of distinct genetic types that have existed for centuries, and all claim (sometimes subtly) to be far superior to the competition. Well, competition is the American way, but the recent proliferation of registries may be too much of a good thing.

Often registration in a breed association is "open" for a few years. That is, animals are accepted if they are of a certain type, or, perhaps, if they have one parent already registered in the new association, and the second parent is of a particular approved breed. Most registries, however, are eventually "closed," which means that registration is only granted if both of a foal's parents are registered. Thus all breeding now must take place within that particular gene pool. This may help assure a purity of type, but it may also stifle infusion of new and beneficial genes.

Another problem is brand loyalty so strong it keeps horse lovers who are devoted to a particular breed from giving a beautiful animal of another breed so much as a passing glance. Your preference may be foundation Quarter Horses, but you should be able to see the beauty in the arched neck of an American Saddlebred, and its owner in turn should recognize the dynamic power in the muscling of *your* horse.

I will not attempt to sort entirely through this huge and growing list of breed registries. Besides, we need to rein back a bit in considering horse breeds. Dr. Deb Bennett has said that there are really only four types of horses in America: riding, racing, carriage/harness, and draft. (She adds a fifth type with some tongue in cheek, the "project type," such as the horse you deliberately train to do something for which its breed is not known, cutting cattle on a half-Belgian, for instance.) These "types" refer to the intended *use* of the horse, the task for which its conformation is appropriate.

Earlier in this book I urged putting trail performance first in your search for the complete trail horse. If trail riding is your passion, why select animals whose primary claim to fame is dressage, cutting, reining,

Western pleasure (decidedly *not* a trail use by my requirements), sprint racing, or distance racing? Why not gravitate toward horses built for what you do; for efficient, smooth, ground-covering ability, and the versatility and disposition to tackle any trail obstacle likely to be encountered? And while there are good trail prospects to be found among all the light horse breeds, all are not equal in this respect. The trail horse I've been describing in this book is decidedly within the camp of the riding type (I like the term "saddle" type) outlined by Dr. Bennett.

Really, we're talking about the horse that prevailed for centuries, the *traveling* horse, the horse that evolved to carry a rider in relative comfort over many miles before decent roads existed. This was the sort of horse that carried our congressmen to the capital in the early years of our nation and took mountain men and their long rifles to America's West.

So here's a very quick look at some of the most populous breed registries today with some candid comments about pluses and minuses for the trail. These days, a touch on your computer's mouse can bring complete breed histories, bloodlines, and practically any other information you desire. I won't reinvent the wheel, but instead will restrict my comments to personal observations, always with trail use in mind.

We'll concentrate here on the best-known "American" breeds, or at least the American version of them, remembering that all originated elsewhere. Horses existed in the Americas during prehistoric times but had been gone for thousands of years by the time the first European explorers arrived on these shores.

## The Morgan

The Morgan horse is one of America's oldest breeds. Its registry, established in 1894, makes it the oldest *organized* breed. Since many books and a popular movie have told the story of the breed's founding stallion, Morgan history is probably well known to most horse-loving Americans. The founding stallion, named Figure, was later given the name of the most prominent of his several owners, a music teacher and composer named Justin Morgan.

The actual origin of this compact, nut-brown stallion, born during the 1790s, has kept equine scholars hopping for a couple of centuries. There is much controversy about that, but no one disagrees regarding the nature of the stallion himself: The horse was beautiful, muscular, short-backed, good-natured, and tough. He could drag logs, pull a buggy, sprint race, or carry a rider with ease down a muddy colonial road. As a stallion he quickly distinguished himself for what is known as prepotency, the tendency to produce progeny that remarkably resembled their sire. If Figure himself, and the successive horses that became known as the Morgan breed, were attached to any one descriptive word, it would be "versatile." No horse has better established itself for its ability to perform many tasks well than the Morgan. In addition, no American breed has contributed its bloodlines to other breeds—the Quarter Horse, the American Saddlebred, and the Tennessee Walking Horse—to such good effect as has the Morgan.

Morgans have been cow horses, cavalry horses, buggy horses, packhorses, and the everyday farm workhorses. In our part of Montana, ranchers crossed Morgans (probably the stallions standing at the

*A trail rider and her Morgan horse. Becky Siler (photo courtesy of the American Morgan Horse Association).*

government remount station) with their Percheron and grade work mares to get a medium-sized work animal that was tougher and more athletic than larger draft horses. Interestingly, many of these early "government line" Morgans had a smooth, single-foot gait, a characteristic still occasionally found. (The Morgan Single-Footing Horse Association, a service organization of the American Morgan Horse Association, researches and promulgates information about these gaited Morgans.)

I cannot claim as much first-hand experience with Morgan horses as I would like, but I grew up with great admiration for the breed. A cherished memory from when I was a young Marine with a day off in Washington DC, is of a conversation with a mounted policeman. I told him I admired his dark-brown horse, and he said proudly that it was a Morgan, that more Morgans passed the stringent police training than any other breed. While we talked, and he, like any proud horseman, extolled the virtues of his mount, particularly its gentleness, a little girl from the crowd walked to the rear of the horse and reached out and touched the animal's hock. I froze, and so did the policeman, but with a smile on his face. The horse, completely aware of the little girl, froze also. "See what I mean?" the policeman said under his breath. Enough said.

There is some division within the breed (as with nearly all others) between those who advocate an extremely refined, spirited, show animal, and those who seek to preserve the breed in its most original form. Perusal of the breed journal shows many elegant animals that resemble more, to my layman's eye, American Saddlebreds than they do my image of the Morgan. About the only negative thing I have ever heard about individuals within the Morgan breed has come recently from clients who have talked about "hyper" show animals that must be worked hard daily to stay tractable.

All breeds seem to face this difficulty to some extent, the downside of breeding for extreme performance. Were I looking for a Morgan for the trail, I can't say to what bloodlines I would gravitate, but I'd certainly look for a tradition of "using" horses, for the durability and versatility that made the breed famous in the first place. And, if the animal had a single-foot gait, the prospect of hitting the trail on him would be all the sweeter.

## The American Quarter Horse

So vast is the American Quarter Horse Association and so varied is the scope of horseflesh registered by the association, that it's quite difficult to talk briefly about the breed. The registry is not only the world's largest—it encompasses twice as many animals as *all other registries combined!* No horse breed can touch the financial success—and the success in terms of sheer numbers of registrants—enjoyed by the AQHA.

Like the Morgan, the Quarter Horse is an extremely old American breed, since the first competitive quarter-milers were bred during colonial times. It is as sprint racers that the animals first became known, their bloodlines a mixture of compact colonial stock, some of it athletic ponies from the Chickasaw tribe, with the English Thoroughbreds imported before the American Revolution. We won't delve into the extremely complex history of the breed (that has been the subject matter of several book-length studies) except to say that *modern* Quarter Horse development tended to begin with the convention in 1940 in Fort Worth, Texas, when the registry was born. Wimpy, a powerful stallion from the King Ranch, was designated #1 in the registry.

An explosion of growth followed. One reason the growth was so rapid was an open registry early on that employed a number of inspectors who traveled far and wide, looking for horses meeting the criteria envisioned by the founders of the formalized breed and then registering them. The Quarter Horse in these early years tended to be known for a blocky, muscular conformation, heavily muscled quarters, a small head with wide jaws and small ears, and low hocks. As the breed grew the registry eventually closed, but only partially: Thoroughbred sires can still be used on Quarter mares to produce foals registered as Quarter Horses. This dipping constantly into the Thoroughbred intensified with the mushrooming of the prize money available in Quarter Horse racing. Talk to one Quarter Horse breeder and you'll hear that the Thoroughbred blood has ruined the breed. Talk to another, and he'll call this outcrossing the breed's salvation.

Today the picture is even more complicated, Quarter Horse conformation tending to mesh with the many intended uses within the breed. There are probably at least a half dozen Quarter Horse types today. Quarter Horses dominate the emerging sport of reining, as well as cutting and sprint racing. The extremely heavily-muscled type of the early registry has given way in many individuals to greater reflection of Thoroughbred blood, although the "bulldog" type is still to be found and is cherished by some groups and several smaller registries that deem it the foundation animal to be preserved.

Within a breed so vast and so multitalented there are bound to be many wonderful trail horse prospects. Were I looking for one, I would tend away from the extreme muscling of the bulldog type, believing that massive quick-twitch muscling is more useful in the roping arena than it is on the trail, where endurance and a loose walk are (at least to me) more important. I'd pay special attention to the feet and cannon bones, making sure both were adequate for the animal's weight, and I'd look for a high-withered build, rather than a downhill top line.

In selecting a Quarter Horse trail horse I'd look hard at what ranchers use, particularly ranchers who have vast, rough-country pastures and forest service grazing leases. Ranchers who work in this sort of country, inaccessible by vehicle, have horses that spend little time in trailers

*A nice high-withered Quarter Horse of Thoroughbred type, owned by a man who uses him extensively in the mountains.*

and much time covering ground. Their recommendations as to blood-lines would be more valuable to me than those coming from the performance arena. I'd pay much attention to the size of the feet and the mass of bone in relation to the animal's weight.

## The American Paint Horse

The Paint is in many ways similar to the Quarter Horse, but with spots and patches, of course. To a degree it is a "color breed," since a certain degree of white hair over unpigmented skin is required. But the association seeks to maintain what they consider a "stock horse" type. Thus to be registered, paints must have two registered parents from among the Paint, Thoroughbred, or Quarter Horse breeds. The breed has grown rapidly in size, to become the second largest breed registry in the US. Part of the fuel for such growth has been an AQHA rule that prohibits white above the knee. Thus many good Quarter Horses could not be registered as such, but could be registered as Paints. In terms of choosing the trail prospect, what we've said about Quarter Horses applies equally to Paints.

During my boyhood in Montana the term paint was rarely heard, pinto being the more common term for spotted horses. Another registry, the Pinto Horse Association of America, maintains that terminology but registers animals of four distinct types: stock, hunter, pleasure, and saddle. Thus a registered Pinto can have sire and dam registered in the Pinto association and/or in one of several outcross registries, as long as it meets the color requirements.

## The Arabian

The Arabian, more than any other breed, has through history been praised by poets for its beauty, and sought by breeders for its genetic ability to improve other breeds. American breeders have kept track of pedigrees for a relatively short time. The desert tribes that treasured the Arabian kept track of bloodlines for many centuries. It is said that when horses were taken in battle, emissaries would return to the vanquished to solicit breeding information on the backgrounds of the horses captured. And, with a wisdom that only the best breeders comprehend, it was the mares that were truly treasured.

Possibly it was the harsh desert environment over so many generations that bred into the Arabian the great endurance for which it is best known. Although other breeds often do well, Arabians dominate endurance events. For endurance purposes they are models of efficiency—relatively light in weight, narrow in build, all muscles contributing to the ultimate goal, none superfluous. Although some lines of Arabians today are bred considerably larger, the horse that made the breed's reputation probably averages between 14 and 15 hands, and 750 to 900 pounds.

Admired by many as well is the beauty of the horses, particularly the distinctive head with concave face. So taken are many lovers of other breeds with the Arabian head, that we're seeing them appear on Quarter Horses, Tennessee Walking Horses, and other breeds as if grafted on, perhaps at home there and perhaps not, depending on your taste.

In looking for the ideal Arabian trail horse, I would find myself doing the opposite from when we were searching among Quarter Horses. With the Quarter Horse, I'd look for some moderation in the most extremely muscled animals. With Arabians, I'd look for a bit more width through the chest and a bit more substance than seen in most all-out endurance animals. (If I weighed 125 pounds instead of 200 plus, I might modify this.) For all their toughness, Arabians, too, are subject to that rule of thumb we mentioned earlier: that 25 percent of a horse's weight is just plenty for it to carry.

I would also look hard at disposition. You have to love the gameness, the sheer energy for which Arabians are noted. But if I were planning to ride up a trail on one, perhaps leading packhorses, I'd look for a relatively mellow disposition.

## The Appaloosa

Originally developed by the Nez Percé tribe, the Appaloosa is known for its several distinctive spotted coat patterns, its sparse mane and tail, and its toughness. Unlike most tribes, the Nez Percé practiced selective breeding, gelding male horses not up to stud quality, and trading away inferior mares. The quality of the animals was well-known and respected by whites, though that did not prevent the disaster that befell not only Appaloosas, but most Indian ponies during early reservation years, when many thousands were slaughtered.

*An endurance Arabian horse.*

The few Appaloosas that survived formed the nucleus for the revival of the breed that began when the registry was formed in the late 1930s, the breed eventually growing to be one of this country's most populous. Much crossbreeding with Quarter Horses, Arabians, and Thoroughbreds was done over the years. Certainly the breed's credentials on the trail are unparalleled, since it was on Appaloosas that Chief Joseph and his tribe made their magnificent, but ultimately tragic, forced march from central Idaho, east through Yellowstone Park and north, nearly to the Canadian border. Interestingly, I am told that a certain percentage of early Appaloosas had a distinctive gait, called by whites who sought it, the "Indian shuffle." This smooth running walk is still found in a few representatives of the breed and has spawned a registry called the Walkaloosa, a cross between the Appaloosas and gaited breeds. The Appaloosa Horse Club itself has discouraged gaitedness in the breed, so remaining "Indian shuffle" genetics are uncommon in modern Appaloosas.

# 4

## The Gaited Breeds

*Upon an amblere esily she sat.*
—Chaucer's Wife of Bath, *The Canterbury Tales*

*Old Paint's a good pony, he paces when he can,*
*Goodbye, ol' Paint, I'm leaving Cheyenne.*
—American Folk Song

I've made enough references to gaited horses thus far in this book that it seems logical to rein back for a moment and examine this thing called gaitedness. Then we'll have a look at some additional breeds, ones usually referred to as gaited. In a way this is a misnomer, because all horses have gaits. The three most common are the walk, the trot, and the canter or lope (which when speeded up becomes the gallop). But it doesn't end there. A good portion of equines have what I consider a genetic gift, a gait faster than the walk that retains the four-beat characteristic of the walk, and is thus much smoother under saddle than the trot. Thus gaited has come to mean that a horse has one or more additional "gears" besides the three standard gaits. (In parts of the American South, gaited specifically refers to one particular breed, the American Saddlebred.)

The regular walk, which any horse can perform, is a four-beat gait. Listen to the hoof beats on a hard surface and you'll hear all four beats in fairly even succession, much like four-four time in music. Footfall sequence can be described as left front, right rear, right front, and left rear. Speed the nongaited horse up a notch and it will normally go into a trot, which is a two-beat gait. In the trot, the left front and right rear hit simultaneously. Then comes a moment of suspension (all feet off the ground) followed by the right front and left rear hitting the ground together. The trot, particularly when fast, tends to be rough, because of its vertical movement and the concussion created as two opposing feet hit the ground together.

Those unfamiliar with gaitedness in the genetics of horses sometimes claim that only the walk, trot, and gallop are "natural," that the other gaits are completely man-made. This is incorrect. Gaitedness has been documented from the earliest times in domestic horse history, though as with other saddle horse traits, these desirable gaits have been enhanced by both selective breeding and by training. Sixteen hundred years ago the Romans invaded the British Isles astride their Barb horses, and saw people riding smooth-gaited native ponies. So impressed were these tough soldiers by the ease of riding offered by these gaited animals, that they attempted to make their own horses perform the same gaits. The Romans invented rollers, chains, and cross hobbles in their attempt to duplicate the gaits they saw (thus considerably predating modern big lick trainers in attempting to do with artificial and perhaps cruel implements, what they should have been doing with selective breeding).

In the British Isles, several hardy smooth-gaited ponies—the Galloway, the Hobby, and a breed which survives as the Connemara Pony—had in common a smooth, ambling gait, while in Spain a hardy horse called the jennet, also extinct today, was sought throughout Europe for its smooth gaits. The mother of these gaits is, ironically, the pace, a gait that in itself is not particularly desirable. Like the trot, the pace is a two-beat gait, only now the two feet on one side hit simultaneously, followed by the two feet on the other. A pacing horse tends to rock from side to side. In some animals the gait is as uncomfortable as the roughest trot, while in others the impact of the hooves is considerably softer.

But an interesting thing happens when the pace gets just a bit out of time. The hind foot on one side hits the ground just before the front one on that same side, breaking up the impact. This "broken pace" sort of gait is often called the amble or stepping pace, and it's likely the gait performed by those sought-after British and Spanish ponies. Chaucer, writing in the 1300s, tells us that his character called the Wife of Bath sits on an ambling horse.

Equine historians here must forgive me for such a generalized account, but it's clear that blood from the Spanish jennet kicked into the horses of the Conquistadores. In the New World this was probably the main source of gaitedness in the Paso breeds, in those Indian ponies that exhibited it, and in those early Appaloosas that did the "Indian shuffle." The British gaited breeds probably were the primary source of smooth gaits in the Canadian Pacer and ultimately in the American Saddlebred, the Tennessee Walking Horse, and the occasional single-footing Morgan.

Between the trot and the pace lie a myriad of four-beat variations. The running walk, single-foot, rack, amble, fox trot, stepping pace, paso, tölt, and saddle gait are terms for variations in cadence and footfall, as performed by different gaited breeds. Studying these gaits is an extremely complex endeavor, made more so because the terms themselves do not mean the same thing among all breeds and in all locations across America. For instance, an entire breed has been based on a very specific definition of the single-foot gait, yet to early Montana cowboys (who sought it) the term applied to any smooth, fast, four-beat gait. All of these gaits do have one thing in common, however: they are virtually always faster than the walk and smoother than a trot of the same speed.

But let's go back to England for a moment. It is said that before 1750 in England no person above servant class would ride a horse that trotted. Gaited horses were the norm. So what happened? For that matter, what happened in the American South; in the mountains of South America? What caused the "Indian shuffle" of the early Appaloosa to be lost? Why, here in Montana, when we first began raising a gaited breed in 1980, did the oldest cowboys in the valley know exactly what we were talking about in describing the running walk, while their sons, daughters, and grandkids looked at us as if we were discussing nuclear physics? And why, now, conversely, is gaitedness returning with a vengeance?

In England, several things happened. Thoroughbred racing became fashionable among the upper classes, and that had something to do with the fading of the gaited horse. Fox hunting, too, was growing in popularity, and the Thoroughbred proved adept at jumping fences and hedges. But the bigger factor was the same scenario played out in other parts of the world. Civilization had been advancing faster than the infrastructure was being built. In other words, there was much need for travel and mobility, but the roads were lousy, if existent at all. The gaited horse could cover ground swiftly and comfortably even over torturous terrain, and particularly through the knee-deep mud to which most roads deteriorated in colonial times. Remember, this is an age when people in every segment of society rode horseback, and they did so out of necessity.

But as road building gradually caught up to the needs of civilization, people sought something even more comfortable than the saddle of a gaited horse. They coveted a padded seat, on a buggy with springs. This was luxury. For most people riding became an occasional sport or pastime, and the nuts and bolts of transportation were taken over by wheeled conveyances pulled by horses. Suddenly the gaits of horses became unimportant. As long as the horse moved forward steadily and efficiently, which many could do at the trot, comfort on the animal's back was irrelevant. True, in the British tradition, a servant boy was mounted on the "post" horse of a multihorse team, but he was a servant and was left to cope as best he could. To keep his bottom less bruised, he developed the technique now called "posting."

Similar scenarios played out in the American South, in South America, and later, in the American West. As long as people had much ground to cover, and had to do it horseback, the gaited horse held on. When buggies became practical, it faded. In the American South, gaited genetics formed the basis for the American Saddlebred, the Tennessee Walking Horse, the Missouri Fox Trotter, and many other smaller registries, along with a host of grade, gaited animals. The swift, gaited horse is given much credit for the early success of the Confederate forces, for their ability to relocate and strike more quickly than anticipated by the Union generals.

Out west, the migration to goldfields and homesteads brought all sorts of horseflesh, but gaited animals were well represented. The historian Francis Parkman, writing of his western trip during the 1840s, tells of a dispute between a Frenchman and his Sioux wife, who insists he buy her a "pacing horse" as a present. The mountain man, Andrew Garcia, left his memoirs in a dynamite box. These became a wonderful book named *Tough Trip Through Paradise*. At one point Garcia is tracked by a notorious murderer and fears the man will catch up with him because of the "swift single-footer" the bad man is riding. In the great trail drive book by Andy Addams, *Log of a Cowboy*, single-footing horses are mentioned as those spotted by the foreman, then nabbed for his remuda.

My wife's grandfather frequently traveled from central Montana during the 1880s to the Crow reservation (in the southeast portion of the state) to buy horses, which he would then train over the winter to sell for profit. He made the trip down on rail, bought the previously untouched horses, and trained one over a few days, then herded the rest of them with that newly trained one the 200 miles back to his home ranch. (This was a feat of horsemanship I would give anything to have been able to witness.) Normally he could find a single-footer for himself from among the Indian cayuses.

This prevalence of gaited horses in the Old West surprises many. But if you view old photographs we mentioned earlier, such as those taken by L.A. Huffman of Miles City, Montana—and for that matter, photos from other parts of the west—you see a horse quite similar, if less refined, to individuals in the gaited breeds. They're a bit narrower, higher withered, and less heavily muscled than today's Western horse. They are built more for endurance and smoothness than for arena performance.

That fact seems obvious, of course, since we're talking about an age in which there were no arenas to speak of, and there were certainly no horse trailers with which to transport your horse to a competitive event. If you helped a neighbor brand cattle fifteen miles away, you rode there. In the South, where horse shows were becoming more popular, you worked your horse all week, sometimes behind a plow, then spruced him up and rode him the miles to town to compete in the show. If you went on a mountain hunting trip, the "trailhead" was at your doorstep. You rode from there. The requirements for horses were simply different, and the gaited horse made sense. Nearly all horses, in those days, were trail horses.

Early Hollywood also used gaited horses, because they tended to take the bounce out of the star's ride and make him look better in the saddle. Trigger, Jr. was a registered Tennessee Walking Horse (though certainly not chosen for that reason, since Roy Rogers was an excellent horseman). Gene Autry's Champion and Mr. Ed were also Walkers. When Alan Ladd as Shane, in the movie by the same name, rides to town for the final confrontation, he is riding a slightly pacey, but smooth-gaited, horse.

Today there seems to be a major resurgence in the popularity of gaited breeds. I suspect there are a couple of reasons, the primary one being the subject matter of this book. Trail riding is said to be the fastest growing American equine activity, and it's clear that gaited horses are mushrooming in popularity for this use. That was, after all, the purpose for which they were originally bred. More generally, people are riding for the sheer enjoyment of it, for the joy of capturing that feeling voiced by the character in *Lonesome Dove,* when he talks about how fine it is to "ride a good horse in new country."

Because gaited horse knowledge in many parts of the US was skipped for a couple of generations (and in parts of Europe for a couple of centuries), myths about the animals run rampant. Those old cowboys who told us back in 1980 that they remembered the single-foot, are pretty much gone now. So is my own father-in-law, prime motivator in our seeking a gaited breed, whose blue eyes twinkled when he said, "You have to ride a gaited horse sometime, Dan. It's a whole different world. You'd never get off." So here is a look at some of the myths.

*Myth #1—Gaited horses are not surefooted.*
For the trail horse, this is the most damning accusation of all. I have never heard it voiced by people who have actually used gaited horses in rough country. History, of course, flies directly in the face of this misconception, for gaited horses have ruled in the some of the roughest country in the world. Indeed, such places as Iceland, Peru, and the

muddy pre-road American South, are the very place gaited animals have excelled.

However, any truth that lies behind this oft-voiced complaint can be laid squarely at the feet of people who shoe gaited animals for shows, who attempt to enhance gait or style of gait by weighted or enlarged shoes. The pads and chains of a "big lick" Tennessee Walking Horse make walking even on smooth surfaces problematic. To put an animal shod this way in the mountains would be torturous for the horse, and dangerous for the rider. Even the "light-shod" show walker is often shod with an inch or two of extra toe in front. If you wear size 9 shoes but were required to don size 13s for a walk through rough country, I expect you would stumble.

Lastly, gaited horse riders tend to enjoy the speed of the animals, and often cruise down the trail a bit too fast for their own good. It's unfair to compare the surefootedness of any horse at 3 miles per hour, with that of one going 8 miles per hour. Regardless of the gait, the horse will be less surefooted at the higher speed.

*Myth #2—Gaited horses are not compatible on the trail with nongaited ones.* There is actually some truth in this one, though the fault lies more often with the riders than with the horses. The standing joke around our ranch for many years has been that if an elk hunter who normally goes to the mountains with a particular group buys a horse from us, one of two things will happen. Either his friends will come back the next year for similar horses or, tired of trying to keep up with the first man, the others will kick him out of their group.

Americans tend to be impatient. Gaited horses encourage tooling down the trail, with little compassion for your companion on a non-gaited animal whose horse is pounding the ground in a punishing trot. For this reason, many of the major trail ride centers, those that cater to large, organized rides, offer separate trails and departure times for gaited and nongaited horses. However, most gaited horses can be taught to slow down. Many don't particularly like it, but most can loaf in a dog walk if necessary. That feature is a desirable one, and should be trained into any gaited trail horse.

*Myth #3—Gaited horses can only walk and "gait;" they can't run, and are thus unsuitable for working cattle and performing other tasks that require speed.* This one has no truth whatsoever. Most gaited breeds possess the same canter and gallop of other breeds, and the American ones normally carry some Thoroughbred genes. In shows, most are required to canter. As to cattle, the working horses of many South American gauchos are gaited. I personally have worked cattle on Tennessee Walking Horses for twenty-five years. Because of their endurance muscling, few gaited

*Elmer's Silver, six-gaited, capable of dragging a bull in from the range, trusted to carry a visiting lady. (Elmer must have been concentrating on the camera, because he warned that low-hanging loops like the rope hanging on this saddle were hazardous.)*

horses will accelerate as rapidly as Quarter Horses do, but I've never ridden one on which I could not catch a cow.

I've written in the past of a horse named Silver, one of Elmer's, known to me only from photographs and Elmer's words. "He had every gait in the book, at least six of them." There was no pedigree, of course, but the photographs suggest old time Saddlebred or Walker breeding. Elmer told of the time he brought a bull in from the hill section on the end of his lariat rope. "There was no herding him, because he just wouldn't move. Silver brought him in."

*Myth #4—Gaited horses are primarily suitable for the old and infirm, for those whose physical limitations make them unable to ride trotting breeds.*
This one is often voiced by people who have little experience either with gaited horses, or with the folks who ride them. It is both a compliment and a putdown. It is certainly true that soft gaits make horseback riding appealing to those who have bad backs or other disabilities, and that is a wonderful thing. However, the opposite edge of the state-

*The smooth speed of a gaited horse nearly always invokes a smile, even from riders used to it.*

ment implies that the healthy and young would have no reason to be interested in gaited animals. That's like saying that young, healthy people would have no interest in a car that rode smoothly. Gaited horse enthusiasts come in all ages and conditions, and many are attracted most to the speed of the animals. Put differently, it is not just the smoothness, but the smoothness at a high rate of speed, that riders find so attractive.

Recently I watched a sequence I've seen played out many times before when a rider has his or her first encounter with a gaited horse. The rider in this case was a young Wyoming cowboy, a man who spent much of his workday astride a horse. He radiated competence, so I let him ride Pride, the young stallion pictured earlier in this book. As the horse arched his neck and accelerated into a running walk, a look of surprise came over the cowboy's face, then a broad smile. I could hardly get him off the horse. That is the typical reaction to a first ride: momentary surprise, sometimes a very brief fright at this strange speed that is unaccompanied by the familiar up-and-down movement of a trotting animal. Invariably, this is followed by the big smile.

If I sound high on the gaited breeds, I plead guilty. Gaited horses have worked my cows, carried my children, and taken me over the high passes of the Beartooth Mountains. They have packed my camps to the wilderness and dragged out elk on snow for our winter meat supply. They have nudged newborn calves down the lane on snowy February mornings during calving. In my hands, and in those that worked our land before me, they have dragged irrigation boards, tended sheep, and carried inexperienced visitors from the city. And, although I do not claim that they are the only sort of horse that could do these things, they certainly are the only sort who could do these things with such comfort for the rider. And because I know their capabilities first hand, I give short shrift to those with scant knowledge of them, who expound on their limitations.

That said, the gaited breeds have also suffered from breeding excesses. Some of the horses within these breeds, too, have been funneled toward types of arena performance that do not enhance the traits we are seeking in the complete trail horse. We will touch on some of those problems in the breed descriptions below.

## The American Saddlebred

In *The Last of the Mohicans* James Fenimore Cooper takes time out from the plot to extol the virtues of a wonderful small horse, a tough, gentle animal with a gliding, ground-covering gait. This horse, the Narragansett, bore the name of both a Native American tribe and a bay in Rhode Island, where its type had been isolated and perfected by plantation owners. Cooper talks of the breed with the nostalgia one feels for something both wonderful and lost, and for good reason: these little horses were virtually extinct by the time he was writing this novel, victims of their own success. So desirable had they become as plantation horses, that most had been exported to the sugarcane planters of the West Indies.

Nevertheless, the blood of the Narragansett and that of the Canadian Pacer, later enriched with Morgan and Thoroughbred blood, became the foundation of another great American breed. The Saddlebred, known in some parts of the US as simply "the saddle horse" or "the gaited horse," has always been known for both elegance and utility. Bred mostly in the Kentucky region, these horses fit the demands of a day when one's saddle horse had to work, but with style. Rugged enough to pull buggies and even plows, the early Saddlebred arched its neck and headed for town, or wherever else its owner pointed him. I always think of the word "elegant," when I think of this high-spirited breed.

When I first knew Elmer he had just two remaining geldings, Brownie, the spirited one, and Tommy, the more plebian cousin, heavily built, from a dash of Percheron blood. Both—on a good day, if spurred forward while being reined back—were capable of dipping their hind ends and striking briefly a thrilling rack, a smooth, animated, powerful four-beat gait. In neither horse was this gait natural enough to be sustained, but it was there genetically. I asked Elmer for the source of this gait, and he smiled.

It seems that a wealthy Montana man had once owned a magnificent stallion of a breed called Kentucky Whip, another nickname for the Saddlebred. A poor man, who claimed to have been wronged by the stallion's owner, took his revenge in a particular way. Under a full spring moon, during the middle of the night, the wronged man sneaked his favorite mare into the paddock of the stallion and let him breed her. The result was a gaited filly, later purchased by Elmer, and she eventually became the dam of both Brownie and Tommy.

I have other western Saddlebred memories relayed to me by acquaintances. A friend watched a proud man emerge from the Bob Marshall wilderness with an all-Saddlebred pack outfit, perfectly matched, his saddle horse and all the pack horses sorrels with stockings, that clipped down the trail. My friend said, "They had obviously been there, were back, and were ready to go again."

Another friend, an old-timer with memories from the early twentieth century, told of a man who mowed hay with a pair of Saddlebreds with flaxen manes and tails. Reminding me that mowing machines were ground driven by the revolutions of their wheels, that they worked better if moved along briskly, the man grinned with the memory. "Yah, he could sure cut down some hay with those two horses, racking along just like they were in a parade, their manes and tails flying in the wind."

The American Saddlebred is a fertile breed for a search for the complete trail horse, but, as with all the breeds, some caveats are in order. Only those liking spirit should apply. If an extremely laid-back disposition is your preference, you may have difficulty finding a Saddlebred that suits you. Since these horses are shown in both three-gaited (walk, trot, and canter) classes and five-gaited classes (which add the single-foot and rack) and are usually bred for just one of the two disciplines, one must not assume that all individuals in the breed today are naturally gaited. Some of the breed are extremely refined, so we'd look for good bone and ample feet. As with any breed, sellers who personally use their horses outside the show ring might be more likely to supply the sort of horse we're seeking. If I have a criticism, it is for the extreme show emphasis, with performance too often enhanced by training devices (such as cross hobbles, chains, and weighted shoes) considered by many today to be extremely artificial.

### The Tennessee Walking Horse

Middle Tennessee, like Kentucky, was the breeding ground for another great American equine development. The Tennessee Walking Horse had roots similar to those of the Saddlebred, its gaited genes probably having both Canadian Pacer and Narragansett origins. Perhaps, too, single-footing Spanish ponies such as those described by William Faulkner, brought up from farther south made their contribution. In any case there existed in Tennessee an everyday work animal that paced and, one can assume, broke that pace into an amble or rack.

There were also in those days great families of horses, often named after a particular sire. These were not breeds in the sense we think of them today, with associations and written records. But pedigrees lay in the memories of people who used horses such as the Hals, the Copperbottoms, and the Mountain Slashers, who coveted blood tracing back to great stallions such as Bald Stockings, Earnheart Brooks, John Gray, and McMeen's Traveler. All of these horses were gaited. All could hit some sort of alternative to the trot, and all had legendary endurance.

Thus although the breed as a type is much older (geneticists have analyzed Robert E. Lee's famous horse Traveler as, for all intents and purposes, a Tennessee Walking Horse), modern history of the breed begins with a Standardbred of trotting (not pacing) bloodlines who for some reason refused to trot. Instead he progressed in a peculiar gait, a sort of walking pace. Later, after his failure at the harness-racing track, breeders found that this black horse, named Allan, when bred to the pacing mares of the South produced foals with perhaps the sweetest gait known to man, the running walk. Allan, later designated F-1 (as the foundation sire of the breed), went on to produce Roan Allen F-38, a striking roan with blaze, stockings, and flaxen mane and tail. Roan Allen was said to be able to perform at least six distinct gaits, including the running walk.

By the time the breed association was formed in 1935, the Tennessee Walking Horse had evolved into a medley of Standardbred, Morgan, Saddlebred, and Hambletonian Thoroughbred, with a dash of good southern gaited work stock thrown in. In those early years particularly, it tended to be less refined than the Saddlebred, with much bone. Traits tend to be a short back, a nice sloping shoulder, and high withers. In shows, Walkers are judged on three gaits, the flat walk, the running walk, and the canter. The last of these, the canter, has the same footfall sequence of any canter or lope, but is truly "rocking chair" in nature, high, floating, and comfortable.

The slowest of these, the flat walk, is performed at 4 to 5 miles per hour. Footfall sequence is left front, right rear, right front, and left rear. This is the gait we'll most commonly ask from a Walking Horse when we use him over rough terrain. Although the slowest of the three gaits, you will find that if you are accompanying a Walker while mounted on a nongaited horse, your animal is probably jogging to keep up. Even at this slower speed the Walking Horse is overreaching with his hind legs, that is, his hind feet reach up underneath and descend in front of the track left by the front foot on the same side. In other words, he's taking larger steps than your horse.

We often have guests on the ranch who bring their own horses. I can tell by the tracks in our lane if I'm following a Walker or a non-gaited animal, even if the tracks were left at a slow walk. The Tennessee Walker leaves hoofprints with approximately even spacing between them. The nongaited horse usually leaves two footprints close together, another pair farther on, and so forth. This is because the hind foot of the nongaited horse comes up close behind the front track, but does not pass it, often landing very close to, almost on top of, the hoofprint left by the front foot.

As the flat walk of the Tennessee Walking Horse progresses into the running walk, several things happen. The footfall sequence remains the same, but this overreach increases as does overall speed. It is not un-common for the hind foot to land a full 18 inches forward of the track left by the front on that side. Additionally, the Walker's head nods deeply, evidence of its "working off his back end," as enthusiasts call it. The result is speed, but with uncanny smoothness. Although the horses can walk much faster, particularly as trained for show, this gait is at its very best between 6 and 8 miles per hour. And at this excellent speed, three out of four feet are on the ground (or at least touching down or taking off) at any one time, a great asset for surefootedness.

In good physical condition, a Tennessee Walking Horse can progress at that speed virtually all day. There is a record of a southern mail car-rier with a route of 60 miles, who delivered his mail six days per week, day after day, on the same remarkable Walking Horse mare.

But as is so often the case, perfection, or something very close to it, is not good enough for humans. In spite of an era of tremendous breed growth after World War II, in spite of a series of thrilling shows that pitted two dissimilar black stallions, Midnight Sun and Merry Go Boy in a series of duels for the World Grand Championship, breeders had to tamper with the Tennessee Walking Horse. Perhaps this tampering was caused by envy for the incredible flash of the Saddlebred in Kentucky shows. Perhaps it was simply the bigger is better syndrome, but during the 1950s Walking Horse show folks decided this jewel among gaits, this running walk, was not impressive enough. To make the horse lift its legs higher in front and extend them farther forward, weights and pads were added to its front shoes, and chains to its pasterns.

Even that was not enough. An insidious sort of abuse called "soring" ensued, wherein oil of mustard was applied to the pasterns, causing continual pain, pain that intensified with each descent of the front hoof. Thus the horse reached higher to escape the pain. Although the practice was eventually prohibited by federal law, I cannot say that it has disappeared. As more sophisticated ways of detecting this abuse have evolved, so have more sophisticated methods for soring the horse. Several alternative HIOs (horse industry organization that regulate horse shows) have sprung up to better detect and prevent this abuse, and we can hope for its total elimination.

Of course, none of this should be blamed on the horse itself. Indeed, it is a perverse sort of testimony to the toughness of this remarkable breed that great individuals within it, some of the best breeding stallions, have survived this callous treatment. The public, too, seems insightful on this issue, for the breed has grown rapidly to become America's fourth largest, with trail riding the primary fuel for this growth.

In looking for a complete trail horse among Tennessee Walkers, I would avoid like the plague horses with "big lick" training and experience. First, there is a good chance that the horse was selected for pacing ability rather than for a natural running walk, because a pacier horse is actually easier to train for the extreme gaits than a more natural horse. The pacey horse, when padded, weighted, and chained, often rewards the trainer with the show gait he is looking for. Secondly, the prevailing psychology among many padded horse trainers is that a horse not good enough for the show ring will automatically be suited for the trail. (We spent some time at the beginning of this book questioning whether rejects from any particular performance activity are up to snuff when it comes to meeting our trail horse requirements.) Lastly, horses in this padded, artificial performance arena are often bred for extreme impulsion, the horse rammed up into the bit, then collected. I continually hear of Walking Horses that will not stand still, that will not relax—hyper horses with hard mouths. I suspect training, more than genetics, is the cause.

So again, look for your Walking Horse trail animal from among those who *use* their horses. Field-trial enthusiasts prefer using-type Walkers to follow their pointers and setters, and these hunters can probably point you in the right direction. Look for horses that walk with plain shoes, that show trust of humans around them, that come from stock used as the breed was intended, to carry you far and wide, with smooth good nature, plenty of go, and little in the way of anxiety. Do look, too, for the bone and feet of the great early Walkers, for strong, capable animals. My faith in the breed is obvious; the majority of horses pictured in this book are Tennessee Walking Horses.

## The Missouri Fox Trotter

A great deal of what I've said about the Tennessee Walking Horse applies as well to its cousin, the Missouri Fox Trotter. The Fox Trotter, too, was developed to fill the need for smooth, enduring horse transportation, in this case in the rugged Ozarks. As with the Walker, Saddlebred, Morgan, and Thoroughbred, all made their contribution to the breed with a later influx of Tennessee Walking Horse blood. The breed is to be praised for its refusal to allow action devices among show horses, weighted shoes and chains being prohibited.

The fox trot gait is a broken four-beat gait, comfortable for the rider and swift over backcountry terrain. Just as the stepping pace is a broken lateral gait (and four-beat version of the pace), the fox trot is a broken diagonal gait, in other words, a broken version of the trot. Although the gait gives the impression of "walking in front and trotting in the back," that characterization is not really correct.

Let's back up a moment. A horse that only trots is completely diagonal in gait, its left front and right rear hitting simultaneously. A horse that only paces is completely lateral, its left front and left rear hitting simultaneously. A Tennessee Walking Horse gifted with a running walk that is completely "square" is, in a sense, exactly halfway between lateral and diagonal. As we have said, this horse's hoofbeats sound like perfect four-four time, each beat having the same interval. A Walker (or other breed) doing the stepping pace, the amble, or the rack is, in effect, breaking the pace. You will hear their hoof beats as da-da space da-da. All four-beat gaits break up the two-beat pattern, keep one or more feet on the ground at any one time, and considerably add to the comfort of the rider.

The fox trot leans to the trot side of the spectrum. It is a diagonal gait, a broken trot, in which the front foot touches the ground a split second before the diagonal rear foot. Then there is a pause, then the sound of the opposite two feet hitting separately but in quick succession. Additionally, the Fox Trotter makes things easier on the rider by sliding its rear foot into the area the front foot has just vacated. The result is a smooth, practical gait, averaging in speed just a tad slower than the running walk, again capable of handling great distances in comfort.

The other two gaits of the Fox Trotter are the regular four-beat walk, with overstride as found in the Walker, and a canter that is more like that of the "using" Walker than of the show version. That is, the Fox Trotter, even in shows, is encouraged to canter without the extreme elevation sought by trainers of the Show Walker.

In truth, both of these breeds tend to be multigaited. I have seen Walking Horses perform the fox trot, and I have seen Fox Trotters perform the running walk, and it's no wonder that the Fox Trotter has grown so rapidly in recent years. (The Missouri Fox Trotter website lists more than 76,000 animals registered as of this writing.) Trail riders have much to like in this breed, and we can only hope its association continues to protect and promote it as the wonderful, natural, functional animal that it is.

## The Peruvian Paso

The Peruvian Paso is one of a group of several South American breeds (including the tough Criollo and the Paso Fino, originally from Puerto Rico) that feature smooth gaits and rugged constitutions. Of them, the

Peruvian Paso seems to have found the greatest toehold among gaited horse enthusiasts in the United States. All these breeds are descendants of the horses brought to the New World by the Spanish conquerors. All have gaited genetics probably primarily descended from the Spanish jennet.

The Peruvian Paso is a powerful horse, not quite as tall on the average as the American gaited breeds, but able to carry heavy riders long distances over torturous terrain. The animal's toughness is probably a gift from its Barb and Andalusian ancestors. Its gait is similar in footfall sequence to the running walk, with one interesting difference. When a Walker overreaches, his timing is such that the front foot is lifted a split second before the hind foot on the same side comes forward to overreach the front track.

Young Walkers, tired Walkers, and Walkers moving uphill sometimes forge, the term meaning that the hind foot strikes the back of the front foot before the front foot can get away. The Peruvian Paso also takes long steps in its gait, but the forging problem is handled a different way. The Peruvian flicks his front pastern outward in an arc, accommodating the need of the rear to move into that space. This action is called *termino*. Another characteristic of the Peruvian Paso (and desired in all the South American breeds) is an arrogant, spirited, look-at-me attitude called *brio*. Brio is equine pride personified. Just as the southern gentleman wanted his Saddler or Walker to head down the road with a high, arched neck and proud carriage, the South American wanted a horse with "attitude." This does not mean the animals are not tractable, simply that they are full of life, proud, energetic, and not daunted by the toughest challenge. It is said that in its Paso gait this animal can carry a heavy man 11 miles per hour all day over rough terrain. It is no wonder that Peruvian Pasos have found favor with many American trail riders, a trend that is likely to grow.

As the resurgence of interest in gaited horse continues, many smaller breeds are growing rapidly. The Spotted Saddle Horse, the Rocky Mountain Horse, and the incredibly capable Icelandic Ponies all have their admirers. To my mind this is a healthy horse trend, for it takes us back to the roots of the saddle horse. Transportation over rough ground that is as efficient and comfortable as possible—strong credentials in our search for the complete trail horse.

# PART II

# A HORSEMANSHIP PRIMER—
# A SURVIVAL REVIEW

# 5

## Reviewing the Basics

*Riding: The Art of keeping a horse*
*between you and the ground.*
—Anonymous

The word "primer" normally suggests something that teaches on an elementary level. The experienced horseman, seeing it here, may be tempted to skip this short chapter. But I really wish he or she wouldn't. Rarely do I talk to another horse enthusiast without learning something, and I hope that something is in turn learned from me. Most of this chapter will be devoted to safety and, as such, it may well be the most important portion of this book. Perhaps my take on the subject will jog the memory of the accomplished horseman, remind him or her of safety dictates once followed but now, in one's hurried routine, occasionally forgotten.

For years I assumed a knowledge of basic safety principles in experienced horse people. Lately, I have quit assuming. I have seen experienced people, including instructors and clinicians, commit the most elementary safety violations, and worse, I have seen them do so in front of students. Recently I watched a riding instructor casually flip the reins over a horse's neck, let go of them, and then, grabbing the horn in her left hand and the cantle in her right, clamber on. She had relinquished all control of the horse during an extremely touchy time, the time during mounting when even the best riders are off balance. Further, she was doing this on a horse she had never ridden, a horse that she did not know. The moment she began to mount she was "driving," but without control of steering wheel or brakes.

Let's start with the obvious: horses are big, far stronger than any human, and fully capable of hurting or killing you. Most of us who have spent a lifetime with horses have, more than once, been hurt by them. Insurance companies, which stay solvent only by their expertise at calculating risk, consider interaction with horses to be exceedingly dangerous. It has been said that all such interaction should be geared toward keeping both you and the horse safe, but let's not put the two on equal footing. Politically incorrect as it may sound, you *must* put your own safety, your own survival, first. (Your very existence is the result of humans having done so in the past.)

Since horses are flight animals, potentially dangerous situations exist whenever we restrain them while their instincts signal, "Flee for your life!" When such a powerful animal gears itself to escape, whether from a horse trailer, a corral, or the hand holding its lead rope, sparks can fly and things can break. Like the logger who carefully studies the potential energy of a tree he's about to fell, the horseman stays constantly ready, constantly aware of that potential energy and its likely path in case of a bee sting or some unanticipated spook.

For all their physical prowess, horses are prey animals, endowed with nearly 360-degree vision, and senses of smell and hearing far more acute than those of humans. They feel, and chase with a twitch, the tiniest fly landing anywhere on their bodies. Humans are predator stock, so at the very least we must show horses the common courtesy of honesty and openness. In other words, we do not sneak up on them. We do not slip behind them silently, and we do not whisper.

Since the horse's primary weapons are its hind feet, closely followed by its front feet and its teeth, we do not approach horses from either the front or rear. Intent on petting noses and giving kisses, pet owners too often go directly at horses from the front, invading their space and the blind spot that exists a few feet out from a horse's eyes. Don't do that! Instead, approach a horse from the side, at the shoulder. Touch its shoulder first. Touch firmly, rather than just tickling. Then slide your hand up to its withers, rubbing them, which is a nearly irresistible touch to most horses. Keep your hand there a while. Stroking the face, particularly just under the eyes, can come in time when the horse, at ease now with your presence, bends his neck toward you to "visit." (Do make sure its purpose in bending its head toward you is friendly, that its ears are forward, that it is not attempting to bite.)

Basketball players, playing in the "paint," (under the hoop) are allowed to touch and rest a hand on an opposing player. As long as they do not impede the movement of the other player, this is not considered a foul. Watch them. They make such contact, because their touch will telegraph the direction and timing of the opposing player's next move. Your touch on a horse's shoulder does the same. You can also feel whether the animal is at ease.

Recognizing that the shoulder is the safe zone, horsemen since Xenophon have advocated training the animal to lead from this position. This is still the best and safest way, the juncture of the horse's

*Whitney showing the safest position from which to lead a horse.*

neck and shoulder just to the side of your own shoulder, the lead rope slack, the horse neither pulling back nor charging ahead. Only recently have I seen trainers advocate the horse walking well behind you, one instructor I know classifying anything else as disrespect. The problem with this position is that the horse is behind you where you cannot see him, where you cannot touch him, and where you cannot control him should something go wrong. A spooking horse is likely to jump on top of you.

I do make an exception for trail horses. Since it may be necessary to lead your horse down a narrow trail, the animal should understand that under these circumstances you wish him to stay behind you. A well-trained horse can quickly make this adjustment.

In walking behind a horse, do one of two things. Either give its rear end an extremely wide berth (best if you have any doubt about the friendliness or attitude of the horse) or, with one you trust, do the opposite: Pass very close to its hind legs, your hand on its rump, your voice reminding the animal you are there. Again, your arm will telegraph any trouble. It is the kick launched from several feet away that has the most wallop. Always watch the horse's ears and face for signs of its attitude.

*With a horse you trust, pass close behind with your hand on the horse so that he knows you are there.*

*Even with a trustworthy horse, groom tail off to one side as is being done here.*

Be extremely careful of loose horses in a group, particularly if you are carrying a grain bucket. Your presence *should* overrule the pecking order, but it often does not. If your horse is pastured among others and is relatively easy to catch, lose the grain bucket. Then, remember the admonition of boxing referees just before a match begins (and this applies to all horsemanship): "Protect yourself at all times!" With your voice, a stick, a whip, or anything else useful, keep a dominant horse from launching an attack on your own horse as you halter it and lead it from the field. An attack on a horse you are leading is just as disrespectful as an attack on you, and it can't be tolerated.

Do not "glue" yourself to a horse in any way or any time. This rule applies both on the ground and in the saddle. A simple wrap of the lead rope around your hand can turn into a half hitch with a sudden pull by a frightened horse, and you could be dragged. To turn the lead rope into a more effective handle, double or triple the rope in such a way that you are holding several thicknesses, but with none of it wrapping around your hand.

Avoid loops of all kinds on the saddle. A too-long latigo hanging with its end nearly to the ground is relatively harmless, but if it be-

*For a better grip, as in handling an untrained colt, Steve doubles or triples the rope and puts his hand around the coils. Do not wrap the rope around your hand.*

comes a loop somehow, it becomes extremely dangerous, ready to snare an arm or leg should you suddenly part company with the horse.

The ultimate nightmare, of course, is to be thrown while your foot slips all the way through the stirrup, then being dragged. If this horror should ever happen, try to have the presence of mind to turn over on your belly, a position in which your foot is more likely to come free. More important, prevent this problem in the first place by riding in proper boots with heels, not in sneakers, and in stirrups large enough so that your feet don't stick in them, but small enough so that your foot is unlikely to slip all the way through. Even better, consider adding tapaderos of the sort that prevent any possibility of your foot going through. "Taps" also protect from brush, moisture, and cold out on the trail.

This whole business of being inadvertently tied to a misbehaving horse must be taken with utmost seriousness. So must the Murphy's Law, which reads, "If anything can go wrong, it will go wrong." At the risk of dwelling on clichés, let's add a few more: "Expect the unexpected;" and, from *Hamlet*, "The readiness is all."

All of the above applied to that day long ago when Rockytop Tennessee, the first colt I raised and trained from scratch, spirited and already 16 hands high at three years old, dropped his nose to graze on the lush timothy hayfield while I stood beside him. I had dismounted to look at a fence that needed fixing and was enjoying the fine day, the breeze, and the brief respite from anything that could be properly considered work. But I was not paying attention. Rockytop was furiously munching. Suddenly my right foot, pulled from the rear by a mysterious, unseen force, began to rise. I could not stop it, and I could not for the life of me assimilate what was happening. Up went my right foot until I was hopping on my left, panic building with the gradual realization that my foot was somehow attached to Rockytop's head, that in another second he would panic and begin a headlong flight through the pasture.

Well, I am alive to tell about it, but possibly only because at the last instant whatever had glued me to the horse came loose. The culprit was a coincidence so unlikely that I still have trouble believing it actually happened. I was wearing spurs with relatively small rowels. As Rockytop grazed next to my foot, the rowel of my right spur somehow slipped through the ring on his bit. He'd realized the resistance and had done what horses instinctively do when a strange force holds them: pulled against that force. Had my rowel not come loose at just the right time, this big, powerful, long-necked horse would have dragged me in the worst possible position, my body under all four of his legs. I still shudder at the thought.

The old-timers often quoted the rather unpleasant expression, "It's the gentle ones that kill you." They were referring to two things. First, all horses are fallible. Strike "bombproof," "kidproof," "spookproof," and other such fallacies from your vocabulary. Second, Hamlet's expression, learned through what he perceived as personal failure, that "the readiness is all," tends to get lost when we're working with gentle horses. It is with them that we let down our guard. And when we do, something happens as freaky and unexpected as the bit/spur incident with Rockytop.

We need to expect the unexpected in little ways as well. When tacking up the Western horse, for instance, when front cinch, back cinch,

*When saddling, check that all is well on the right (off) side as well before cinching.*

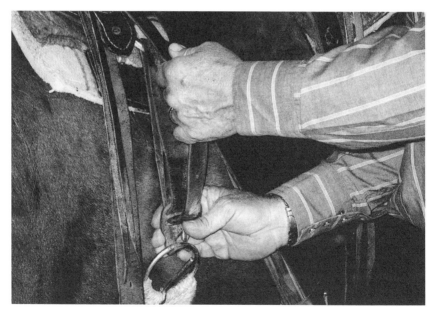

*The main cinch always is fastened first when saddling and unfastened last when unsaddling. The author likes the old-fashioned device called the "tackaberry," resting above his right hand. Note hand under the tackaberry and cinch ring to prevent horse's hair from being caught and pulled.*

and breastcollar all need to be attached, keep in mind the possibility of a spook during the tack-up process. Thus, there's a proper order. Fasten the front cinch first, because it does the holding. Then progress to back cinch and breastcollar. In unsaddling, reverse the process. In other words, the front cinch goes on first and off last. Why? We do not want the saddle only half attached. If you fasten the breastcollar first and something should spook the horse, or a bee should sting it, the result might be a saddle hanging upside down around the animal's neck. Again, most wrecks happen when something is off kilter, but still attached to the horse.

Riding styles and traditions vary widely, but certain safety principles apply to all disciplines. All riders are vulnerable during mounting, particularly as the years add pounds to our physiques, while stealing strength. Whatever method is used, and with whatever sort of saddle, the rider is not fully in control while climbing up. Anything we can do in terms of physical conditioning and simple practice, anything that helps us mount speedily and smoothly, is good. Mounting smartly reduces that vulnerable time. All well-trained horses should stand like rocks during the entire mounting process and not move until signaled to do so. Work toward that end on your own horse. But with other horses, and even with your own, be prepared for some contingency that might move the horse at the worst possible time.

So, it's important the horse be under your control throughout. Key in mounting is to keep the left rein slightly more taut than the right. With your left hand, clasp both reins, all slack removed from the left one, and, if possible, grab a handful of mane as well. Assuming that you're using a Western saddle, grasp the horn with your right hand, insert your left foot into the stirrup, and mount. For strong, well-balanced individuals mounting horses that aren't too tall, this is the best method. Your body is angled forward, and the horse's nose is tilted toward you. If he should take a step, his bulk moves in your direction, a better scenario than having it move away from you.

Tall cowboys on stocky, 14-hand horses make this look as easy for them as stepping into the cabs of their pickup trucks. But add some height to the horse and some weight to the rider, and this approach can be difficult. Just as good, assuming you are tall enough, is to grasp the

*The preferred mounting method if you're physically capable of it, left rein more taut than right, right hand on horn.*

*Here, the right hand reaches across to the right side of the pommel for more leverage than on horn, left hand still grasping mane and reins, the left rein more taut than the right.*

reins and mane with your left hand as stated but to put your right hand on over to the far side of the saddle's pommel (to the right of the horn). Grasping there changes the angle of pull slightly and gives you more leverage.

Less desirable (but most often seen) is to grasp the horn with your left hand and the rear of the saddle (the cantle) with your right and climb on. There are several disadvantages. First, your body is at right angles to the horse, not angled forward ready to go. Second, this method seems to pull the saddle sideways more severely. Last, because your left hand (we're hoping it still holds the reins) is farther back at horn (or withers) position, and your hand is locked around the horn, you really can't move the reins until you're mounted. Watch people mount with this method. Until they're fully seated they can do nothing but speak to their horses, and the horses, having learned this, often take a step or two, or drop their noses to graze.

*This method, left hand on horn and right on pommel, is most often seen, but tends to pull the saddle to the side and doesn't allow control of the reins while mounting, since the left hand holding the reins is locked to the horn.*

Conversely, with the first method, the rider mounting with left hand along the neck grasping the reins, right hand pulling him or her into position from horn or pommel, can check the horse even while mounting. The ability to bring the horse around, to circle him, is central to our next survival topic, the one-rein stop.

Fundamental to most horse training is teaching the horse to yield right and left. I do not mount a colt for its first ride until it yields readily, allowing its head to be brought all the way around to the side. In this position a horse can neither readily run, nor buck well. The one-rein stop should be your built-in, gut-trained reaction to any horse's attempt to run away or to buck you off. When a horse tries to run away you've no doubt already attempted to stop it by the usual pull backwards with both hands, hollering "Whoa!" while you do so. If this has not succeeded, neither will additional pulling. Or, it may work *too* well, causing the horse to rear or even go over backward on you. The one-rein stop means that you pull on one rein so hard that you bring the horse's head gradually all the way to your knee. This is survival, so you must momentarily forget the welfare of the animal's mouth. Remember, too, that you must give slack with the other rein for this technique to be effective.

Practice this gently with your trained horse. Say "whoa" and bring its neck around. A horse that won't let you do this is probably not safe to ride. Do remember, both in practice and in emergency, to give slack the instant your horse stops or otherwise does the right thing. Be ready, though. The panicked horse may stop running or bucking when his head is pulled around, but resume when given slack, so be prepared to repeat the process if necessary.

Of course, the one-rein stop is only feasible if you are ready for it. You will notice that I refer to "light rein" often in this book, that I don't use the currently in vogue "loose rein." Ideal rein tension for the Western horse is for the reins to be slack enough so that the horse moves its head freely right up to the end of that natural, telescoping movement made by a horse's neck as it walks along. At that farthest extension, I like to see the horse just nudge the limits allowed by the reins. In other words, the horse is not impeded at all, but there is also no excessive slack.

But I see many instructors today preaching loose rein to the point of what the old timers would call a "belly in the reins." This riding style features reins so slack they make a big, looping belly downwards. This rein position may be just fine for certain arena events and demonstrations, but it is dangerous on the trail. Slack, flopping reins can catch on brush. More important, when a bear appears directly in front of you on the trail, your horse *will* spook. How quickly can you effect the one-rein stop when you have a yard of extra rein to reel in? The horse has at least one free, unimpeded jump on you before you can exert control of any kind.

Always watch transitions with any horse, and be ready. Horses are creatures of habit. For the most part they dislike and distrust anything new. Furthermore, their mindset is easily changed by an obstacle or difference in terrain. You might be ambling casually along, come to a small ditch, and decide to let the horse jump it. But be ready. That moment of airborne freedom might feel awfully good to the horse, and you may well get a couple more stiff jumps or crowhops when he comes down on the other side of the ditch.

Watch particularly the transition of a new horse from trainer or former owner to you as the new rider. Always go back a few steps. Let's say you've ridden the horse on the farm of its previous owner, watched its trainer or owner ride, and determined the animal to be at a certain stage of progress. Don't take the horse home and start right in at that stage. The animal is likely to be a bit upset at its change of surroundings. Since nearly all horses will occasionally test their riders, this, from the horse's point of view, is probably an opportune time to see whether you enforce your cues as firmly as its former rider. So ride the horse first in a safe corral or arena, no matter how experienced he or she is. Get your signals and cues straight. Then, gradually move toward the level of performance to which the horse has been trained.

Before mounting any horse that is the slightest bit new to you (or perhaps *any* horse), move it around a bit after saddling. Longe it a little, or at least take its left rein and turn it in a couple of tight 360s, then do the same to the right. The purpose isn't to wear down the horse, but to remind it you are in charge while you inspect the way the saddle is riding. This is the time to spot any stiffness or any of what the cowboys call "a hump under the saddle."

Since few horse owners today have the luxury of being able to mount their horses at the stable and immediately hit the trail, trailering has become a way of life. Particularly with small trailers, it's better to train your horse to load by walking into the trailer ahead of you. With many two-horse trailers, this is a must. You just don't want to be trapped in a dead-end space, locked between steel in front of you and 1,000 pounds of horse behind. Training the horse to enter the trailer alone is easily done by the long lead rope favored by "natural" horsemanship, and by other methods of driving the horse in front of you.

In large trailers the only practical way of loading may involve leading the horse aboard, but make sure you have an escape route in front. During unloading from a large trailer, many riders allow the horse to turn around. If you do that, make sure you're either on one end of the horse or the other. I watched a friend break several ribs by being casual and distracted, his body passing along the side of the trailer just as his

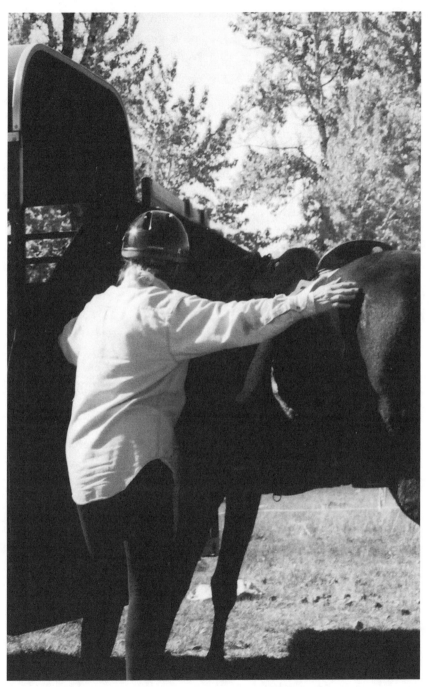

*Whenever possible, send your horse into the trailer rather than leading him in.*

large mare turned around, slamming him into the trailer wall with her chest. To avoid this, use a long lead rope, get completely behind the horse, then cue him to lead around. You'll be out of harm's way as he turns around.

Far better, in my opinion, is to train the horse to back out, even if it's a large trailer. The horse that backs on command from the ground can be readily taught, and the exit is certainly safer.

The idea is not to fear but to respect, to gradually gain a feel for, an understanding of horses. Their body language, the position of their ears, the very looks on their faces (yes, horses *do* show expressions on their faces) usually telegraph behavior to come. As experience with horses grows, these things become more readable. Meanwhile, safety procedures must become as automatic as the clicking of the safety belt has become to most Americans when they sit down in an automobile.

## A Safety Checklist

1. Do not apply such words as "bombproof," "foolproof," or "child-proof," to any horse.
2. Approach horses from the shoulder, not from directly in front. Always let them know you are there. When passing behind stay out of kick range or, with a horse you know and trust, stay very close with one hand on the horse's rump.
3. The safest position from which to lead a horse is with your shoulder approximately at the juncture of his neck and shoulder.
4. Both from the ground and in the saddle passionately avoid anything that "glues" you to the horse. Do not wrap the lead rope around your hand. When leading two horses, unless one is extremely dominant it is often safer to lead both with one hand, leaving your other hand free for balance and for opening gates.
5. When helping another person work on a horse (i.e. grooming, vaccinating) both of you should work on the same side of the horse. Horses are always more comfortable if they do not feel trapped.

6. Dress appropriately; choose clothing that matches climate and terrain, erring in the direction of greater protection; wear boots with enough heel to guard against a foot sliding completely through the stirrup. As further protection (also from cold and wet conditions), install tapaderos that absolutely prevent a foot from going all the way through. Should you ever be dragged by one foot caught in a stirrup, turning over on your belly will increase chances your foot will come loose.

7. When saddling, fasten the main cinch first (before back cinch, breastcollar, or crupper), and when unsaddling, unfasten the main cinch last.

8. Avoid loops of all kinds hanging off the saddle. A too-long latigo hanging down is not a problem unless you make it into a loop, which could trap a limb and fasten you to the horse during a mishap.

9. Always control the reins while mounting. If you ride with a Western saddle (or other high-pommeled type) mount with left hand on the neck holding the reins (the left rein more taut than the right), the right hand on the horn or pommel.

10. The one-rein stop, pulling the horse around to one side, is the basic escape technique should the animal try to run or buck. (However, it works only in horses well trained enough to yield to direct rein pressure, and it is not foolproof.) On the trail, ride with a light rein, not a "belly" in the reins—too much slack can be dangerous.

11. Trailering is safer if the horse is taught to load in front of you and to unload by backing out, rather than by turning around in the trailer.

12. Improving your own physical conditioning helps safeguard against accidents. Leg strength is crucial to ability to stay mounted.

13. When going uphill, lean forward. When going downhill, stay erect or lean slightly forward (not backward).

14. It is usually better to go straight up or down short, steep slopes such as ditch banks, rather than slanting up or down diagonally.

15. If you must turn around on a narrow trail, turn the horse toward the edge (or more dangerous side).

# PART III

## TRAINING FOR THE TRAIL—AN OVERVIEW

# 6

## Approaching the Task

*Behold, we put bits in the horses' mouths, that they may obey us; and we turn about their whole body.*
—James 3:3

Writing about training horses can be rather intimidating. From Xenophon to Tom Dorrance, from classical dressage to reining, the subject itself is vast, and so is the range of writers who have tackled it. From ancient times until now, training horses has been fascinating for many. As shown by the quotation above, even St. James, in Biblical times, held beliefs about horse training. But never has interest been more acute than it is today.

Across the land, training arenas entertain weekend clinics to which horse owners flock for greater insight into the mind of the horse, or for a technique to solve the latest glitch in a horse's behavior. Videos of training gurus fast-forward off shelves and into the libraries of knowledge-hungry equestrians. Equipment and jargon go with each training method, proponents talking proper code to brothers of the faith. "Yes, I've got him hooking on," says one of them, and the other asks whether her friend is using the "carrot stick."

There is much good in this. Horse owners today are a conscientious lot for the most part, anxious to do the right thing and avoid the wrong thing, sensitive to the well-being of the animal, gravitating toward gentle methods. Their interest spawns research into equine behavior by scholars at universities, and stimulates marketing of many useful products. "Horse-clinic junkies" (as a friend describes herself) assemble much useful information that hopefully translates into improved relationships with their horses.

There is a downside to modern attitudes about horse training, however. One unfortunate trend is the consignment of horse training to the mysterious, the metaphysical, the nearly unattainable. The movie *The Horse Whisperer* did much to jump-start that trend. After release of this tremendously popular film, the news media was loaded with stories of various "whisperers," all of whom, we were told, practiced methods vastly superior to those of the past.

A common release was old footage of cowboys roping and snubbing a colt to a post, handling it roughly, contrasted with footage of the whisperer quietly working his horse in a round pen. The message, often from a narrator who knew little about the subject, was that horse training in the past was categorically bad, while that of this modern trainer was gentle and good. What was missed is that while rough training occurred in the past (and still does today), so did sensitive methods. Horse training is an accumulation of knowledge and methods over many centuries. Among our forefathers (who relied on horses for their survival) there were many practitioners of horsemanship on a level we should study and emulate, not condemn with scant knowledge.

Some scholars believe that the term "horse whisperer" meant something in the past that was quite different from its connotation today. Several prominent horse trainers in England and America made it their business to straighten out seemingly impossible "outlaws" that had injured and even killed their handlers. Such men insisted on working in private, often in walled stalls, and refused to discuss or share their methods. The secrecy of their approach gave way to the term: people whispered and speculated about their methods. The term had nothing to do with whispering to horses.

But perhaps the most unfortunate side effect of today's fascination with horse training is its removal to the realm of the strange, the mysterious, the unexplainable, the stuff of experts only, nearly impossible for ordinary people to achieve. If these things were true, our civilization would not have survived. Most horse owners today use their animals for weekend recreation. The horsemen of the past used a saddle horse (or work team) to take the children safely to school, to farm the fields, to deliver milk up the urban alley, to ride into battle, to move belongings a thousand miles west, to take a herd of cattle a thousand miles north. This could not have been accomplished without superbly trained horses. And this training was accomplished by *ordinary* people.

So we've come full circle. In the past the cowboy or the mountain man or the farmer would eyeball a colt in March, think he'd need that animal soon, and say, "Well, I'd better get him broke." It was no big deal. Today, the horse jigs a little on the trail and its rider says, "I'd better take him to a clinic or two, buy some videos, and get some professional help." In some cases all the horse needs is *more riding*! I'm not knocking clinics or videotapes or professional trainers. They're wonderful educational tools. But a first-rate clinician once told me that, while it was nice people gave him credit for the tremendous progress students made with their horses over a brief weekend, much of that progress actually came because they spent more time with their horses during his weekend clinic than they normally would have in several months.

I recall a sunny spring day during which my father-in-law Elmer stood leaning on a pole corral, squinting down our lane toward Butcher Creek. He was watching a rider and mare. The mare, fat and sassy with spring grass, jigged along, crowhopped a couple of times, and attempted to turn back toward the barn. Her frustrated rider cursed and yelled. Elmer pushed his hat back and said, "The trouble with most horses nowadays is they're just not *used* enough."

Elmer had hit upon the greatest difference between life with horses a century ago, and life with them for most riders today. Elmer had lived his life with "using horses," horses with daily work to do. During irrigation season he rode in rubber boots, avoiding the Jeep because of the ruts it would make in the flooded fields. Twice daily, his horse took him on inspection tours through those wet fields, looking for dry spots that needed attention, Elmer riding with reins in one hand and his irrigation shovel in the other.

After each inspection he used his horse to help him change the canvas dam that stopped the water and flooded it over the bank of the ditch onto the field. First, the 20-foot long soaked canvas was pulled from the ditch, rolled up, and flopped onto Brownie's back behind the saddle. No flinch came from the horse when the cold, wet tarp slapped against his body because all this was old hat to him.

Then Elmer carefully stacked the boards that leaned against the heavy pole, used as backing for the dam. He circled the load with three half hitches, and put a fourth around the long pole in such a way that all knots would tighten when the load was pulled. Finally, he'd take up an extra notch on the cinch latigo (he did not use a breastcollar), and warn you to remember that extra notch and release it after the pull for the comfort of the horse. Then he'd mount and dally the rope around his horn. Brownie would lower his head and lean into the load, skidding the several hundred pounds perhaps a hundred yards down the ditch bank to the point of the next "set." This twice-daily routine during irrigation season was just one of a host of tasks Elmer performed on horseback.

Brownie was no cold-blooded work type. He was a classy, arched-neck, spirited horse of what Elmer called "Kentucky Whip" (Saddlebred) lineage, mixed with Western grade stock. I often wondered just what Brownie would have been in the hands of a lesser horseman than Elmer or someone who used him every third weekend and let him stand looking over a fence the rest of the time.

The point is that today there is an invaluable body of training information and assistance available to us all. The flip side is that today we really *need* it, because, in most cases, we don't use our horses the way Elmer did. So we begin this section on training for the trail with this admonition: *Use* your horse! *Ride* your horse! It's amazing how the horse that is in constant use gradually learns things from you (and you from him) without your being aware of teaching them.

There will be no attempt here to write a comprehensive training manual or a set of instructions for starting a colt under saddle, though I'll outline ways I sometimes approach that task. Many such books (and videos and clinics) exist, some good, some not so good. What are more rare, unfortunately, are readily available teachers who have worked with horses and lived with them, not in arena spotlights, but in their daily lives. What I *will* try to do is show something about my approach to the business of training, then concentrate on training tips that directly relate to the trail horse, the horse that must take you safely cross-country on varied and sometimes treacherous terrain.

Training horses is complex, yet simple; mysterious, yet explainable; humbling, yet rewarding. When you embark on it, you're in for the duration, because the learning will be life long. But training horses, in my estimation, has much more to do with behaviorist psychology, often best employed by horsemen who may scarcely have heard of the term, than it does to extrasensory communication, religious incantation, voodoo, or (dare I say it?) whispering. Training horses is primarily instilling desirable habits into an extremely habitual animal while not instilling undesirable ones. It's primarily a matter of positive and negative reinforcement, the negative used sparingly and within seconds of any infraction. These techniques have been known through the ages. The best horsemanship continues to emphasize them, while asking us to pay special attention to the *nature* of the horse, and, whenever possible, to see things from the horse's point of view.

Horses are marvelous, extraordinarily sensitive animals. Their senses are extremely acute. You may think a response from a horse came without communication, but the animal's superior senses have probably picked up a signal you do not know you sent. For instance, we're told that our perspiration smells different when we're frightened than when we're simply overheated. A horse can easily differentiate, and its response to you may well reflect that knowledge.

Training and education are not the same thing, and this is true in humans as well. Both involve learning, but training stresses acquisition of these desirable habits, these ingrained reactions that allow acting without thinking. The policeman, the emergency room nurse, and the Marine are trained to respond in certain ways. Although these responses become so automatic they are sometimes called instinct, that is a misuse of the term. Instinct means a response without the necessity of any sort of learning.

The policeman, the nurse, and the Marine have education as well as training. So does the horse. But training comes first in making the animal a safe, willing partner on the trail. There comes a time in the life of a well-trained horse whose leader is a sensitive rider, that the pair cross over into the domain of education, a state of mutual simpatico, a joy on the part of *both* horse and rider. But basic training must come first.

Deeply instilled, desirable habits, allow a horse—or a human—to act without thinking, which is necessary when action must be immediate, decisive, and safe. Psychologists tell us that the hardest habits to extinguish are ones reinforced intermittently with a random schedule. Thus the slot machine pays (or reinforces) frequently and randomly, and trains humans to continue inserting coins. Similarly, if you use grain to catch your horse every time you need him, and then quit doing so abruptly, the desirable habit of coming to the gate will stop relatively easily. However, if you use grain occasionally and on a random schedule, the good habit will hold on more stubbornly.

The reason a well-trained old horse is almost always more reliable than a well-trained young horse is that the older one has simply had more repetitions in his acquisition of desirable habits. Its habits can be thought of as more deeply ingrained. The good habit in a well-trained horse of walking quietly past a new and potentially frightening obstacle controls his instinct to flee. The young, green horse may test its rider by trying to turn around and head for the barn. The old, well-trained horse may only make a slight move in that direction, one that requires just a touch of the rein and tightening of the leg to counteract. But the rider without the knowledge or ability to do even that may successfully untrain (allow to become extinguished) the desirable habits of even this older, well-trained horse.

Careless treatment, incomprehensible signals, and lack of will among human handlers can all extinguish desirable habits meticulously ingrained by careful training. Thus the "owner problem" trainers constantly mention: it's often easier to train the horse than to train the owner. Or, in the western jargon of my father-in-law, "It takes six or seven years to really break a horse, but any fool can ruin one in fifteen minutes." By "break" Elmer meant train or even school, which brings up another point. Political correctness has invaded the world of horse training. The old-timer said a horse must know that you are boss. The current, politically correct word is "alpha." The meaning is identical. (I personally do not use either, preferring "leader," which *does* mean something a bit different.)

Nowhere is the Ecclesiastes line that "there is nothing new under the sun" more true than it is in horse training. This is because horse training operates with only a few principles, but with a myriad of methods. Methods change and come into and out of favor. But the principles (and the horse) do not change. Most trainers today can read Xenophon's *The Art of Horsemanship*, written twenty-three centuries ago, and find little with which they disagree. (An exception is the conformation advocated by the writer to provide comfort for the bareback rider in a day before saddles.)

An example of a principle that has not changed is that of pressure and release. Nearly all good horse training is based on it. Pressure is applied to get a response from a horse. Hopefully the pressure used is as light as it possibly can be to elicit the desired response. When the response occurs, pressure is immediately released. A horse is directed to back, and, if you notice—whether from ground or saddle, no matter what school of training is being advocated—some sort of pressure is applied to the horse, whether by halter, bit, stick, body language, voice, or lead rope. After even one step to the rear (or with a beginner, the suggestion of a step) pressure is released. The pressure leads or directs. The release rewards.

All good horse trainers from ancient times have used pressure and release. Another principle, closely allied, is that of making it easy for the horse to do the desirable thing, but more difficult to do the undesirable thing. Put another way, the training situation is comfortable for the horse when it does the right thing, uncomfortable when it does the wrong thing. Xenophon outlined this principle, yet I recently saw a famous modern trainer credited for having developed it. Beware of the hype!

Psychologists use the term "shaping" for gradually edging a trainee in the direction of desired behavior by positive and (less desirable, but sometimes necessary) negative reinforcement. You've probably heard the story of the psychology class annoyed by its professor's constant pacing as he lectured at the front of the classroom. They decided to "shape" the professor to stand in one place toward the exit door while giving his lectures. This was accomplished quite simply. As the professor paced to his left toward the door the students became more attentive, took notes, and laughed at his jokes. When he lectured from other areas they tuned out, let their minds (and eyes) wander, sighed, and generally acted less interested. This was done subtly by students who, one suspects, were drama majors. Soon the professor was delivering his lectures from the desired spot by the door, the place that garnered him the most positive reinforcement. He was never aware that he had been "shaped."

Notice the word "art" in the title of Xenophon's ancient work. Good horse training is never cut-and-dried, never mechanical, never identical in the horse you train today with the one you trained last spring, and we don't want to make it sound that way. It is amazing how many of today's would-be horsemen view horses in the same way they view four-wheelers or computers, machines with buttons you should be able to punch with nearly foolproof results. Unfortunately, some modern trainers imply virtually the same thing by insisting that every horse be approached identically.

Yes, horsemanship is art, but before you can compose music, you must know the theory, the notes, the scale. Before you can paint impressionistic portraits you must know the basics, the tools, the techniques of representative art. So, as we said regarding crossing over that line between training and education, horsemanship can eventually become art for you. Train with firm sensitivity, with clear, intelligent signals, and you'll eventually know the art. Now, however, we'll emphasize the safe and the practical for which psychology applies. Watch practitioners of virtually every method now touted as the proper way to start a colt, and you'll see applied behavioral psychology at work.

If pressed, I would classify my training orientation as eclectic. There is much to be learned not only from the various masters, but also from the old man next door, who talks of training work teams for logging back when he was young. A broad, open-minded approach fits our concern with the trail horse, because we are asking the animal to be broad as well, to handle a spectrum of eventualities on the trail. And, ideally, this training begins when the horse is very young.

## Beginnings

In the selection section of this book we mentioned choosing future trail horses from stock that is confined little during these early, formative years. The stall-bred horse, the horse raised only in a small, smooth paddock, simply has less exposure to the spooks of this world and will thus take more time to overcome them. The colt raised in the open, with creeks to cross and hills to climb, also learns how to handle itself, learns to watch where he puts his feet, and begins developing the muscles needed to carry a rider over rough country later in life.

It is not likely that you will have witnessed the birth and initial hours of your future trail horse. Even if you own the mare, you're likely to miss the birth itself, because the horse is one of the few mammals that can actually hold up labor for a while if she's uncomfortable with your presence. Determined to be in on the birth, you put your cot by the mare's stall, but doze off for an instant, and the foal is next to its mother when you awaken. It's a common occurrence.

But if you're lucky enough to be involved in your foal's first few hours, training your future trail horse should begin then. The technique of early desensitization called "imprinting" was popularized by Dr. Robert Miller, the well-known veterinarian. It consists of rubbing the foal, picking up its feet, satiating it with human contact, all within the first few hours of life. Much literature and several videos are available to help you learn these techniques.

I do have a caution, however. If you are actually present at birth, do let the foal bond with its mother *first*. We do, after all, want this animal to be a horse, not a human. Some owners rush in so quickly that the mare stands up prematurely and breaks the umbilical cord. It's best to leave the cord attached as long as possible, because through it the mare is pumping rich, oxygenated blood. Similarly, give the foal some time to get on its feet and nurse. Don't watch its early, unsuccessful attempts and conclude it must have your help. Actually my best advice if you've witnessed the birth is to make certain the foal's nostrils are free of the sac and that it's breathing. Then, check to see that it's positioned in a way safe for the mare, that she's unlikely to step on it in while rising, and make sure the mare has seen and sniffed her offspring. Then go to the house and make yourself a pot of coffee and a big breakfast!

If it's not breakfast time, still take a break. Leave them alone for just a bit! I've had many new foal owners tell me that the foal was weak at birth and had to be helped to nurse. I've asked at what point they've helped and learned they concluded that, since the foal had not risen to nurse within half an hour, it obviously required human help. Give them some time! The spills and missteps are part of education, part of development, part of life for us all.

The term "imprinting" originated in the biological world, primarily regarding birds. It refers to a certain phenomenon, a sudden "hooking on" between infant birds and their mother, which causes the birds to follow her anywhere. Scientists discovered that they could step in with an artificial object, a substitute for the mother, at just the right time, and the baby birds would imprint on that object, following the object instead of the mother.

While I respect and use the techniques, now termed imprinting, with foals, I've always felt these efforts were misnamed. We do not want to substitute ourselves for the foal's mother, to replace her in that role. What we are doing is desensitizing, making the foal comfortable with our presence, our touch, our smell, and the sounds of our voices. We rub the foal all over, stroke its ears, and pick up each foot. When it is just a little older, we put on a halter, but are very careful not to pull on its head. A soft, cotton rope around its rump and threaded back up

*The first step in imprinting a foal is to simply cradle it in your arms until it becomes calm.*

*Stroking the ears of a foal seems to prevent sensitivity in this area later in life.*

through the halter ring allows any gentle pulling to be distributed behind, where it won't hurt or endanger the neck or head.

This early training with a rump rope can have dividends later. After
all, we'll be teaching impulsion, going forward, as the very basis of use-
fulness to human beings. Several months ago a friend called me, somewhat frustrated. His gelding Blaze refused to load. Seven years old and a
veteran of many trailer rides, the horse had been loaded into a smaller
trailer several days earlier and had bumped his head. Horses have wonderful memories. Blaze had transferred the pain he felt upon jumping
into one trailer to this other larger trailer, and he steadfastly refused to
get hurt again.

I had raised Blaze here on the ranch, and I was quite certain that I
had used a rump rope on him sometime during his infancy. When I arrived to help I saw a very resistant horse, sweating, eyes showing white,
legs braced. I gently placed a large lariat loop around Blaze's hindquarters, and he stepped briskly into the trailer. Interestingly, his fear de-
creased at the touch of the rope. It was familiar to him. It seemed to
represent not a tool of punishment, but a touch of security. He had re-

*Teaching the foal to lead with a soft cotton rump rope.*

called that touch over all the intervening years, remembered that coop-eration with it did not get him hurt. That memory overcame the fear of the trailer. This is why we handle our foals.

No, we can't claim that the eventual horse will be superior to one that had not been imprinted. That would be exceedingly difficult to prove. A well-known equine department at a major university once scheduled a summer session on imprinting, then cancelled it, because they realized that as a scientific institution they could not make claims for imprinting that had not been proven. I understand that they've undertaken the massive project of raising several hundred foals in two groups, one imprinted, one not. Comparisons will be made at various ages and, after many years, conclusions drawn. The results should be interesting. Meanwhile, at this writing a similar study at the University of Texas has reported no documentable long-term superiority of horses that were imprinted as foals to a control group that were not. The report I read, however, cautioned that more research was needed and that university scientists were not suggesting people quit imprinting.

Emily and I imprint foals because it makes future tasks simpler. Some of the natural fear is gone. But I do maintain that there comes a time to let the foal be a foal, and that time is, perhaps, after it's a week or two old. Certainly we should continue to handle it from time to time, but we should avoid making it into a little human or into a puppy or a cat.

Notice that I refer to the newborn horse as a foal. I try to avoid call-ing it a "baby." It is not a baby. It is a newborn horse. It has its own identity, its own species, its own dignity. We live in a world where peo-ple make their dogs into little humans (which I've always found a bit demeaning to the animal), and some of these people attempt the same thing with horses. But the species involved are vastly different. The dog and the cat and the human are all predators, all with focused vision. The horse is a prey animal with nearly 360-degree vision. Its first reaction to the unknown is to attempt to flee. It is big and strong, with muscles that dwarf yours or mine. If badly handled it can and will hurt you.

Too many backyard foals become training nightmares. The nuzzling for sweet feed turns into biting. The playful pawing becomes rearing up and striking, and this behavior, dangerous in *any* horse, becomes progressively more so as the young horse grows. The owner, too often doting on his or her angelic "baby," fails to recognize these developments as serious, as threats that can endanger not only humans but the future well-being of the horse as well.

Of course, it does not have to be this way. Owners can nip antisocial behavior in the bud. But even if they're willing to do so, one can argue that the foal is not really ready for serious training, that early discipline, when needed, should be dished out by the dam. Let *her* do the early training, teach the respect for elders (albeit equine ones) that can later transfer to human leaders.

Foals are traditionally weaned at around six months of age, though the recent trend is to wean considerably earlier. We like to complete halter training at weaning time, and handle the foals during worming and vaccinations. We take time to teach the foals to stand while being groomed and rubbed, but we do not dote on them. Since we raise a number of foals, it is rare that one must be alone. We let them form their own society. As in all groups of horses, dominant animals arise in the group, and a pecking order forms, but this is natural and not damaging in any way. When serious saddle training commences, we'll remove our future trail horse from the group and change its focus from interaction with its buddies, to interaction with us.

I like to think of the time from weaning until about two years of age as a sort of latency. Yes, some training can occur. We handle the foals periodically, paying much attention to their feet, preparation for the future farrier. We pick the feet up, hold them, and tap on them with a pebble, simulating the shoeing that is likely to come.

Halter training can be perfected during this time. The rump rope is no longer needed. What works best for me is a gentle version of pressure and release. Instead of pulling hard on the lead rope, I go off at a slight angle and simply take out the slack, then apply a small amount of pressure. Then I wait. It takes patience, but wait, just wait, and eventually the foal will make an adjustment, a slight move that puts slack in the lead rope, rewarding himself for doing the right thing (moving toward you). Praise him. Then move just far enough to establish tension on the rope, and wait again. Most young horses catch on quickly, the total training time probably less than with harsher methods, the reward not only halter training itself, but the beginnings of reward-in-release, the essence of training.

Sometime between weaning and two years of age, the stud colts will likely become geldings. In the past many owners waited until the colt was two or even three before castration, the belief being that allowing some stallion characteristics to develop made for a more attractive and perhaps more physically capable horse. The latter of these is probably incorrect, the former, appearance, probably a matter of taste. In any case, few owners now feel that the risks to both the colt and other horses (and in some cases, to people) can best be avoided by taking care of the stallion problem before it arises. Thus, most colts are now castrated before puberty comes at around two years of age.

Incidentally, there is evidence that castrating a male horse before puberty results in greater height at maturity than if the colt were left a stallion. The flood of testosterone that comes during puberty is related to the capping of growth. Remember the concerns regarding teenage athletes taking steroids? Artificial as well as natural steroids can cap growth. This principle also explains the common scenario of the smaller stallion that "throws big," that produces male foals that mature taller than their sire. Castrating before sexual maturity prevents the concentration of testosterone associated with natural maturity and allows the gelding to continue to grow.

At what age saddle training should commence has been (and probably always will be) controversial. If the physiology of the colt were the only concern, we would delay saddle training until at least three, or perhaps four years of age. It is said that full maturity does not come to the average horse until around age six. Physically, colts are still works in progress until that age, their skeletal structure more prone to damage than it will be at maturity. Unfortunately, economic realities tend to make delayed training unrealistic for many breeders and trainers. Carrying the animal those extra years before it becomes "productive" (able to be shown, raced, sold as a pleasure horse) is expensive.

On the other side of the argument, there are certainly some advantages to earlier training. The two-year-old is not quite so large, not quite so powerful, and, perhaps, not quite so strong willed as he would be if left to himself a couple of years longer. I strongly believe, however,

*The stallion Pride was so well developed at 2½ years old that the author had no qualms about starting him under saddle.*

that any saddle training at two should be done with extreme care, avoiding the jerky things, hard stops and starts, prolonged work in a tight circle (excessive longeing), and all-out galloping. Yes, this flies in the face of many things currently done with young horses, track racing being the first to jump to mind. But, sadly, soundness of the horses late in life is probably not a great concern to those in the racing world. Your partner on the trail, however, is another story. With him or her, you have a personal relationship, years and dollars and emotional attachment invested. Take it easy early, have patience, and you'll add years to your horse's useful life.

We have had good luck starting two-year-olds under saddle without injury using what we call "incremental" training. We train in short, easy stretches of a couple of weeks, with turn-out times in between for the colt to rest and grow. The first increment might involve ground work and a half-dozen light rides in round pen or arena. Then the colt is turned out on pasture for a month or two. The next increment might involve more advanced riding in the arena, the beginnings of neck rein and side-pass, and a few outside rides. Then, again, the colt is turned out.

Is there some slippage using this method, some forgetting, some need for review? Perhaps. But the small amount of extra time spent is worth it to us. Furthermore, among our horses, there seem to be many ready and willing to take up right where they left off at the end of the last session. Indeed, we occasionally swear that a colt has progressed during his time off, has learned and advanced without our help. If that actually occurs it is probably because we've started him in the right direction, and his advancing maturity in itself helps reinforce the earlier lessons.

Besides the obvious physical advantages in this long, slow approach, there are mental pluses. A young horse, like a small child, has a shorter attention span. Perhaps, like a child, the horse needs time off, weekends, holidays, and summer vacations. I confess that in training several of my own horses I've taken this long and slow approach to extremes, stretching to a full year what a professional trainer would do in sixty days or less. Perhaps this would not work with some horses, but it has produced for me several of my very most reliable trail partners. I believe that the lack of mental or physical stress and the advancing maturity of these particular horses has made for a confident outlook, an ease under saddle, that I often do not see in animals that have undergone a more intensive training regimen.

Of course, this approach does not fit in well with a society that demands instant gratification. This drive to see maximum accomplishment in minimum time has not, unfortunately, bypassed the world of horses. Clinics are held in which the teacher does ground work, saddles and rides a previously untouched (or so we're told) young horse in a matter of hours, or even minutes. He or she may tell us not to try this at home, that it would be better to take more time, but the lesson is clear by what the clinician does, and the lesson is an unfortunate one: get to the end result just as quickly as you can. But has training really taken place? Is the colt really "green-broke" when the clinic is over, or is he simply overwhelmed? Were you to work with him on Monday, how would he act?

My father-in-law used to chuckle about the athletic young cowboys hired to demonstrate horses in the sale ring. Slick as snakes, they would vault to the animal's back, spin, stop, slide back onto the rump, dismount over the tail, then slip quickly under the horse's belly, emerging on the other side. "You can see she's gentle as a dog," the announcer would say, "gentle for anyone." And, of course, that same mare, if you bought her, would start her work on the ranch by trying to buck you into the middle of next week. In the sale ring, scared, intimidated by strange sounds and sights and smells, having no time to think about her situation, she had allowed the cowboy his demonstration. But it meant little.

# 7

## Starting a Young Horse Under Saddle

*Remember that the most important*
*gait of the hunter is the halt.*
—William P. Wadsworth

Most readers of this book are likely to purchase their trail-horse prospects already trained, or at least started under saddle. We'll spend most of our time refining and finishing that horse for the trail. Again, I won't attempt still another how-to treatise on starting a colt under saddle, but perhaps I should satisfy any curiosity about my approach. That, in itself, is a bit difficult, because I have no single approach. I can honestly say that when I join a colt in the round pen I have no plan whatsoever. I've laid out a few things I may or may not need: a halter and lead rope, a longe whip perhaps, a long cotton rope, a saddle blanket, and maybe an old, very light saddle that I use for familiarization but which is not fit for riding.

As I've said, in the world of horse training, I distrust absolutes. There is no single, best way to train all colts, because, like humans, they are individuals. Anyone who has taught school or trained dogs or started many horses under saddle, must respect individual learning ability, must know that the same learning methods do not work equally well for all. Thus I distrust blanket statements and any "one size fits all" approach.

And so when I introduce myself to this pretty filly in the round pen, my first effort is really simply getting to know her. Yes, I do use a round pen, while acknowledging that thousands, perhaps millions, of horses have been well trained without one. My father-in-law and his father used any corral compartment handy, usually a square one, because among frontier cattlemen, building a corral was hard work. A round one was useless for cattle, so you built a square corral first, and, meanwhile, there were horses to train! We are told that the Plains Indians, lacking corrals, used whatever natural restraint they could find, a small box canyon, perhaps, in which horses could be trapped. Sometimes they worked them and rode them first in deep snow, or in a couple feet of water. (It is hard for a horse to buck or run effectively in either.)

Unlike some trainers, I don't particularly care for the 60-foot round pen. It always seemed to me that the larger pens just required you to work harder. The first one I built was quite small, perhaps only 35 feet in diameter, and I told my farrier, Ralph, that I probably should have built it larger. "No," he said, "that's just fine. With it small like that, you won't be tempted to stay in it too long. You'll soon get the colt out into the sagebrush where you'll really get him trained."

Today, a pen about 45 feet across suits me just fine. Just what I do in it depends on the filly. If she runs like a scared rabbit the minute I appear, I'll do very little. She would need to learn first that she could coexist with me within that space without being killed and eaten. I would look on the good side—she already knows about impulsion! With as much patience as I could muster, I'd let her run in a circle around me, canceling all other commitments for the next couple of hours. I'd try to make myself small and nonthreatening, looking for signs of fatigue, or at least boredom. Probably, though, I would not let her slow at first, using my body to keep her moving. With this sort of animal, no aid, no extension of my arm such as the whip or flag or the long lead rope popular with "natural" horsemanship is even needed. As she runs left, I extend my right arm to press her and back off to ease up on her. Wild as she is, she is soon responding to me in her own particular fashion.

But what if, when I enter the corral, this other filly, someone's backyard pet, walks over into my personal space, bangs her head against me, and attempts to look into my pockets for treats. This mare, unfortunately, meets a very different Dan. I turn bigger instead of smaller, I'm all elbows and rough edges and guttural language, and she's soon gotten a strong message to back off. With her, my problem is precisely opposite. Because this filly has learned no respect for humans, not even the sort we as humans expect from other humans, since she makes no acknowledgement of my personal space, I must teach that first. Then our aim is for the same general effect—we want the filly to proceed around the corral at our command, to understand impulsion, the first and most fundamental thing we must teach. If a training aid is needed, that's what we'll use, not being afraid to give her a sharp spank to get things going.

It's easy to see from the two above extremes why I eschew formulas for training. Formulas tend to funnel you into a certain sort of behavior, while the two fillies above are demanding opposite treatment. One needs to learn you're not such a bad or threatening being after all, that all you really want her to do at this stage is move in the direction you indicate, then eventually slow up, and even move toward you when you're nice enough to ease off on the pressure. The second filly needs to learn that she must move when told, that you turn quite unfriendly when she does not cooperate, that she likes the friendly Dan better, and that to make Dan friendly she must behave a certain way.

I mention impulsion first, because without it you have nothing. The horse must move when signaled to do so. I avoid the term "asked," because I find it a bit hypocritical. Yes, we start by asking, but using the term implies we give the horse a choice. Ultimately, that is not what the trainer does. The "ask" is followed up, if the horse refuses, by something stronger, and we might just as well get that reality out in the open from the beginning. True, we do what we can to make the desired choice an easy one, and it certainly can initially be framed as a request. But some authority lies behind it.

Most of us have some sort of supervisor in our day jobs. He or she may frequently ask us to do something, but we are quite aware of the authority behind the request. If our supervisor is a dictatorial boss, we probably comply, but we may also be sending out resumes, looking for an alternative. If she's a good boss, we find ourselves only too anxious to comply. The difference is called leadership, which enlists loyalty and creates a sense of cooperation.

In less hectic days I used to enjoy canoeing down a magnificent river we have here in Montana called the Yellowstone, the longest free-flowing (free from dams) river in the lower forty-eight states. It was tempting to sit in my canoe and simply drift with the rather rapid current and watch the scenery go by. But if an obstacle suddenly appeared, a tree branch extending from the bank, I had to scramble to get on course. Why? A canoe, like most boats, only steers well if it is moving through the water, in this case faster than the current. If you're making such headway through the water, a paddle thrust below the surface at just the right angle produces an immediate response—the turn away from the treacherous tree branch. And a saddle horse is of value to us, and is able to perform desired maneuvers and tasks only if it is trained to first move forward. I always combine this directive (whether a leg cue from the saddle or snap of a longe whip from the ground) with a sound, a clucking or kissing or the old-timer's "giddup."

Second, but equally important, the horse must learn to stop. "Teach whoa, whoa, whoa," the old expert wrote me when I expressed concern about a spirited stud colt I was starting. First and foremost, he said, a horse must know when to stop. "Whoa" means not only stop, but to stay stopped. It is the equivalent of "sit and stay" taught to your puppy or the "halt" followed by "at ease" of the Marine platoon sergeant. It is *not* a command to slow down, a fact of which I constantly remind inexperienced riders on the trail. (We use "easy" for that.)

Because of the importance of "whoa," we avoid using any other English word sounding like it. We're used to saying "No!" to our children and our pets, but we excise it from our vocabulary when talking to horses, because distinguishing "no" from "whoa" is a tall order. For a generic "stop what you're doing" command, I use a sharp "quit!"

Now at this point I will bow to the myriad sources you already have available and perhaps to the loyalties to schools of training from which you have already learned. There are many approaches and many tools. Round pen training has been so thoroughly taught to the horse-owning public that it has seemingly become an end in itself. To those who get stuck there, to those who are still spending more time in the round pen with their horses than they are out on trail, my backcountry orientation kicks in—as in that sentence from my farrier while he studied my new round pen—about getting the horse out into the sagebrush where he'd really learn something.

In my memory I can compare two excellent round pen trainers and their work with two respective colts on occasions separated by years. One trainer was a classic whip trainer, using the tool not for punishment (for it rarely if ever touched the animal) but as a signal. The whip's crack created zones of discomfort, such as when the animal's rear end turned toward the trainer. Absence of the whip created zones of relaxation. Desired behavior was thus shaped, and soon a relatively wild colt was facing and walking toward the trainer, allowing the whip to be passed over its body and accepting the halter while relaxing with a sigh.

The second trainer's choice of tools was the halter and the long lead rope favored by many today. The long, loose end of the lead was used instead of the whip. Although the technique was somewhat different, the results were similar. There was certainly no difference in severity, in level of kindness or gentleness. Both trainers used no more pressure than necessary and gave immediate slack when the desired behavior was achieved. Both trainers used their tools of choice with consummate skill, with timing that made their directives to the horse easily

*Impulsion on command underlies all training. This colt needs only the author's extended hand to signal pressure from which he moves.*

understood. Many beginners in the round pen, lacking these skills, inadvertently signal the opposite of what they desire, sometimes hurting the horse in the process.

As we've said, many things work. Beware of the contention that one tool is humane, another cruel. Differences in whips, lead ropes, bosals, spurs, and bits are merely differences of leverage. Tools with more leverage must be used with lighter, more sensitive hands (or feet). It is not the devices, but the manner in which they are used, that determines severity.

I have no quarrel with any particular school of colt starting that is used, as long as it is firm but kind, while being based on sound principles and with the horse's point of view in mind. How do I personally do it? As I've said, I walk into the round pen with objectives in mind but with no pressing timetable for accomplishing them. Yes, the horse must allow catching and haltering, but there's a good chance that has already been accomplished. We'll be teaching impulsion as well as "whoa," and we'll be showing the horse that when it reverses direction it should turn toward me, not away from me. The rear end is the loaded one, the end sometimes shown us in a threatening manner, so turning to face the trainer is fundamental.

Yet, though fundamental, even *that* principle is not absolute. I believe that the horse destined for harness use should not be taught to turn and face the trainer whenever it gets confused and seeks direction. I had quite a tussle with a Belgian-cross gelding that had been round-penned to death. A nervous, touchy horse, Nip turned to face me whenever he was in doubt about what was coming next. He had apparently been taught to drive by simply hooking him next to a steady partner in front of a wagon, and if you could get him that far, you were okay. But he could not even be ground driven, either alone or with a partner. Several times during attempts to ground drive him in harness with another Belgian, this horse turned all the way around to face me, apparently concerned that he was about to be whipped on the rear for the offense he was sure he had committed, that of turning his back on the trainer. Thankfully, my other Belgian, Lefty, was steady enough in each case that I was able to back him through a 180-degree arc around Nip's rear, so that they were again facing the same direction. (I leave to your imagination what sort of a wreck was thus avoided.)

As we've said, we avoid absolutes in this business of horse training. Very possibly other horses could more easily have transferred from round pen training to harness work, where all direction comes from the rear, than Nip was able to do. Nonetheless, a Western trainer whose clients increasingly ask for their horses to be trained for both harness and saddle tells me she has quit asking horses to turn and face her. "I want them to simply stop in place and look at me from the side," she says. What is important is not necessarily the position of the horse's body but that of his mind. His attention must be focused on you in order to learn from you, and for this he must be watching you. But a horse can do this from positions other than facing you, and my friend feels she has that attention when the horse stops broadside to her and looks at her.

I will get to know this filly in the round pen, and she will get to know me. I will be prepared to approach her in ways I've never used before and learn from her, because she is an individual, and if ever my book is closed to further learning as a horse trainer I will quit training. I will introduce myself as her leader and not be ashamed of that role. Yes, that includes domination, but the good, supportive kind, not the tyrannical kind.

I will respect her herd instincts but will not mimic them, and I will not impersonate the dominant mare of a herd with feigned ears laid back (currently in vogue). She is not a wild animal but a domestic one, a horse, not a zebra, and there is much evidence that our domestic animals have within their genes a certain simpatico with humans. She will, by the end of the first session, understand she is to keep her attention on the "dominant Dan," not a dominant mare.

Thus I'm preparing this young horse for things her "natural" background did not include. Nothing in her nature as a horse has prepared her to walk by a frightening object with a rider on her back, to carry a child safely, to pull a cart, to help rope a calf, or run a dressage or reining pattern. All horses are domestic; there are no truly wild ones, only feral ones, returned to wild living conditions. All horses are, by breeding and human selection, products of mankind. This is the reason, not a trainer's impersonation of wild conditions, that they readily accept good human leaders. But the world lying ahead for this young horse is a new one entirely, one for which she needs the leadership and support of a human.

Yes, the filly will be introduced to discipline, but let's remember that discipline is not the same thing as punishment. Punishment is an act of retaliation for an infraction. Discipline is a system, and the word is still used in this way by the academic world. (You ask a professor which discipline he follows, and he says, "economics.") You, too, have accepted discipline. You succeed at your job because of training and education, of accepting consequences both good and bad for your actions.

I know a trainer who likens his first few sessions with a colt to boot camp, although I must note that this trainer has never been through a boot camp. I have been, have survived one of the toughest, and I don't like the analogy. Too many people emerge from boot camps hating their handlers. Hopefully, human intelligence lessens their tendency to generalize that hatred. (They don't forever hate all sergeants—only the particular ones who made them run lap after lap and do push-up after push-up.)

And yet, there is a legitimate analogy here. We're trying to create the perfect trail horse. We will send this animal into dangerous situations, to places where the very lives of humans will rely on him, perhaps onto ledge trails with hundred-foot drop-offs inches away from its hooves. Now, would we be doing a favor to a human civilian if we said, "Look, we must send you into combat, so we'll put you into a Marine uniform, but just skip the training, because it's so tough, all that discipline and hard work, you know?" No, given the mission ahead, the more humane thing would be a system of training and education, of discipline, of true preparation for the demanding world that lay ahead.

In the round pen I will move the horse around, perhaps with a longe whip, perhaps with a flag or merely my arm. I'll teach whoa by backing off and making it easy for her to stop. (If I've raised her, she already has a concept of "whoa," because every time I've stopped while leading her I have said it to her, even when she was a tiny foal.) I will desensitize her to my touch, make it pleasant instead of frightening, scratch her withers, rub her. I will saddle her, maybe during the first session, maybe during the fifth, depending on her nature. Yes, I will punish infractions by a sharp signal, a sharp word, maybe a sharp spank if required, remembering that unless I react within a few seconds the response is useless and harmful.

I will require her to watch me. Sometimes I prefer to work her on a line, other times free, the round pen and my body being her constraints. Always I will remember the most basic precepts, pressure followed by quick release when the desired response is achieved (even by the merest suggestion), making the right thing easy to do, the wrong thing harder.

I carry pressure and release farther than many modern trainers, doing some old-fashioned things that I'm convinced pay dividends down the trail. I tie a soft cotton rope to her pasterns, one at a time, and teach her to lead by each foot. It's really quite easy. Take the slack out and wait. Most colts readily figure out that movement toward you removes the slack. This is the beginning of leading. Take the slack out again. Once she leads by that foot, try another. Your farrier will someday love you for these lessons, and you'll pat yourself on the back as well, when your grown horse sticks her foot through a fence wire and, instead of struggling and tearing herself, she gives to the pressure and waits for help. And, the horse that can be led by each foot will easily adjust to being picketed out by the front foot during that future overnight trip to the mountains.

I also tie up each hind foot in turn with the same cotton rope, using a loop around the base of the neck tied with a bowline (the only safe knot I know of for the purpose, and one every horseman should know). Why do I do this, particularly with a horse I've already taught to give each foot regularly? Let's call it insurance toward the day when something occurs for which I can't train her, perhaps the snout full of porcupine quills, in a mountain clearing far from horse trailers and veterinarians. Taking a foot away may provide the restraint necessary to allow me to pull the quills, and this advance preparation in a safe environment may prevent an explosion of surprise when the restraint is later imposed.

In all cases I will attempt to teach this filly just one thing at a time, being satisfied with our progress if that task is learned. Whenever possible I will quit before either of us is tired or frustrated. I will try very hard to never lose my temper.

*Teaching a colt to lead by each foot not only leads to easy work for the farrier, but reinforces the business of pressure and release. Total time to teach this colt to lead by each pastern in turn, using a soft cotton rope, was about 20 minutes.*

I prefer to teach the elements of guidance by ground driving. Many other approaches work just as well, I'm sure, but ground driving works well for me and seems to accomplish many things. I keep saying that some day I will spring for a bitting rig, but I haven't done it yet. My working saddle has several D-rings through which I can thread the same long lines with which I drive my work team. (Lacking D-rings in the past, I simply threaded them through stirrups adjusted rather short, connecting the stirrups to each other under the horse's belly with a leather strap to keep them from flapping.) Driving begins after the filly is thoroughly accustomed to the saddle and cinch, to the usual slapping of stirrup leathers on each side. By the time I put my good saddle on her, I've normally let her wander around the round pen during several sessions wearing the light, old, "sacrificial" saddle. This gives her some time to train herself to the creaks and slaps of saddle leather.

I start driving by threading the long lines through my saddle's D-rings and attaching them to the side rings on either side of a regular

*Ground driving with long lines, first with halter, then snaffle (shown) is author's preferred method for teaching "whoa," yielding right and left, and backing.*

web halter. For driving I prefer this sort of halter to the rope type, because it does offer these rings for side attachment. A pull on the rein attached in this fashion more clearly tells the filly that she's being asked to bend in that direction. Toward this end—that of making her give easily in each direction—I've already done some training by standing many times on each side of her, bending her head toward me with the lead rope, then immediately releasing when she "reins" toward the pressure.

The filly, already accustomed to facing me and walking toward me, may be initially confused by her trainer's position behind, holding the long lines, but I will use the vocal commands she's already used to, reinforced if necessary by a snap of the whip behind her. Initially the driving may be more like two-rein longeing, circling the round pen, but that's okay. The difference now is that we'll turn and stop her with the reins. At first, quite a bit of pressure may be required, but again that's okay, as long as the pressure is released the instant the response is correct. The objective is to be able to walk quietly behind the animal, guiding it by direct reining, turning in each direction, stopping, and backing. As we've said, earlier work on the ground will have hastened success in driving, but we still won't expect to accomplish all in the first session.

Driving a young horse does many things in addition to teaching direct reining, and that is why I like it. The long lines touch the filly everywhere, get under her tail, slap against the saddle, and occasionally tangle a hind foot. That's just fine. The tolerance so essential for the trail horse is beginning now.

Just when I first ride a young horse is impossible for me to predict, but her accomplishment while being ground driven has much to do with it. After a few driving sessions I switch to the snaffle, first letting her wear it a while before attaching the long lines. Each session she's better, soon graduating from the round pen to a larger corral and arena. When she direct reins smoothly in each direction; when she stops on a dime, rewarded instantly by slack in the reins; when she backs with little pressure, again rewarded; when, after each driving session, she does not mind my standing up in a stirrup on each side of her in turn; when all these things have happened, and she seems willing and at ease, then perhaps it is time to climb aboard. I've had this state occur after just a couple of driving sessions, and I've had it come much, much later.

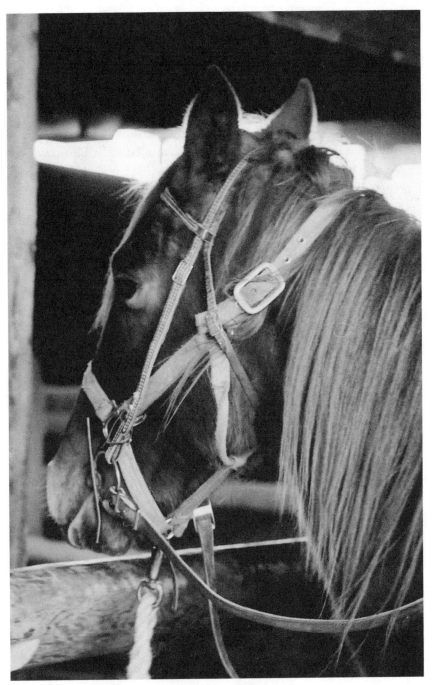

*The author's ranch-built training bit.*

I have much respect for the hackamore tradition, but it does not happen to be mine. Similarly, I have no quarrel with those who ride young horses with rope reins, but I was influenced strongly by a different set of preferences. Elmer, my father-in-law, liked slim leather reins, kept supple with neatsfoot oil. Yes, the filly, for her first ride, needs something a bit stronger (because things *can* happen), and a slightly heavier rein is easier for her to feel on her neck, important because I will begin teaching the neck rein almost immediately. Thus my preferred rein for starting colts is a single, fairly wide, braided leather loop, connected to the snaffle ring on each end.

There is nothing special about the bit I happen to use, except for the way I got it. It is a plain ring snaffle with a vertical bar welded to each side, the ends of the bars smoothed and turned slightly out so as not to gouge the side of the horse's face. The idea of the bars is to distribute a side pull over a larger area than the ring alone would do. Basically this is a full-cheek snaffle, available commercially, but this particular one was made by a neighbor. He was watching over the corral fence as I trained the first colt I ever started from scratch, decades ago. The tall, spirited sorrel gelding was a bigger handful than I knew at the time, and Mike said, "I have a good bit for starting colts. I'll bring it by."

I used the bit, and when I decided Rockytop could graduate to another, I told Mike I should give it back to him. "No, hang onto it a while. You might want to start another colt or two."

"Okay," I said. "Just holler if you need it back." Well, I have started dozens of colts with this bit, and perhaps I should jog Mike's memory, but he has never "hollered," and the bit continues to work extremely well for me, so I stick with it. Much of horse training is this way. Something works well, so you keep doing it, refining it and becoming more skilled at applying it. Although you shouldn't close yourself to other approaches, it seems silly to throw out things that work well because they don't correspond to the latest trend. The horse-training world is much influenced by fad and fashion. The truths, the principles, the things that work well, remain the same.

Somewhere along the line, before I expect the filly to carry me, I will probably teach her to pack. As a rancher, I have genuine work to

*Packing is extremely effective training, teaching the young horse to carry weight and to toler-ate contact of the load with its body. Here a filly carries a sawbuck packsaddle and 100 pounds of stock salt for a training ride that includes a bridge and stream.*

do with horses, including taking salt to the cattle periodically. This involves a brief trek of several miles, a pretty good hill, and a trail through a pine-studded coulee. For training I use a sawbuck (crossbuck) pack-saddle (we'll cover packing techniques later in this book) and nylon panniers, into each of which I load a 50-pound sack of salt. Salt, being dense, rides low in the bags, and is soft enough to be comfortable against the horse's flanks.

I introduce the packsaddle in the round pen first, let the filly get used to its breeching. That's a new wrinkle, because it fits around her rump under the tail. The panniers come next: empty, orange cloth bags that tend to flap as I move the filly around the pen. When all is going well, I load the salt sacks into the bags, and the young horse feels for the first time what it is like to carry weight.

The next step is to saddle a gentle older horse, one used to the task, and pony the filly up to the high hill pasture where the cows are graz-ing. Such a task teaches worlds of useful knowledge for the future trail horse, knowledge that no amount of arena work can simulate. The young horse feels the load, bumps the packs against trees, hears new sounds, and learns to stay on the trail. And, if you are not a rancher with work to do, such as I have, you can approximate it out on the trail with a pack setup and a couple of bags of oats, ponying the colt along on a day ride.

And so, eventually, time for the first ride arrives, and I confess that much preparation as we've done, I usually feel a little tightening in my stomach at this point. So, no doubt, does the filly. Many times I will have stepped up on her in the stirrup while bending her head toward me, doing this on each side, petting her neck all the while. I will have simulated the feel of a boot dragging across her rump by rubbing my hand across her croup behind the saddle. (And, of course, any packing we've done will have accomplished wonders in this direction.) She is at ease with all of this, but actually crossing my leg over to the other side always seems a big step.

But she knows that "whoa" means to stand until allowed to move on, she has come to trust me, and so I mount, swing over, and slide my right foot into the stirrup, keeping her head bent to the left, anticipat-ing that if a fright occurs I will keep her turned toward me. Most often,

A

B

C

*First ride on a colt named Jed. (a) After warm-up, author shortens left rein that he grabs along with shock of mane in his left hand, then grasps horn with right. (b) Aboard, author keeps colt bent left until he relaxes. (c) Relaxation; Jed's life as a trail horse is about to begin.*

nothing happens at all. The horse that does move off has been well trained enough on the ground that the movement is in a tight circle, any tendency to ease rewarded, as always, by a slight slackening on the rein, but for safety purposes, until we're quite sure that there will be no bolt or buck, the circle maintained. If the filly does not move at all, that's okay for this first mounting. I pet her, rock the saddle from side to side, make sure that she knows that my whole body is up there. If she seems willing to walk off, that is also fine, but I keep her in the circle left, practice stopping her, and then, very soon, get off. We have just had an excellent first ride, and I expect no more. She gets unsaddled, curried, and rewarded with a bite of grain.

Successive rides in the round pen simply build on this first one—short, simple, the filly being checked around to one side sternly if she tries to buck or run, rewarded with slack for doing the right thing. Some young horses refuse to move at first, even though they've been well schooled from the ground, your weight feeling so strange to them. (This problem will likely have been averted by our trip to the hills packing salt.) Often turning the horse's head in one direction and cueing hard with your foot on the opposite side will start it moving. Sometimes a tickle behind is required. The timing is crucial. Always, we'll use pressure only to get the desired result, then slack off.

We will leave our filly here, because you probably know the sorts of things that come next. We'll stay in the round pen until we can go safely in each direction, stop well, back, and stand with slack reins while we talk to a visitor over the fence. We'll eventually move to a larger corral or arena, then take our first ride out, preferably with one reliable friend on a gentle, well-trained horse. We will, within the limits of our personal safety parameters, ride much alone, for it is on such rides that we both really learn.

# 8

## The Neck Rein

There is a dimension of starting young horses where perhaps I buck the trend. Had you asked me twenty years ago to name the single element most indicative of the Western-trained horse, or, for that matter, a backcountry horse anywhere, I would have said the neck rein. If you've never known the sweet balance, the sheer joy of a horse that you ride with both reins held lightly *in one hand*, a horse that requires only the slightest movement of that hand in whatever direction you want to go, you've missed something.

Furthermore, backcountry riders of all sorts, past and present, need one hand free. The cowboy needs one hand to swing his lariat rope, while the mountain man (in the day of rifles too long for saddle scabbards) needed an unencumbered hand for his flintlock. The packer must have one hand for the lead rope of his front packhorse, and the trail rider needs a free hand to fend off the hazardous tree branch. In the arena and the horse show, different riding styles prevail, but in rough country and in the world of true using horses, one-handed riding is the norm. In the Alpujarra mountains of Spain I noted cattlemen who rode with just one rein, their horses direct reining in one direction, neck reining in the other, the man's free hand clasped around the long cane they favor over lariat ropes in that part of the world.

I certainly won't quarrel with anyone who takes to the trails riding English. For a recreational ride down a tree-lined trail, there is nothing wrong with a riding style that requires both hands on the reins. But *use* that horse in the backcountry, and the advantages of the neck rein will quickly become apparent.

I take time to point this out, because I fear that fashion today is de-emphasizing the sweetest thing about the Western horse. Everywhere in the West and in Western magazines today you see two-handed riding. A direct-rein approach that would have been reserved for only the first few rides on a green horse in the American West of the past, now prevails into the horse's maturity. Indeed, I watched a rural television cable network on which a trainer in an arena demonstrated the "Western" horse while his daughter rode an English horse. The trainer compared and contrasted the two styles, all the while riding with one rein in each hand, thus ignoring the traditional essence of Western riding.

Understand, now, that in teaching neck reining for the trail, we are not seeking the neck rein of competitive reining, that athletic arena activity growing currently by leaps and bounds. For the trail we do not want a horse that spins 360 degrees at the slightest touch, or that "stops" by sliding its hind feet while it continues to trot with the front ones. We want a horse whose steering is so light and so automatic that we never have to think about it, and we want the horse to require just one light hand on the reins to accomplish this. The good news is that teaching the neck rein is extremely simple. But here's the part that bucks the current tide of fashion: The trail horse can begin learning the neck rein from its very first ride. Furthermore, if you buy a trained horse that does not neck rein, you can begin teaching it regardless of its age.

So let's go back to the filly in the round pen. I have taught her to direct rein, primarily by ground driving. By direct pull (rewarded by release of pressure), first on a halter, then on a snaffle bit, she has learned to turn in the direction I signal. Fine so far. So how do I translate this direct reining to my ultimate goal, an immediate turn whenever she feels the weight of a very light rein lying on her neck? I do not do it with gimmicks, by crossing the reins under her neck, or by special bits and expensive pieces of gear prescribed by a clinician. It is all far too simple for that.

From the very first ride the filly feels three things, not just one, every time I signal a turn. For a left turn she feels the direct pull of the left rein on the left side of her bit (or bosal, or halter). Secondly, she feels the right rein contact the right side of her neck. Lastly, she feels a leg cue on her right side at or in front of the cinch line. (All this is opposite for a right turn, of course.) We make each cue just as crisp as possible, so that she associates them only with turning. Later, we can use this same yielding to the leg to teach the side-pass and other maneuvers, but now we're riding two-handed, the filly primarily turned by the direct rein, but becoming more and more aware of the other two cues, the rein on her neck and the rider's calf and heel pressed into her side. Again, and I can't emphasize this enough, we are not teaching *reining*; we are teaching the *neck rein*. The two are not the same. Reining is a competitive arena sport, very complex and very specialized. Trainers adept at it have an entirely different regimen from the approach I'm advocating here.

By signaling a turn with three cues each time, we gradually train the horse to respond to, first, any two of the three, and eventually, any one of the three. Soon the leg alone or the neck rein alone cause the turn. Since the neck rein is our ultimate goal, we apply light rein to the neck first, then the leg cue, and finally the direct rein as an enforcer if needed. It is amazing how rapidly colts pick up a neck rein when taught this way and when we remember to apply all three cues every time we turn.

During these early two-handed sessions we are applying the direct rein and neck rein very deliberately. There comes a time to change this, however. For the Western horse, two-handed riding is a crutch, and there comes a time to move on. Not long ago someone commented on the neck rein of a black gelding I was starting, and asked what my "secret" was to putting such a nice neck rein on a colt so early in training. I said I did not really have a secret, but that one key was what I did with my right hand. (I most often handle the reins with my left, switching occasionally for relief.) Holding the reins in my left hand, I raised my right hand into view, then very deliberately placed it in my vest pocket. "Your horse won't really be neck reining until *you* are neck reining," I told the bystander.

I went on to explain that there comes a time when, in order to move on, you put the extra hand away and ride the colt with just one. You force yourself to go each way around the arena, to stop, to back, without ever touching the reins with your second hand. The colt cannot

*Early direct-rein riding on Pride with snaffle bit. Two-handed riding should be a brief stage of training for the Western horse, because a free hand is needed for many trail-riding tasks.*

learn to do this unless *you* learn to do it. Cheating a little by putting one or more fingers between the reins is just fine. Many Western riders always do so, and the advantage is that with one hand you can both neck rein and give the colt a little inside (direct) rein that way.

After the clinic mentioned above, a woman told me, "I was sure glad you said it was okay to put one or more fingers between the reins. At the last clinic I attended I was told it was wrong to do so." The "wrong" probably came from show rules in some breed associations that prohibit fingers between the reins. What a pity. A clinician (who advocated two-handed riding well into a colt's maturity) had steered this woman away from an important transition technique, one that allows the colt to still receive some direct rein in the early stages of neck reining.

However, for quite some time we will feel no shame in reverting to two hands whenever the filly needs a refresher, when she balks at a trail obstacle, when she shows some sign of barn souring, or of any problem where enforcement is required. Sometimes she needs a reminder of her earliest training during those first ground drives, and going back to two

*Three ways to hold split reins in one hand. a) provides maximum sensitivity; b) reins coming out of the bottom of your fist has maximum leverage; c) one or more fingers between the reins allows giving the colt that is making a transition to the neck rein a little direct rein along with the neck rein.*

hands will accomplish this. But try the leg cue first. If you've applied it faithfully, the leg cue may be all the enforcement you need.

In the open western country where I'm privileged to live, we can often ride across vast spaces off any trail, through sagebrush flats dotted with small coulees, rock outcroppings, and other obstacles. Steering a colt through such country is a wonderful builder of the neck rein. Usually, sage flats provide many avenues for passage, but you choose them, you don't allow the horse to do so, and you constantly neck rein the animal through this opening or that. Similarly, moving a herd of cows requires constantly riding back and forth behind them, pushing the stragglers. It is wonderful work if you can get it, great for a colt and fine for its rider, as well. I have seen a colt that knew only the plow rein (direct rein) go out on a cattle drive in the morning and come back that evening with a pretty decent neck rein. If you ever have an opportunity to volunteer your help moving cattle, do so; your horse will learn volumes that are difficult—or impossible—to teach in an arena.

*Driving cattle on horseback is one of the best possible situations for teaching the neck rein.*

Beyond that, once out on the trail we continue to teach the young horse to neck rein by constant repetition. Even while following another horse's tail up a winding tree-lined trail, where our horse would know to follow around the bends without any guidance from us, we still gently neck rein at each turn of the trail.

I once took a couple from Florida on a mountain ride, explaining that the older geldings they would ride were so completely Western in training that they would not understand direct-rein, two-handed riding. The couple assured me they rode both English and Western, and indeed, they did quite well. However, occasionally after a rest stop, when we had allowed our horses to face this way or that, I heard the gentleman having a quiet argument with Major. Each time this happened, I looked back to see that the rider had taken a rein in each hand, that he simply couldn't believe that a light touch of rein on neck was all Major needed to turn 180 degrees and head down the trail in the right direction. He knew about neck reining, could ride that way, but didn't fully trust it because he hadn't ridden a finished Western horse.

A horse that is finished in the neck rein is a joy on the trail. He has progressed past any dependence whatsoever on direct reining. Meanwhile, you reap those liberating benefits. Your second hand is free to hold the lead rope of a pack horse, to push a branch away from your face, or to handle a camera or binoculars. You can begin to train your horse for advanced trail skills such as dragging a dead snag of firewood back to camp or ponying an unruly colt, even roping if you incline in that direction. You have your partner one step further in the direction of "Complete Trail Horse."

# 9

## Training on the Trail

*What a horse does under compulsion he does blindly . . .*
*The performances of horse or man so treated are displays*
*of clumsy gestures rather than of grace and beauty. What we*
*need is that the horse should of his own accord exhibit his*
*finest airs and paces at set signals . . . Such are the*
*horses on which gods and heroes ride.*
—Xenophon

And so, we have a horse to ride. Although this book has spent some time on training the young horse, most readers will have acquired their horse already trained, and have probably purchased the horse before buying this book. Our worry now is not whether this horse is the best possible choice for the trail. Perhaps if we had it to do over again, we would have chosen a slightly different conformation, smaller or larger size, a better natural walk, or perhaps even a horse of another color or another breed. But we rather like this horse to whom we are a bit attached, and are not about to sell him or her and look for another. Instead, we really wish to fulfill the potential of the animal we have. Delmar Smith, the great trainer of gun dogs, would nod in approval. Not 10 percent of hunting dog owners, he says, realize the potential of their dogs, and the same is certainly true of horse owners. To borrow from a past US Army motto, let's work to make this horse "be all it can be."

Most horses can be taught to walk better, spook less, carry a pack, and go boldly forward on a light rein, whether in the front, middle, or back of the group. If sound, most can be conditioned to carry a rider all day through rough terrain. Most, in other words, though they may never fit our ideal, can make safe, satisfying mounts for the backcountry.

So, let's focus on the horse we have, on our relationship with it, on the present and on what lies down the trail. That said, we can not totally ignore the animal's past. While not falling into the trap called "the abuse excuse" (all deficiencies in the animal's training laid at the doorstep of alleged mishandling by a former owner), we do need to look critically at the horse's past environment and ask whether it was "trail deficient." Has the horse known only stalls and small paddocks, his past devoid of deer, streams, bridges, or any of the frightening stimuli he's likely to meet on the trail? Has the horse known only the heat of competition, never knowing relaxed, steady work in the hands of a human? Has the horse been oppressed with some show affectation, like the padded big lick Walking Horse, who wears elevator shoes on its front feet, whose muscles and tendons have grown unused to walking plain-shod down a backcountry trail?

In a perfect world, my prescription for all three of the above would be a turnout of six to twelve months on a full section (square mile) of western range. There the stall-bred horse would find stimuli aplenty, see the deer and rabbits, hear the coyotes howl, cross the coulees, and thread through the sagebrush. The competition-weary animal, jaded by the clock and the impatient demands of human handlers, would learn to simply be a horse again. Priorities for him would be food and water and survival; natural things. The padded big lick Walker, shoes pulled, would learn to realize his physical potential (extensive, in most representatives of his breed), learn to climb the hills and negotiate the rocks. All three would come out of this pasture vastly more ready to be trail horses than they were when turned in.

Of course, it's not a perfect world, and providing such an experience for the horse that truly needs it may well be impossible. Lacking such an opportunity for natural rehabilitation, we just do the next best thing—train for the trail in whatever ways our particular horse seems to need.

But there are good reasons I have chosen to title this section "Training *on* the trail." Yes, to a degree, we can simulate trail conditions in the arena. We can set up obstacles and scenarios that will help the horse during later encounters with the real thing on the trail. Many of these exercises can be performed in any small pen, or even in parking lots.

Ultimately, however, it is on the trail that the trail horse is made. Trail accomplishments in the arena, even in competition, do not always translate readily to equal confidence on the trail. Even the horse that wins trail classes in shows may become unnerved when confronted with the real thing out on the trail. Perhaps the arena obstacles are simply not realistic enough, the arena trail bridge lacking the same hollow sound and the water rushing underneath. Maybe the horse senses the vast difference between the protected arena environment and the great outdoors. Since the horse may not associate the simulated arena obstacle with the real thing, we'll apply as many lessons as possible out on the trail as follow-up for the arena introduction.

However, the large organized trail ride, with many riders, is in my opinion one of the *worst* scenarios for training the trail horse. It's simply a terrible teaching situation. Your horse, sandwiched between others, may well cross the creek or the bridge, and it may learn in doing so, but it also may not. Pressured by herd instinct, the horse may forget fears that readily awaken when you're attempting the same obstacle on your own. Worse, large trail rides have a collective mentality, often slightly competitive and impatient. Is this big group of riders going to wait while you overcome your horse's fear of a muddy crossing or a creaky bridge? If the answer is "yes," you ride with an exceptionally patient and sensitive group.

It is far better to hit the trail with just one other rider, a patient friend mounted on a steady, seasoned trail horse. Make sure your friend is clued in. She must fully understand that the object of this ride will not be to cover a given amount of ground. This is not a pleasure trip, but a training exercise. You'll be asking your friend to let you lead part of the time, but also to wait patiently while you and your new horse work out difficulties with obstacles.

*A trail bridge in an arena can be a useful teaching tool, but don't count on it preventing resistance at the real thing later on the trail.*

## Obstacles on the Trail

The business of obstacles, or things the horse perceives as obstacles, seems most problematic for many horses and their riders out on the trail. Horses are the archconservatives of the animal world. Anything strange, new, funny looking, reflective, or out of place in any way can be a potential spook, a barrier to overcome. I've taken strings of horses through treacherous territory, past moose and through bogs, only to have the whole string act upon return as if the sign at a trailhead were some sort of monster ready to bite. I've seen urban horses unnerved because the trail crossed a highway, and the pavement under their feet felt so different from the rest of the trail. They were used to pavement, but found it out of place in this particular setting. Big reflective boulders on the side of the trail often look menacing to a horse. A backpacker, human outline altered by the shape of the load, can appear to be a scary creature.

The least serious of these cases are simply problems of perception. The horse is afraid merely because his senses haven't assimilated the true nature of the object. Remember, too, that the sense of smell is a huge part of the animal's reality. My seasoned gelding Little Mack, recently leading a pack string loaded with supplies for a Forest Service work camp, was afraid of only one thing during the entire 32-mile round trip, and he was afraid of it both times, coming and going. The object: neatly stacked and banded timbers from a bridge the crew had torn out. The crew had built a new trail bridge and had sawed up the old one into lengths short enough to put on pack mules. Off to the side of the trail, muted in color, the piles still looked unnatural to Mack, and more, they gave off the sharp scent of creosote. If I could smell it, the odor must have been nearly overpowering, and out of place, to the gelding's far more sensitive nose.

Since perception *is* reality to the horse (and to you, too) we must respect it and not dismiss it. Give the horse some slack. He's frightened of these things because he genuinely fears them, and telling him he should know better is no more helpful than telling a child that his or her fear of the dark is stupid. With the least serious of these fears, often just shifting the horse on the trail far enough that he sees the object from a slightly different angle, is enough to deflate the fear. The sign loses its reflection, and the rock again looks like a rock. In the case of the back-packer, speaking to the person as soon as you're within earshot often does the trick. "How are you doing? How's fishing?" is not only friendly (important during these days when there is sometimes friction between riders and hikers), but it is likely to bring a reply. "Oh, I haven't caught much yet," the backpacker says, and suddenly your horse realizes this a human being.

Likely to be more serious are obstacles that involve crossing some-thing, particularly water and bridges. The horse may anticipate the chill of the stream around his pasterns and the hollow sound of his hoofbeats on the bridge planks, but his reluctance to cross has more to do with the way he sees the objects. Witness the fact that many horses cross wide streams quite readily, while narrow ones, or even puddles, result in stiff front legs, white around the eyes, and threats to bolt. The nature of the large stream is quite evident to the horse. For some reason that of the smaller one is mysterious and threatening.

There are two basic approaches to getting your horse past or across an obstacle at which it hesitates. The first, the one known by most horsemen, is to simply *drive* the animal past or over. The horse has been taught impulsion for his first training, whether from the whip or the long lead rope. Much of his training has been centered upon moving forward on command. You have no doubt seen demonstrations of trailer loading that involve using either the long lead rope or the whip to make every place *outside* the trailer rather hot for the horse, the inte-rior of the trailer thus becoming a sort of refuge, the horse loading be-cause he perceives the trailer as a safer and better place.

The trained saddle horse has been taught to go forward with a squeeze of the legs or a touch of the heels and no longer needs such stimulus from the ground. So, the average rider, when confronted with his horse's reluctance to cross a stream or bridge, kicks the animal mightily or uses a riding crop on its rear end. If the horse is well trained, perhaps this succeeds. Helped by the example of other horses in front of him and the herd instinct to follow the others through the obstacle, the horse may do its rider's bidding.

So, with this first method, "success" is gained if you measure success only by whether you are now able to continue down the trail. But has the horse learned anything? Will he be less frightened of the object the next time, simply because he has crossed it once? I have seen it go each way. His real reason for hesitation in the first place, you see, is genuine fear. Because you as rider are proud of your animal, think he or she is better than this, should be above such silly fear, you've spurred him over, hoping other riders didn't notice. You've satisfied your Type A side, but you haven't trained your horse. Worse, you may fail completely with this approach, no kicking, slapping, urging, or cursing convincing the braced-legged horse to budge. Perhaps someone in your party has a horse capable of dragging yours across with a lead rope dallied around the horn, something I can't recommend, but which could get you down the trail in an emergency. (We would hope you would get off while this is going on, since the potential would be huge for a halter or lead rope letting go, and the horse coming over backwards on you.) And, again, the horse would learn little and would perhaps be even more frightened of that same place on the trail next time.

There is a better way. There is an approach that will take less time in the long run and will result in true learning on the part of the horse. Unfortunately, though I knew better, I didn't take time for it recently while riding a delightful three-year-old I've been training. Skywalker had progressed so quickly that I had successfully led two organized trail rides with him, one on the ranch and another in the mountains. So when I took a visiting couple on a ride and approached a bridge the horse knew well, I was surprised when he hesitated, stopped, snorted, and did a quick 180-degree spin in an attempt to head for home.

I really should not have been so surprised. Two days earlier a huge cottonwood tree had fallen during a windstorm, straddling the road on the other side of the bridge. I had managed to chainsaw my way through its massive base, then move it with a tractor so that it lay parallel to the road, out of the way. I piled most of the larger broken branches into a stack nearby, but small ones still lay strewn about on and beside the road.

For the young black gelding, a scene he knew intimately had been sharply altered. A big shade tree was gone, resulting in unaccustomed visibility to the left on the other side of the bridge. To the right was a horizontal tree, its leaves wilting, its smell one of cottonwood sap. Anything new is potentially dangerous from a horse's point of view, and he had stiffened predictably. His handling the spook by turning around and attempting to leave was, of course, unacceptable, but his fear was understandable. I, however, refused to acknowledge it.

Perhaps a bit embarrassed by the behavior of a colt I'd been bragging up to my guests, my reaction was the typical "you know better than that." My heels, legs, and ego took over, and I forced the colt over the bridge and past the downed tree. He went a tad sideways, wide-eyed, but he went, and so the ride resumed.

But it doesn't end here. A few days later our excellent trainer Travis had occasion to take a client out on a horse he had been working for her and needed a gentle horse to ride along. "Take Skywalker," I said. "He's been doing well, and it's about time he learns that someone other than me can be on his back." Tending some barn chores, I looked up a bit later and watched the party arrive at the bridge down the lane. I saw the black colt stiffen, attempt to turn around, and saw Travis's reaction, identical to mine, the colt dancing across the bridge, eyeballing the fallen tree.

To this point, I realized, the colt had learned nothing about the inoffensive nature of the altered scene by the bridge. Both of us, with a job to do, had not given him credit for a genuine fear, had not taken time to let him overcome it. Both of us know better, but had not practiced what we preach; both of us use the other, better method.

And that method, the second and better one, is really very simple. It merely involves respecting the horse, giving him or her some understanding and realizing that the horse's perception is its reality. We, too, have fears of the unknown. Who hasn't felt a tightening in the stomach when walking into a strange office for a job interview? Our training probably overcomes our desire to flee, but best of all is a smile from the interviewer, followed by a short chat that helps us discover the he or she isn't a monster, but a human like us.

So, back to Skywalker and his third encounter with the scene that had suddenly grown so frightening for him. Now I ride him briskly down the lane in that glassy running walk that makes him such a joy. He is completely at ease until we get to within 50 feet or so of the bridge, when I feel a suggestion of reluctance, his legs a little stiffer, his pace a tad slower. "Whoa," I say. We stop. I keep him looking at the bridge. He does not attempt to crop a bite or two of the tall timothy that grows on the edge of the lane, but were he to try, I would not let him. Our job right now is to look at the bridge.

In less than a minute Skywalker lets out a sigh, then fidgets. He is used to going and likes it, for he has never been a stand-around sort of horse. This fidgeting is good. Since he feels relaxed I cue him forward. He takes a few steps toward the bridge, eyes it, stiffens again. I stop him, pet him, hum a tune, and act as if we have all day (which we do, because I've now prioritized this little training problem, as I should have done in the first place). Now it takes an even shorter time for the colt to signal he that he'd just as soon move. I don't let him move for a moment (I *am* the one in charge, after all), and then we walk just to the edge of the bridge. Now he looks across and gets genuinely scared. He's not ready to bolt, but he's very uncomfortable. He has learned to back quite well, so I back him up two steps. He relaxes again, but only for a moment.

Having had time to really study the situation, Skywalker has himself decided that the downed tree is nonthreatening, that this whole routine is rather boring and silly. As with humans, the knowledge that we acquire ourselves, through our own direct experience, has the most weight. Skywalker, now having *learned*, responds to an ounce of pressure released on his reins and walks briskly across the bridge, past the fallen tree with little more than a passing glance, and down the road. The problem has been solved and the resistance is gone.

Now you understand why I consider the large, organized trail ride to be a very poor training situation for the young trail horse. Do you know a group of twenty-five riders, anxious for the miles ahead, eagerly anticipated the previous week in their stuffy offices, who would have cheerfully waited even the few minutes necessary to complete this little routine with Skywalker?

As to actual time spent, as noted trainer John Lyons articulates, this second method takes less time in the long run because the horse actually learns, and you do not have to fight the same battle time after time. But in the short run, few groups would have the patience to wait for you, and with some justification. A trail ride leader must keep the group together, keep the morale up, and look to safety. He or she can't allow individuals on the ride to hold up the group.

*One trusted companion, on an older, steady horse, is the safest and best training scenario for the trail horse. Allow the young horse to frequently take the lead and figure out obstacles without help from the patient companion, who hangs back.*

Your good friend with the steady horse is thus the best company, but if it's within your safety threshold, riding out alone can be the best teaching situation of all. How about using your new trail horse's natural tendency to follow the horse in front, to cross the obstacle because of the lead horse's example? We've all done this, and I think it is perfectly fine, just as long as you remember that learning may not have taken place. This is why it's important to periodically switch places with your partner, letting your horse lead. If he stops at an obstacle while you are in the lead, resist the temptation to beckon your friend forward. Use the method outlined above, while your friend hangs back.

This second method we've described for confronting obstacles works equally well when there is water to cross. Again, it is often the very small stream that confuses the horse. Lyons emphasizes insisting that the horse look at whatever spot you've chosen to cross. Do not allow him to look elsewhere, but use the same technique of waiting for

*The stand-and-relax method of meeting an obstacle. a) colt tenses, ears back, at trail bridge so he's allowed to study it until relaxing; b) threat removed in his mind, colt walks across bridge; c) reverse direction is easier; he's now parked on the bridge briefly while he further relaxes; d) proof of the pudding later on the trail: colt walked boldly across actual bridge.*

complete relaxation. Then move the horse forward to the point where anxiety begins, back off a step, and continue to stare. Eventually your horse will walk into the stream. Once there, let him drink if he wishes. Don't rush him across. If it's safe, shallow water, walk him upstream a few steps. The whole experience should be relaxed, the smell of the stream sinking into the horse's memory bank for future reference, plus cool, quenching water if he's thirsty.

The bridge and the creek have something in common from the horse's point of view. Like all large animals, horses are extremely afraid of falling. Thus they are conscious of their footing and worried about any that seems suspicious. All bridges, even very large ones, sound and feel hollow to the horse, the fall of each hoof causing vibrations that

A                                                                                              B

*a) Emily uses the same method teaching Redstar to cross water. First he's allowed to stop but required to stare at the crossing place until he relaxes. b) Then he walks across.*

the horse can detect. The horse senses and anticipates this, just as he does the liquid medium that he'll feel when stepping into the creek.

But if there's one sort of footing that justifies fear in the horse, it's the muddy, boggy area. Maybe this is why horses often balk at small puddles, but step into large, rocky streams quite readily. Off maintained trails, we'd better respect a horse's judgment when it comes to an area that looks suspiciously boggy. Although we, as riders, fancy ourselves

*Teaching a horse to walk calmly over a noisy plastic tarp teaches that he can trust your judgment on unaccustomed footing.*

to be always right, this is a subject about which the horse may have greater wisdom.

Many years ago I was hunting alone with a steady gelding named Marauder, many miles from any potential help, when he balked at crossing an area between two trees that looked perfectly normal to me. I urged him across, becoming pretty forceful about it, then felt my stomach sink as his feet broke the surface. All four of his feet dropped into an unseen bog caused by one of those springs that surface inexplicably in our mountains. Marauder gave two hard jumps and was free, fortunately too quickly for the full horror of the possible consequences to sink in. I apologized profusely, hoping he could understand.

Horses evolved neither on high, rocky mountain slopes nor in swampy, tropical areas, but on vast, grassy plains. They do not handle bogs very well at all. Watch a cow, a species that is native to the wet areas of the world, cross a boggy area. She'll take her time and will not panic, cropping a mouthful of grass even while sunk to her knees. Her large, split hooves spread wider for traction in the wet stuff. Even bovines do sometimes bog down, but everything about them—including temperament—is better suited to the swamp than horses are.

The horse, though it becomes accustomed to both, is not inherently comfortable either high in the mountains or deep in the woods. Its preferred environment is open with plenty of space around, security against a sneaking predator, with room to run and escape. Much of the spookiness we must overcome with trail horses, along with their reluctance to cross obstacles, is completely natural, built into the essence of the critter. Marauder's sense of smell, so superior to mine, had picked up the scent of water under a normal-looking surface. Maybe his ears, also superior, could actually hear the gurgling of a spring under the crust of benign-looking soil. I had not deferred to his judgment, and it almost cost both of us dearly.

There is always a fine line, of course. Horses *will* learn to take advantage. We, as their riders and leaders, must learn to distinguish a justified fear, such as Marauder's fear of the bog, from one in which the horse's perception is giving him information we can overrule. The horse that learns he will get out of any task that appears to frighten him will become a problem indeed. He'll eventually use his "fear" as an excuse to rest and balk, or for even more serious misbehavior such as rearing or attempting to return to the barn.

The log or tree trunk straddling the trail represents one sort of obstacle for which you can prepare in your home arena. Stepping over poles strewn on the ground is a good start. Progress to cavaletti (or a pole elevated by ends set on wood blocks or buckets). The idea is *not* to jump. Although there may be times you prefer to have your horse jump (I like to train them to jump on command), for the most part it is safer for the trail horse to calmly step over the log. Stepping over minimizes chances of injury, is less likely to jar any gear we happen to be carrying, and is less likely to surprise a relaxed rider. In crossing logs we're not normally training a horse to overcome something he fears, but simply building physical confidence. Crossing ground poles, then elevated poles, stepping over low barricades in parking lots—these things become mundane, and so, likely, the log on the trail will be equally easy.

*You can even practice in parking lots. The idea is to step calmly over the log, not to jump.*

However, be careful of just what you ask your horse to do out on the trail. That log may be a bit higher than an angled view judges it to be. How is the footing on the far side? Is the trunk smooth enough to rub against the horse's belly without causing injury? (I heard of a terrible accident caused by a rider whose lack of scrutiny caused the death of the horse, its chest penetrated by an unnoticed snag.) If the log is high or bristling with branches, look for a route around one end of the tree, and get off if necessary.

Montana's forests were ravaged by fire during the summer of 1988. Starting approximately five years later, the standing, burned trees began to fall. A single windstorm often resulted in literally hundreds of trees straddling a stretch of trail. Many of our favorite national forest trails threaded through these burns. Those of us who volunteered as members of Backcountry Horsemen of America to help the US Forest Service clear these trails learned much about a type of saw known around here as the Oregon pruning saw. This light, curved tool that cuts only on the pull stroke is remarkably effective. Today it's common to see at least one rider in a party carrying such a saw on his horse, usually in a bright-colored nylon case.

Having such a tool along is an extremely good idea. First, we can fulfill our obligation to improve the trail wherever possible, whenever our capabilities allow. The small sapling or snag on the trail can probably be removed quite readily. It is both good trail etiquette, and good training for your horse, for you to dismount and take a few minutes to make the trail just a bit better and safer for everyone. Your horse will watch you work, appreciate the rest, and perhaps learn that there is more to this trail horse business than putting one foot in front of another. In the case of a tree too large for you to saw, the pruning saw may allow clearing a place on the trunk free of protruding branches so that your horse can step safely over it.

If you choose to lead your horse over or through any obstacle, such as a small stream, ditch, or log, be extremely careful. A frightened horse can become totally absorbed in worries about the obstacle and decide to jump, and, if you are in front of him, nail you right between the shoulder blades. At age fourteen, working my first summer on a ranch, I had to return with the boss to the ranch buildings, down a steep slope in darkness. We dismounted and led the horses in. This was open Montana ranch land, so we were not on any particular trail, but had to cross several small irrigation ditches on our way down the hill. "Hold the reins off to the side of you at arm's length when you lead him across," the boss told me. "That way if he jumps he'll miss you."

Again, with all obstacles the best method is the one that allows the horse to learn that the object is benign. Let him look at it long enough, walk closer when he's ready, and his fears will usually dissolve. If the object is to the side of the trail, do not feel you must take the horse all the way to it for a smell. It's enough that he walk quietly by.

## Spooks on the Trail

It is the nature of the horse to spook. Were the instinct to jerk into defensive flight within a split second not built into horses, they would not have survived. The horse that is truly spookproof is rare, if not nonexistent. Certainly police horses come very close, yet I suspect that some of them, so masterful in their city environment, might jump if they were suddenly transported to Montana range and had a frightened baby calf leap from its bed, let out a bawl, and run up underneath them. A sudden stimulus apart from the horse's usual sphere of experience is nearly always cause for a spook. I recently rode a steady, aged gelding many miles in the mountains. Grouse, deer, and roaring rapids got from him not even a second look. But once, during a long, hot lull, when the trail had grown uninteresting, I suddenly and loudly sneezed, and he gave a good stiff start. He had heard humans sneeze hundreds of times, but in that mountain context on that trip, the sound was somehow totally out of context, and he reacted. Knowing this particular horse, he probably felt foolish about it afterwards.

Accordingly, we're not going to worry about making our trail horse truly spookproof. We ourselves, after all, are not spookproof. No matter how "trained" we are, a prankster surprising us from a dark corner by jumping out with a huge "boo," will get a reaction. However, you are well "trained" enough that the spook will be momentary and will not cause you to run out of the house and onto a busy street. Similarly, we'll concern ourselves with two things: minimizing spooks by exposing our horse to many stimuli and, as with obstacles, showing that they are not dangerous; and insisting that our horse spook only in proper fashion.

Let's take the second one first. Yes, there are both proper and im-proper ways to spook. Improper spooking includes using fright as a li-cense to run away, buck, rear, or balk. "Proper" spooking might just be a slight jerk running through the horse's body, a quick tightening of the muscles, or a slowing of the walk. Depending on the severity of the fright, we could probably give a horse a good grade on his spook when he stayed in position and did not do anything particularly antisocial.

I asked a cowboy not long ago whether he had worked cattle yet with the colt he was starting. "No," he said, "not enough handle." What he meant by "handle" was simply the level of control over the colt at this point. Yes, he could lope the animal after a cow, but could he turn him? In the excitement of the chase, could the cowboy keep the colt from trying to buck or to run the wrong direction? Wisely, he was rid-ing the colt in less stressful situations until he felt his "handle" was up to the task.

"Proper" spooking is pretty much the result of "handle." Training to a large degree is the horse's acceptance of restraints, of limits. These re-straints become habitual and gradually override the natural tendency to flee from whatever frightens the animal. The spook happens, but it is si-multaneously controlled by the strength of training. Although it would be a stretch to apply Freudian psychology to horses, Freud's terminology is handy here. He described natural impulses as the id. The first control-ling impulse is the ego, which puts restraints on the id, but without really knowing why. The superego is a higher, rational controlling power. So if another person says something extremely nasty to you, your id might tempt you to throw a punch, your ego might just as spontaneously hold your arm back, and your superego might say to you, "I can't stand this guy, but it's not worth having assault charges levied against me."

Now, it is debatable whether horses ever are educated to acquire something like the superego, but it is altogether possible that in those higher stages of training, those we call "education," they indeed do. Until then, training is installing something akin to Freud's ego. When the rabbit runs out from the bush the horse does not rationalize. He does not say to himself, "I'd really like to turn around and run home, but I can't because my rider will punish me." But, just the same, probably after a slight jump, he stops himself from running home and goes on up the trail. His training has overcome his desire to run.

So are we saying that excessive spookiness is a shortcoming of the horse's training thus far? Yes, with this caveat: horses vary immensely in this respect, some by their very nature being particularly challenging. Emily and I raise twelve to fifteen colts each year. After weaning, the whole bunch run in a large corral with adjoining paddock. Each year one or two of the group lead the small herd in spooks. If you observe closely, when a sudden noise causes the bunch to retreat across the corral, the flight is led by just one or two. These colts are not leaders in the sense of dominance, but merely the first to jump at something unexpected. The rest go along out of herd instinct.

Sometimes hay is pitched over the corral fence. Though eager for the feed, one or two individuals in the group find the motion made by a laden pitchfork arced overhead toward them from across the fence to be particularly intimidating, but gradually, the spook leaders have less pull on the group at large. The others, anxious to eat, eventually learn to accept hay pitched from over their heads, wait for it to land, and begin to eat without making the ritualistic flight across the corral. The spook leaders, however, take a long time to figure out that this "scary" motion is benign and in fact beneficial.

I'm sure you could not prove the correlation, but I sometimes think that the extremely spooky horse, the one you've raised with others that don't show this trait, may be less intelligent. He simply takes longer to learn that certain objects, sounds, and actions are harmless. Perhaps there is another cause, such as poor vision. Still another reason could be a dam, herself spooky, passes the trait to the colt, not necessarily genetically, but through early learning: The mother jumped often, and the colt learned to do likewise. Or, perhaps in its way, this particular animal is more intelligent, at least in the sense of survivability, its instincts of self-preservation more sensitive.

Last are horses that fake-spook, that jump at things with which they're familiar simply because they feel good or are bored. Competitive trail riders and endurance riders who carry heart monitors for their horses sometimes say they can tell the difference between a fake spook and a real one by a spike in the heart rate. A real spook causes the increase, while a fake one does not. Sometimes a stern word to the seasoned horse is enough to get him to knock off this sort of horseplay.

Whatever the cause for the serious sort of spooking, we must deal with it. We have already discussed getting the horse past an obstacle that frightens it by giving the animal time to study things out and become relaxed. With spooks, however, we're dealing with something a bit less rational: the horse's handling of a stimulus that prompts him to jump or run. Initial training of the animal should have addressed those spooky things that come from saddle and rider. Certainly during basic training the horse should have gone through some sort of "sacking out" (old-timer's term) or "desensitization" (college-educated, politically-correct clinician's term). Yet, there are "trained" horses that still jump if their riders make a sudden move to retrieve a slicker from behind the saddle. A horse is never too old to step back in training and learn a little more or to address a deficiency.

One way to desensitize a human or an animal is to flood it with the stimulus that scares it. Psychologists call this "implosive" therapy. A friend, who is a good horse trainer, watched with horror as his wife's horse suddenly bucked, frightened by the sound of an approaching all-terrain vehicle. The woman was tossed into the barrow pit of the county road and thoroughly bruised. My friend was convinced it was the sound, not the sight, of the four-wheeler that scared the horse, because the vehicle had been approaching them from behind and was over a slight rise, out of sight, when the mare spooked.

This trainer's version of implosive therapy was to put the mare in a stout round corral. He removed the blade from his lawnmower for safety, parked it in the middle of the round corral, started it, and went about his business while keeping a distant eye on the situation. In the hour or so the mower ran, the mare progressed from panic to simply running around the perimeter of the pen to standing and watching and eventually to walking up to the noisy mower and touching it with a front hoof. This was a rather extreme approach to desensitizing the mare, but my friend, who had just seen his wife unceremoniously dumped, felt extreme measures were called for. Whether the procedure made the horse absolutely small-engine proof, I cannot say, because the mare was lost to an illness not long afterwards.

Another implosive approach is to saddle a colt and hang all sorts of noisy but harmless stuff from the saddle—a slicker or plastic tarp, milk jugs, anything that makes a lot of noise and bounces around but is unlikely to cause injury to the colt—and then simply turn it loose in a round pen. Some refer to this as "bombproofing," one of those terms I avoid. Still another was the old-timer's sacking out, often performed on a colt whose hind leg was tied up, the tarp or blanket slapped repeatedly all over its body until it elicited not so much as a twitch in response.

There are, however, some dangers in the implosive approach. A certain small percentage of horses will simply lose it. These are the ones that try to crash through the side of the round pen, go over it, or die trying. This sort will injure themselves (and possibly bystanders) when frightened that badly. The second problem is that the trainer must be willing to stay the course. Cancel all appointments, dinners, and recreation for the next few hours. If you choose an implosive approach, you have no idea how long it will take, but you must push through until the horse is thoroughly desensitized and thoroughly calm with the stimuli, or you will have done more harm than good.

Sadly, many horses classified as trained by the folks who sell them have never undergone a thorough desensitization. Show horses and those destined for a particular performance activity are often channeled only toward winning in that sphere, their trainers believing they can budget no time for anything "nonproductive." An older horse that is still "goosey" about saddling, ropes touching it, or movement by the rider needs some retraining. For the spooks that come from above—from the rider, the saddle, from donning a slicker or grabbing your hat when the wind tries to blow it away—my own favorite approach is to teach the horse to pack. I do all the usual things during basic training, with some extras thrown in. I slap stirrup leathers until there is no reaction, pass ropes and blankets all over the horse's body, tie up feet, lead by each foot, and play a loud radio while riding in the arena.

But for building future reliability on the trail, I'm convinced that one trip carrying a pack is equal to many, many arena sessions. And, in a perfect world, I wouldn't hesitate to prescribe for the older, spooky horse a summer of service in an outfitter's pack string. Every colt I start gets at least one trip to the hills packing a sawbuck pack saddle before he carries a human, the panniers loaded with 100 pounds of salt for our cattle. In the section on starting a young horse I mentioned packing as part of this initial training, but it's equally valuable for remedial purposes. Here is a bit more detail.

Of course, some skills and equipment are involved. You also need a good, steady horse, one experienced at ponying another and capable of handling some resistance to a lead rope dallied around the saddle horn. But you certainly don't need a ranch or cattle or an actual job to do. Any trail you would ride recreationally is just fine as a training ground.

For training purposes the sawbuck saddle and a pair of soft (cloth) panniers are simplest. I introduce the horse to this new equipment in the round pen. The sawbuck should feel to the horse pretty much like a riding saddle, but with one major addition—the breeching that goes behind its rump under the tail. Stand to the side as you lift the tail over the breeching, and expect a reaction. Then, without panniers or loads in place, work the horse in the round pen for a bit. When he seems used to the saddle, add the panniers, which normally hook by looped straps over the top of the sawbuck. A strap between the two panniers goes under the belly and secures the two together to prevent flopping.

Again, work in the round pen. Longe a bit, and then move the horse around. When all is going well, add the load, my favorite cargo being a 50-pound sack of granulated stock salt per side. The salt is dense, so the weight stays low in the panniers, and it is a cheap, practical, and expendable load even if you don't have salt troughs to fill. Again move the horse around, then if all is going well, mount an experienced horse, grab the packhorse's lead rope, and head for the hills.

In the packing section I will again be reminding you of safety. You do not tie the pack horse's lead rope to your saddle in any way, and you do not wrap it around your hand. In the course of a good ride the packed horse will learn many things. The breeching around its rump, which helps hold the load back when going downhill, will soon desensitize the horse to touch in that particular area. The packs will rub on trees and brush, making sounds and touch sensations that will surprise initially, but then become routine. The horse soon learns to give trees a slightly wider berth to avoid bumping the packs, which will help spell future safety for your knees while riding.

Overcoming spooks is more than desensitization, however. As we said earlier, it is also a matter of training, of discipline, of instilling in the animal that automatic check on its impulse to flee. Again, I must emphasize the importance of teaching that "whoa" really means whoa, that the word means to stop and stand still and not move until allowed to do so. As we've also said, this command should *never* be used when you want the horse to merely slow down. This command should be so strongly instilled, that the horse obeys it even under the stress of extreme fright.

Not that many years ago, most of America moved behind horses in harness. The basic team of two horses owned by the typical rural family was both tractor and automobile. The workhorses were also constant companions, usually much loved. Strict as schools were in those days, the death of a work team member was considered cause for mourning on the part of the children and a legitimate excuse for absence from school.

When a horse is pulling a wagon down a narrow road with deep ditches on each side, no "one-rein stop" is possible. There is no refuge in spinning the animal when it acts up. Terrible accidents were quite common, the horse-and-buggy days having been far from the stereotyped sedate times. The US Government issued pamphlets on horse training, suggesting various methods for correcting bad habits and making transportation with them safer. Some of the methods and equipment seem quite harsh by today's standards, but when you put your family out on a road or trail behind animals capable of running away and overturning the wagon, you made one thing certain above all else: The horses had to stop when commanded to do so. Today it is easy to judge the training used as cruel, forgetting that the lives and survival of one's family often relied on absolute obedience by horses. And, as we have said, it is not usually the method itself that is either harsh or humane, but the way it is applied.

The "running **W**" was a favorite device for teaching the draft or buggy horse an absolute "whoa." The letter "**W**" describes the pattern made by a long rope that led from the wagon seat to a ring on the side of the horse's harness at his shoulder, then down to a hobble half on one front pastern, then up to a ring at his chest, then down to the second pastern, and finally back up to the horse's other shoulder where it was secured to the harness. The term "running" is used here just as it is with the running rigging on a sailboat, to mean a rig that is not static, a rig through which the line will move.

To avoid hurting the horse, this device was normally used in a soft, plowed field or on ground blanketed by snow. The young horse was taken out, put into a brisk walk, and told "whoa." If it stopped, fine. If it did not, the driver's assistant pulled back on the running **W**, taking the animal's front feet away, and putting the horse down on its knees. Usually only one or two treatments were needed, the horse's innate fear of falling asserting itself, and the whoa becoming absolute. This training was very similar to the electronic collars used on hunting dogs today. If you watch a professional dog trainer use one of those, you will be struck by how subtly the dog can be just tweaked, just signaled that he is near the allowable boundary.

Watching an old-timer use a running **W** struck me the same way. I had thought of this device as a sort of hair-trigger tripwire, but found that quite the opposite was true. The same thing that gives the device its great leverage, the effect of a block and tackle, also means that much line must be pulled in for relatively little movement down at the pasterns. The horse I watched was never made to fall. The driver's assistant pulled just far enough to spell out to the horse that it was very close to being tripped, that it had better mend its ways and listen.

Few trainers remain today who have first-hand knowledge of the running **W**, and most of us would not tackle enforcing "whoa" in that particular way. I take time to describe this method to remind you that among people whose daily lives absolutely relied on safety with horses, an unquestioning stop upon command was the highest single priority. Whatever round pen method you have learned for teaching whoa, the same will work for enforcing it, making it stronger, and teaching the horse to stay facing you and any spook that might happen to come his way. Enforce whoa and then introduce minor spooks, a tarp, a cap pistol, a bicycle. Keep the horse facing the thing that frightens him.

From the saddle, practice whoa as much as you practice all other maneuvers involved in riding. Stop frequently for no apparent reason, say "Whoa," and do not let the horse move until he stands and relaxes.

Use pressure and release as always. The horse moves and you tense the reins; he stops, and he gets slack reins in the way of reward. Enlist the help of a friend in setting up trail situations that might frighten the horse. Keep it mild at first. You are not eliminating fear, but teaching the horse how to handle it. You are building another positive habit, the habit of stopping on command to view a possible spook but staying standing in place, facing what frightens the horse. Have your friend ride up on a four-wheeler or a motorcycle, taking it easy, of course. Stand safely off to the side of a road and watch traffic go by. (A fence between you and the road is an added safety comfort.)

Working hand in hand with "whoa" is the horse's training to flex laterally. The horse that handles a spook by taking the bit firmly in his teeth and running away needs retraining for the trail or any other purpose. The one-rein stop is still your protection against the spook that is out of hand, the one that overcomes whoa.

Working steadily in this manner, you are both desensitizing and training the horse to handle its fears. Every new potential spook to which you can introduce your horse is a spook you may well have diffused. I must add the "may," because objects that the horse deems harmless around the barn in familiar territory can still prove scary on the trail. When llamas first became popular as backpackers' companions, many horses that met them on the trail were terrified. An outfitter friend purchased a llama to run with her packhorses in the hope they would become desensitized to them. It worked fairly well, but not entirely. My friend says that she's still cautious when meeting llamas on the trail because some of her horses still haven't made the connection between the friendly llama in their pasture at home and the pack-laden ones led by backpackers that they sometimes meet on the trail.

Beyond this, work to prevent spooks by continuing to board your horse in a place with varied terrain, sights, sounds, wildlife, people, and livestock. Avoid, if you can, boarding your horse in a stall and leaving it unridden for long periods of time. Ride, ride, ride. How at ease would you be behind the wheel of a car if you drove on the freeway just one hour per month? It's asking a great deal of a horse, particularly a spirited one, to live in confined quarters, rarely getting out, and then be anything but snorty when you hit the trail.

Lastly, don't be afraid to simply get off the horse, hold it by the reins or halter rope, and let the crisis pass. When you see a truly dangerous spook coming, a truck or a train, or when you feel tension build in the horse that edges toward true panic, put self-preservation above any training objective, and dismount.

## Laggards and Chargers

The complete trail horse is neither a laggard nor a charger. He should, for my own taste, have the spirit and natural "go" to be a charger if you let him. But you should not let him.

Think of the complete trail horse as a vehicle with an automatic transmission and cruise control. On a gravel road you prefer to go just 25 miles per hour, so you set the cruise at that speed, and its engine and transmission take care of the rest. Swinging onto the freeway, you accelerate and reset the cruise at 70. You need do nothing to maintain that speed.

All finished saddle horses should have this ability. You should be able to put one "in gear," then ride and enjoy without either holding the animal back or urging it forward. I'm amazed at how many people tolerate laggards and seem content to kick them every step just to get them to plod along. Similarly, others ride charger types with hard mouths, horses that keep the reins string-tight the entire ride and return their riders to the barn with aching arms. Though the two types might be dissimilar in disposition, they have something in common. Usually, each has been made the way he is by bad riding, and, in the case of the charger, incomplete training.

Trail-ride leaders tend to despise laggards, for such animals gradually open up a big gap between themselves and the next horse in front. Eventually, probably of their own volition rather than because of the ignored cues of the rider, they decide it's time to catch up. They lope forward so as not to be left behind, and a whiplash effect is created. Put two or three such horses (and riders) in a group, and the tail end of the snake will be trotting or loping half the time and nearly stalled for the rest of it.

Chargers, by contrast, often insist on being in front. In that position, they often quit being chargers. Interesting! Who has trained whom?

As a youngster working out on various ranches, I came to know many laggards. The ranch hand at the bottom of the chain of command does not draw the best horse. I usually got the lazy ones, and worse, the ones that guarded their right to be lazy by crowhopping if work was demanded from them. Possibly these horses were truly lazy in disposition, but their behavior had been made worse by riders like me at the time: relatively green, easily bluffed out by a truculent reaction. Laggards can smoke out in a very short time just what sort of rider is on their back. With the green rider they laze along, steal bites of grass, and thoroughly enjoy doing anything but meaningful work. On another day a real horseman climbs aboard, does anything she wants with the critter, and says afterwards, "What a nice horse you have here."

I don't believe there is any particularly kind way to correct the laggard. If you find that you have brought one home, do make sure first, that there is nothing physiologically wrong. If the horse's feet hurt or if he is weak and malnourished, we cannot expect him to be energetic on the trail. If, however, he is hale and hearty yet shows himself—long before there is any reason to be tired—inclined to let the distance to the rear end of the horse in front gradually lengthen, we probably have a laggard. By then you've probably already noticed you're keeping your heels into his sides, that the insides of your thighs are tiring from applying leg pressure.

Something may have been missed during round pen training. We can certainly go back there, and probably should. Basic lessons in impulsion should involve this same requirement that the horse maintain whatever speed you ask from him. Whether your tool is the longe whip or the long lead rope favored in "natural" horsemanship, it should be applied as necessary to the horse's behind to remind him in no uncertain terms that he's required to work.

But the confirmed laggard has probably been made that way under saddle, and that's probably where you'll have to correct him. If you have ethical problems with the course I'm going to prescribe, I understand and respect your opinions. But I also doubt whether you are going to correct the horse that has been hardened into selective laziness by poor riding.

The old-timer's tool of choice was the quirt, a short, fairly heavy, braided leather affair with a loop that lets you hang the tool on your wrist when not in use. A short whip will also do, as will a willow switch in a pinch. What about spurs? Yes, they'll work in many cases for this sort of correction, but I hate to recommend them. I like spurs as tools of finesse, not enforcement. I like them because they allow my heels to be even lighter and allow me to isolate my leg cues even more precisely. More on that later.

First, quit continuously kicking the laggard. It means nothing to him and certainly is not hurting him. (If it were, it would probably be having some effect.) Also, when we do anything continuously, we're removing—from the horse's point of view—any possible reward for doing the right thing. This horse is used to being kicked all the time. Big deal. Instead, as the animal begins to lag, we say or cluck perfectly gently and quietly whatever command we usually use to "giddup," and we just touch him with our heels. Nothing will happen, of course, so within a second or two we land a major whack on his rear end with our tool of choice. Do be ready for consequences. You may get a big jump or a crowhop or even worse, so if you don't feel confident to handle such a response *don't do this!*

Most likely you'll get a jump forward and a picked-up pace, which is what you want. So, reward the horse by keeping your heels completely off him. The selective laggard, the one that only lags with certain riders, may be cured. Oh, he'll probably try it once or twice more on the ride, but he's figured out that he can't take advantage of you, that you are one of those riders for whom he had better work.

But the chronic laggard will not be so easily cured. He will find it hard to believe that he cannot train you to let him laze along, just as he has all those other riders. Persistence, however, will usually pay off. Again the principle is that same basic one of pressure and release. When he keeps up with the horse in front of him he gets no pressure whatsoever. When he does not, he gets warned first by a squeeze of the legs, a touch of the heels, and sounds from your mouth that tell him to pick up the pace. If he ignores those, the major pressure comes quickly and just as quickly disappears. In the long run this rapid reminder is probably a more pleasant life for him than plodding along with heels dug into his sides at every step.

The charger, by contrast, is a horse we must love for his heart and willingness to work. Many have potential to be the very best kind of saddle horse, but they, too, have taken advantage of riders in their particular way. They like to go, which is great. Most, too, have much endurance, part of the reason they have become chargers. But they have been successful in getting what they want by ignoring the consequences, by a willingness to take the discomfort of pressure on their mouth. Often riders have tried a succession of bits, progressing toward the most severe. The charger has simply adapted.

Watch a charger being ridden, and you'll often see the rider making the same basic error as the one mounted on the laggard, that of applying continuous pressure. Just as the rider of the pokey horse kicks it at every step, the rider of the charger continually hauls back with hard, steady pressure on the reins. "I'm just holding him back," the rider will say, but really he or she is cueing the animal. (*Everything* you do while horseback is a cue of sorts.) Unfortunately, the horse is returning the pressure, and has adapted the cue to mean "Go down the trail at whatever speed you want." In training horses from the very first, we should try to avoid steady, hard pressure because the animal's natural reaction is to press back in the opposite direction.

Just as some horses choose to be laggards on a very selective basis (notice how they almost never lag when you turn back toward the barn), many chargers are often playing a con game. On gaited horse rides, where everyone is used to clipping right along, a high percentage of the riders will tell you that their horses really want to be in front. The horse plays the part of a charger when he is back in the ranks, but put him in front and he behaves. He now has the primo position, and likes it there. In most cases, so does his rider.

So where do we start? The very first thing is to try very hard to remove the continuous "cue" and replace it with something that rewards the horse for the correct behavior. Our goal, remember, is to have a horse we can put in whatever gear we choose. It's fair to point out, however, that horses have been bred for different purposes. Most gaited horses have been bred to move out. Even their slow walk, sometimes called a dog walk by gaited horse enthusiasts, is often long-striding enough to be the same speed as the trot of heavily built, nongaited animals. If you're consistently riding a Tennessee Walker with companions mounted on slow-walking nongaited animals, your horse's genetics are agitating to move out.

That's no excuse to let him, however, and if your arms ache at the end of ride it's time to change something. Try a tactic similar to that we used with the laggard. Tell the horse "easy," then give the reins a pronounced jerk, followed immediately by release of pressure. That bump back on the reins is likely to cause a very brief slackening of pace, while your release of rein pressure during that moment is a reward. Timing is everything here, since the confirmed charger may only give you a second before he resumes his thrust forward.

I recommended this tactic to a woman who owned a Quarter Horse with the charger problem. She was exhausted at the end of each ride from holding the horse back. "But won't I hurt his mouth?" she asked.

"I think he's well beyond that. If the bit were hurting his mouth, wouldn't he slow down? He's pulling against your arms with all his might. The jerk, however, is sudden and uncomfortable, and the lightness you give him immediately afterwards is a reward for doing what you want, not what he wants."

I'll be the first to admit, however, that this tactic will work only with some horses. Like the laggard, the charger missed some training lessons essential for the complete trail horse. Or perhaps he learned them, only to unlearn them with the help of poor riders. I've never had to tackle correcting the most extreme cases, but if I were cornered into doing so, I'd go back to the round pen and a snaffle bit. The horse would be treated like a colt again. The snaffle would not be chosen because it is any more "humane," but because this horse needs to relearn lateral flexion, to give to the bit, which can be most easily taught with the snaffle because of its direct side-pull effect.

One of the first things I would do is the old-timer tactic of tying the horse by a rein from the snaffle to the cinch ring so he is flexed to one side. Modern trainers often discourage this tactic, but I think that's because it's been terribly misused. The misuse is due to the old American idea, "If a little is good, more must be better." Thus trainers bend the animal's neck nearly double and tie him off. But the whole point is for the horse to learn to give to the pressure. If his neck is tied so far around that he can bend it no farther without extreme discomfort or pain, the entire point has been missed.

The secret to getting results by tying the rein off to one side is to tie the rein just tight enough so that the horse takes up all slack and pulls the rein fairly tight when he puts his nose straight forward. If you've tied him off to the left, he's unable to bend right. The rein is just tight enough to make him uncomfortable with his nose straight ahead. So what does he do? He bends to the left, gives himself slack, and removes the pressure. He has learned something, and from his point of view, he has learned it himself. Self-discovery is always the strongest kind.

It takes some horses quite a while to discover how to give themselves slack, but others learn it virtually immediately. I am now starting a delightful two-and-one-half-year-old gelding named Jed. The day after I introduced him to the snaffle bit I tied him around to the left in the manner described above. Jed made several circles in that direction, but by the time I had walked across the small round pen, he was standing watching me, his head bent left a little, the rein completely slack. The right side went equally quickly. Jed, I suspect, will train into a "fingertip" horse.

The charger often does not know these basics. Whether you could reform one by starting from scratch in this manner and working toward lightness, giving laterally, circling, and backing, I do not know. But to save a good horse it would be worth a try. Meanwhile, smaller things might help. Assuming the horse has a good "whoa" (if he's a charger and does not have a good stop, I wouldn't be riding him outside an arena), stop frequently for no good reason. Make the horse stand. If necessary, turn him all the way around to face the opposite direction. Pet him. Get off and take a break. Ride him in deep snow and terrain where he doesn't quite trust his footing. If it is within your safety standards, frequently ride the horse out alone. It's possible that a herd effect, the collective personality that unites any group of herd animals, is partially responsible for his behavior. Perhaps when alone he will listen to *you*.

Trite as it may sound, prevention is the best cure for either the laggard or the charger. As you develop your trail horse, concentrate on its cruise control. This is one scenario where a few sharp, decisive cues are better (and probably kinder) than many little ones. Don't be a nag.

Don't kick every step or continuously pull back on the reins, but demand work of the horse that shows any inclination toward laziness. The horse should be punching in on its time clock when you climb aboard. Work has begun, and, yes, we'll try to make the job pleasant, but any breaks taken should be at the boss's direction, and that boss must be you. Do not let a disrespectful horse laze along; do not let it eat while walking, and do not let it stop for no reason.

The higher-spirited horse, the one with natural go, should not be discouraged in his ambition, but merely constantly reminded who is in charge. If his preferred gait is a trot (or running walk or rack), that's fine, but practice the command "easy," and frequently bring the animal down to a walk. Occasionally make him dog walk even if he (and perhaps you) detests going so slowly. Maintaining a steady gait at your command is a matter of proper, trained behavior, just as important as refraining from bucking, spooking, or running away.

# 10

## Advanced Trail Training

You are training your horse on every contact with it. Horses, like people, learn their entire lives. Long after initial training, horses can learn both positive and negative things. They can always get better. You may not think of yourself as a horse trainer, but if you are riding you are training, so why not make it a goal to improve your horse just a little bit every time you ride, to teach it something new?

So you have now a trail horse that is very satisfactory to you. The horse rarely spooks, holds the gait you prescribe, crosses streams and bridges readily, and performs quite comfortably both singly and on large group rides. He works all day on a light rein. When thunder rumbles in the distance, you can stop, slack the reins, reach back, untie your slicker, and put it on. He tolerates traffic around the parking lot at the trailhead, even motorcycles that pull in to turn around.

But how is his walk? If he's of a nongaited breed, does he break into a trot at speeds slower than you walk yourself? Does he understand leg cues? Is his neck rein so complete that you haven't had to touch the reins with a second hand in many rides?

I've already expressed my belief that the complete trail horse neck reins. I've also expressed my dismay at the loss of this sweet trait of Western riding. A writer for a horse magazine visited and rode with me recently. I pointed out that the gelding he would ride was a finished Western horse, that the animal would have no idea what the man wanted if he took a rein in each hand and reined with direct pressure.

The man assured me that he "rode Western" and that all of his horses neck reined. But when he mounted, he immediately turned the horse by beginning the neck rein, then reaching down with the other hand and pulling the rein in the direction he wanted to go. Several times I told him he was confusing the horse, that all he had to do was to move his one hand in the direction he wished to turn. After several such corrections, my instructions took hold.

I believe our modern clinicians could do a better job in this area. In teaching colt-starting with a direct rein, they don't emphasize that direct reining is a means to an end, not an end in itself, at least for the Western horse. So proud are they of obtaining lightness on the end of a heavy rope rein tugged directly, that they dwell there. Some discourage students from graduating toward the neck rein, reserving that for an advanced level. But, as we've discussed in the colt-starting chapter, training toward the neck rein can and should begin immediately. I have no desire to head out on a pack trip or a fall hunting trip on a horse that requires me to ride with a rope rein in each hand, a style of riding that denies me a hand to hold the lead rope of a packhorse, snap a picture, or check out wildlife on the other side of the canyon with my binoculars.

The basics of starting the neck rein were discussed earlier, but I'll just remind you that my approach teaches three cues for the turn, and teaches all three from the beginning. Going left, I direct rein with the left rein, lay the right on the colt's neck, and cue fairly far forward with my right leg. Surprisingly quickly, the colt will learn to turn with just two cues, the neck rein and the leg. One-handed riding follows, several fingers between the reins allowing you to give slight inside pressure when needed. I also encouraged you to not be overly religious: Go back to two-handed, direct-rein riding if necessary at an obstacle or some sort of trouble point. Eventually that will be unnecessary.

Constantly improve the neck rein of your trail horse by deliberately but subtly neck reining at each bend in the trail. Yes, he would stay on the trail around that turn anyway, but lay the rein lightly on his neck just the same. So strong will the association eventually become, that the need for a second hand on the reins will become a distant memory for both of you.

Leg cueing and the advanced maneuvers made possible by leg cue-ing are just as important on the trail as they are in the show ring. Your first thought may be that a maneuver like the side-pass is of no real im-portance to the trail horse, but let me give you a scenario. You are rid-ing on a trail 3 feet wide. On your right is a cliff nearly straight down for several hundred feet. On your left is a cliff nearly straight *up* for sev-eral hundred feet. (A US Forest Service trail just like I've described ex-ists within 20 miles of my house.)

Now, your mare, Fearless Fran, has no apprehension whatsoever over this situation. She's enjoying herself. So much does she like the view, that she keeps thrusting her head 6 inches farther to the right than nec-essary so that she can better see around the bends in the trail. Further, she enjoys walking on the extreme right-hand edge. Yes, she stays on good footing, but your right foot is actually dangling over the edge of the cliff. So, while Fran marches up the trail with a horse-smile on her face, you are petrified. And I don't blame you.

Were you riding the plow-reining gelding you just bought, the one you (thankfully) left home today, the horse that turns whatever direc-tion you pull him but has no clue about leg cues, your only option would be to put pressure on his left rein. Seeking the safer inside por-tion of the trail, you'd want to get him left, but all you'd be able to do would be to rein his head left. Yes, his head would go over to the secure side, but his body might just stay on that outside edge of the trail. Even worse, too sharp a pull on the left rein and his hindquarters just might move to the right, a normal compensation. That, of course, would be the last thing you want.

Luckily, you spent some time in the arena teaching Fearless Fran all about leg cues and side-passing. You tell her that much as she enjoys dancing with death, you'd just as soon seek the safe side of the trail, thank you—you'd really like to live to collect social security. So you press your right leg into Fran's side, not reining her either direction and, like the good mare she is, she moves left and begins hugging the "up" cliff instead of the "down" one. Whew!

No skill is more useful for the trail horse than the ability to move laterally with a light leg cue from the rider. Not only is it crucial for situa-tions like that described above, it is handy when another rider slides up just a little too close to you for comfort while your horses drink from a stream. When you meet another rider on a narrow trail, and the woods are too thick to allow getting off to the side of the trail, being able to press your horse to one side is an asset. Again, in such a situation, the plow-reining horse that knows only to follow the way its nose is pulled is likely to make little more room on the trail.

Much has been written about teaching the side-pass. My particular approach is rather simple. Standing on the ground next to any horse, old or young, I constantly practice cues. These consist simply of moving the horse with the command "over," by pressing my fingertips into his sides. I may use a harder object, such as the handle of a curry or the rowel of a spur, for a thick-skinned horse. A cue back toward the flank moves the horse's hindquarters, while one forward of the cinch moves its forehand.

The horse's understanding that it should yield to pressure from the side coordinates with the approach we've described for teaching the neck rein. Again, we've been turning the horse with three cues: the direct rein (early, and only when necessary), the neck rein, and a leg cue fairly far forward. Now we ride the horse up to a solid fence or wall, go back to two-handed riding, and do not allow him to bend in either direction. Sometimes it is best to slant toward the wall at an angle. The horse is looking for a rein cue to turn left or right, but gets instead only a stern leg cue at the cinch line to keep moving, but to now move sideways. If you've been able to keep his momentum, all the better, slanting left toward the wall, prohibiting a left turn, but cueing on the right side. I accompany the cue with the command, "Pass."

Don't expect perfection quickly. The horse has every right to be confused. You've been teaching him to do all these pretty turns, and now you're refusing to let him turn, insisting instead that he stay facing the wall. Keep the horse calm and remain firm, but low-stress, so that the spirited horse is not tempted to handle the pressure by getting light in the front end. You can almost sense how the smart, well-dispositioned horse thinks in this situation. As with all new lessons, a small step in the right direction is cause for celebration, for rewarding with strokes on the neck. A side step with both forehand and hind end, even if not simultaneously, is a victory.

A                                                     B

*a) Author starting the side-pass to his left on Pride with left leg cue while neck reining to right (to prevent left turn) while saying "Pass." b) Pride responds with a crossover of front legs to his left. A good side-pass takes some time to develop and should begin with the snaffle, riding two-handed.*

Once your horse has taken those first steps he has indeed side-passed; everything from here on is simply perfecting the maneuver. Soon you'll get several steps to the side, then equal success going the other direction. Once you can go smartly sideways down the wall in each direction, begin side-passing out in the open, without having the wall or fence as a crutch. Eventually your horse will take beautiful sideways steps, in which his legs cross as he performs a maneuver not normally within the natural repertoire of a four-legged animal.

For quite some time you will hold onto two-handed riding for the side-pass, but the day will come when your horse can perform it with just your one hand on the reins. And very early in the game, he'll have learned that a leg cue on one side while walking up the trail means to ease in that direction.

Many years ago I decided that I had little interest in any backcountry horse that could not walk as fast as I can. Saddle horses are supposed to be efficient tools of transportation, and the need to break into a trot at 2 or 3 miles per hour does not seem very efficient. Some horses have reasonably smooth trots (though virtually never in league with the intermediate four-beat gaits of the gaited breeds), but many do not, and the idea of posting on an all-day backcountry ride seems a ridiculous expenditure of energy.

But there is more to walking than comfort. The walk is the basic backcountry gait because of its ease for the animal and its surefootedness. As we've said, the walk places three of the horse's four feet on the ground at any one time. The trot, however, is a two-beat suspension gait, alternating between two opposed (one front, one hind) feet on the ground, then suspension (no feet on the ground), then the other two touching down. Obviously, feet on the ground are an asset for surefootedness.

Gaited horses handle this problem in two ways: first, with a smoother four-beat gait that replaces the trot; but, more importantly for the trail, with a regular walk that is loose and efficient. Even the slow walk of most gaited horses reveals hind legs that reach up and land forward of the track of the front foot. Translated, this means the steps it takes are simply longer, the reason a Tennessee Walker can seem to be loafing along, but still put its nongaited companions into a trot in order to keep up.

Virtually all horses, including the gaited ones, can be taught to walk better, but we're primarily talking here about the nongaited animal that trots the instant he's asked to speed up from an extremely slow walk. His genetics may be partially to blame. Perhaps the horse is the result of several generations of breeding for arena activities where the walk is irrelevant, or an extremely slow walk desirable. The animal's conformation, as discussed earlier, might favor the trot and the gallop at expense of the walk. But training usually has contributed to the problem, training during which the animal was never required to walk out briskly. The trainer has been attentive to every other performance issue, but has never cared much about the animal's walk. Perhaps he thinks of the horse as primarily an arena creature, not as one that he ever personally plans to ride long distances in the backcountry.

One way to tell whether a problem with the walk has originated in training, rather than from a genetic or conformational defect, is to watch the horse after it has been turned out. In the paddock after the ride, relieved of saddle and rider, some horses stretch out into a nice walk toward the feed bunk. They have the physical ability to walk better, but have never been required to. With no rider on their backs, they do what comes naturally, a nice, looser walk, whereas under saddle, they trot if asked to move faster than a snail's pace.

I have been too-long spoiled by fast-walking horses to claim expertise, but I can make a few observations. First, adjust your own thinking. If this mare is to be your complete trail horse, her barrel-racing background is of no particular help. True, her sprinting ability might come in handy should a mama grizzly take issue with you on the trail, and her athletic ability is certainly an asset. But we have to upgrade the importance of the walk. If you habitually longe the mare, do so at all three gaits, not just at the trot or lope. Each gait should have a vocal command as well, so that a sharp "Walk!" will grow to have meaning.

Under saddle, practice, practice, practice. Continually urge your mare for greater speed in the walk, then check her the instant you feel a transition to the trot. Try a little impulsion combined with collection. Do not work for a low head carriage, because an extremely low carriage rarely goes with a snappy walk. It's a fallacy that a "peanut-roller" position is better for the horse's ability to see the trail. Indeed, the extremely low head carriage probably locates the trail squarely in the middle of the horse's blind spot. Note also that horses allowed to run free in rough country rarely have particularly low head carriages.

A good walk is usually accompanied by some nod of the head with each step. A more pronounced nod means you are making progress, because it signals a longer reach up underneath by the hind legs, "working off his back end," as it's called by gaited horse folks. The result of such reach is a longer step and better speed.

Try, too, to ask your horse to pick up the walk on "iffy" footing, such as mud or deep snow. Either substance makes it a little more difficult for a horse to trot. Having three out of four feet on the ground seems sensible to the animal that has some fear of falling, so the horse may well answer your cue with a more robust walk. Keep trying. None of this effort will work in a session or two, but a good horse will tend to make your priorities his own. Constantly emphasizing and being conscious of the walk is the first step toward improving it.

An advanced and extremely useful skill for the trail horse is the ability to pull a load from the saddle horn (which assumes, of course, a Western saddle). It's nice during pack trips to be able to saddle Major, find a fallen dry snag for firewood, and drag it back to camp. It's even more comforting to know that Major could yank a horse to safety were it to sink into a bog, or, if there were no other way to get the animal to move, pony a reluctant mule. A horse with this ability can pull kids on a sled or your spouse on his skis. Even if you are quite certain you will never need these skills, the horse that can drag something has added to his repertoire, having thoroughly demonstrated its ease with ropes and strange moving objects coming along behind it.

Dragging is another new skill that I approach cautiously, and first try in the arena. Obviously, your horse must neck rein and must be completely controllable with one hand. Here are a couple of rules. Never tie the drag rope fast to your saddle horn. Take at most two wraps (dallies) of the rope around your saddle horn so that you can very quickly disengage it. Second, keep the thumb of your dallying hand upwards to keep it out of trouble. (A disconcerting number of ropers are missing thumbs and other fingers.)

You'll want a breastcollar on your saddle so that most of the pull comes from the horse's shoulders. Assuming your horse is thoroughly desensitized to ropes—and it certainly should be by now—start by dragging the rope alone, turning this way and that so the horse feels the rope dragging against his hip. If you've taught your horse to pack during training, this will come more easily. Switch sides occasionally. Then add a little weight to the end of the rope. I use a small tire without a rim discarded from a compact car. Now the horse has a little resistance, which makes the rope lie more firmly against his hip. More disconcerting to some horses is seeing in their rearward vision a strange object moving along seemingly of its own volition. The horse at first has no idea that he is the one causing the movement.

Once the horse can drag the tire safely both on right and left, progress to heavier and noisier objects. Although pulling from the horn is not nearly as efficient as pulling with a proper harness and collar, it is amazing how much a horse can pull this way. Many Western horses get their baptism under fire by pulling out field-dressed deer and elk for hunters on snow. A field-dressed elk can weigh well over five hundred pounds. The horse must tolerate the smell of blood and the sight of a strange, brown critter seemingly trying to catch up by sliding on the ground behind him. The horse that does so on the first try and without much fuss is a good one indeed.

Never quit training your trail horse. Always push the envelope just a little bit further, challenging your horse to get better. If you are short and light, teach your horse to park out for mounting, a stance that lowers his back several inches. Perfect leg cues and the side-pass to help you with such tasks as opening gates on horseback. Introduce the animal to gunfire by starting with a cap pistol coordinated with a reward of grain, then progressing toward louder percussion. You may not hunt, but others do, and some day you may well be riding near a group of pheasant hunters (or firecracker-wielding boys). Look for possible trail contingencies in the areas you ride, and work to prepare your horse for them. Look also to your own pleasure, to things you can teach your horse that will make time on its back more enjoyable for you.

And do remember that if you are not training the horse, the horse is training you. Bad habits start innocently enough, but then progress. The "kiss" becomes a nibble, and then a bite. The quick snatch of a mouthful of grass without breaking gait becomes an abrupt stop, the head yanking the reins from your hand as the horse bullies its way toward something tasty. The horse begins to use you as a rubbing post for its sweaty forehead whenever you dismount. Your morning ride has the same turnaround point day after day. Soon the horse turns there without your cue, and the day you have time to go farther, puts up a fight because he has decided it is his right to reverse at that point. And in all these cases you must do what leaders always have to do, even when their subordinates are friends. You must lay down the law.

But with strong, considerate leadership and clear signals, such occurrences will be rare. A simpatico will build between you, improving with each mile, eventually giving true meaning to the slogan "Happy trails!"

# PART IV

## HITTING THE TRAIL: ETHICS, EQUIPMENT, AND TECHNIQUES

# 11

## A Room in Our House

*It is remarkable how easily and insensibly we fall into a
particular route and make a beaten track for ourselves*
—Henry David Thoreau

To our ranch in south-central Montana, come many visitors. When
Emily and I think a hunter or fisherman or horseman or hiker
needs a little reminder of how we would like to see the land treated, we
put it this way: Pointing to our rather modest house we say, "We do not
live in that house. We live on this ranch. Yes, we cook and sleep in that
house, but we live on this ranch. Every pasture, every sagebrush flat,
every hayfield is another room in our house. Please treat the ranch just
this way, just as you would the rooms in a house you were visiting." This
usually does the trick. Few of us are so boorish, after all, that we would
throw gum wrappers onto the floor of the living room in the home of
another. Few of us would damage the shrubbery by the front door or
stamp out a cigarette on the patio.

Although our ranch is "private" land, owned by us in the legal sense,
we are realistic enough to know that we're really only its custodians for
a sliver of time. We think of it as a home we share with livestock,
wildlife, all things that grow, as well as with the humans whose generations will follow. The metaphor holds true for all land on which any of
us venture, whether public or private, whether deeded to you or to
someone else. Wherever we ride our trail horses, we are riding through

the home of someone or something. Whether the land is owned by a private individual at whose pleasure we enter, or by a government entity whose ownership we share, the land is never ours to abuse.

Certainly it is love of the outdoors, not just an affinity for horses, that takes us out onto the trails in the first place. Perhaps we feel a special connection with nature when our mode of transportation is an old and traditional one, a flesh-and-blood creature rather than a mechanical device such as a mountain bicycle or a noisy ATV. Perhaps, too, we feel a connection to humans of the past who have ridden these trails: Native Americans, mountain men, homesteaders, and explorers. A two-track road that runs across the east range of our ranch is visible evidence of the old Bozeman Trail, and we can't ride it without thinking of the wagons and people who once passed there. How did it look then, before power lines and fences?

We who love to ride the trails face some extremely grim realities. The land available for doing so is disappearing rapidly, either ceasing to exist because of pavement and development and subdivision, or being closed to us by private landowners and government regulation. What remains of the land is thus more precious than ever. And we who venture onto it in the company of horses must treat it as we would the immaculate living room of a beloved friend. We must do this for two reasons: It is the *right* thing to do, and always has been; and, to do otherwise is to hasten the demise of an essential ingredient in the good life for many of us, that of going to the backcountry on horseback.

The United States, because it offered such seemingly limitless land to the flood of immigrants, created several extremely careless generations. Believe it or not, there really are places in this world where *no one* throws a soda can out of a car onto the roadside. Our country, even today, is not one of them. Along with careless and messy motorists, there were, and still are, careless and messy horsemen. Many of our most beautiful wild areas contain evidence of careless horse use. There are cupped-out areas around trees from extended tying and the pawing by horses such restraint encourages. Trees are also scarred from tying. Areas where livestock was held on soft, easily eroded ground have been beaten until nearly devoid of vegetation. Riders (and hikers) too impatient to follow the trail on switchbacks have made new trails and caused erosion.

Many of the closures to horses on public land can be laid at the feet of those who use their animals without regard for the impact they make. But not all the blame lies there. Our culture, too, has changed. A couple of generations ago much more of America was rural, and even many inner-city folks were just a generation away from the farm. Until the 1950s many smaller towns and cities in the US allowed livestock within the city limits. The chicken coop, milk barn, and stable were parts of everyday life. A neighbor up the street often had fresh eggs and milk to sell. The good things that came from domestic animals were cherished, and the droppings they left behind were not considered a problem.

Today government agencies are sometimes staffed with folks who have had no connection whatsoever with horses. Similarly, some of the people who hike the trails are put off and perhaps intimidated by all sign of horses. If that were not enough, many other groups, such as mountain bikers and all-terrain vehicle enthusiasts, are competing for trail use.

What do we do? First, we make our use of horses just as low impact as possible. We'll be dealing with ways to do so throughout the remainder of the book. To leave only tracks, as few and as shallow as possible, will be our goal. Second, we must be proactive. We must be aware of proposed land and trail closures to horses (with government land, public notice is normally given, along with a comment period) and be quick but reasonable in our response by letter, phone, and email. Finally, courtesy to other trail users will go a long way toward easing tensions. You may detest meeting a bicycle or ATV on the trail, but all users of the outdoors must minimize their differences and band together to best accommodate all.

Several organizations can help. The group with which I am most familiar is Back Country Horsemen of America. (Incidentally, despite the name, women were heavily involved in naming this group and have often been the prime movers within it.) This organization, which began in Montana, has spread rapidly, with chapters in many states and several Canadian provinces. Members fight trail closures in two ways. First, they work as a political action group to prevent horses and pack stock from being squeezed from areas they traditionally traversed. Second, they volunteer "sweat equity" and their expertise as packers to support the Forest Service and other government agencies in maintaining trails.

In support of the Custer National Forest, the Back Country Horsemen club to which I belong has installed culverts under trails; built water breaks (slanting logs embedded into the trail to funnel water over the side, which prevents its coursing down the trail); installed gates; built hitching rails and other improvements at trailheads; and, when the agency's budget has allowed hiring of a trail crew, packed in supplies as well as furnishing camp cooks. Rewards for all this have included tasteful signs at trailheads crediting the club for such support and, more importantly, much good will from other users of the trails. When a backpacker realizes horses and mules packed in the timbers for the new

*Author leads Major, packing four plastic culverts, and Monty packing tools for Back Country Horsemen project in support of US Forest Service. Culverts were duct-taped together, then loaded on Decker packsaddle with basket hitch, and installed in wet areas of a wilderness trail to prevent bogs. Work projects such as this improve trails and remind the public of the indispensable abilities of pack animals in the backcountry.*

*US Forest Service personnel giving seminar to Back Country Horsemen on techniques for packing timbers into backcountry. Heavy lumber is required for building bridges and for water breaks to prevent water running down trails.*

trail bridge crossed an hour ago, any anger over occasional horse droppings on the trail tends to be mollified.

Such public service, spiced with a dash of political activism, will help to safeguard our access to this country's trails. But the most important safeguard, and the most satisfying, is our impeccable behavior in that field of flowers, that grove of pines, and that "livingroom" by the lake. And, since our horses are hardly housebroken, we, as their leaders, must keep their presence as delicate as possible.

# 12

## Equipment for the Trail

### Shoes and Saddles, Bridles and Bits

Since our horse will be doing most of the work, it is only right that we look to his well-being first. We might just as well start at the critical point where his body meets the ground. "No foot, no horse," said the old timers, often reciting that ditty about loss of the nail, then the shoe, then the horse, and so on. And indeed, it has been iron shoes, nailed to the outer rim of horses' feet (to the painless portion that corresponds to the part of your fingernail you frequently trim) that has protected them for many centuries.

The protection was not illusory. Horses, after all, were being put through all sorts of things for which nature did not prepare them. Creatures of the grasslands, horses had evolved with a remarkable hoof, but not one prepared for cobblestone streets nor for the extra weight imposed by a heavy rider, perhaps equipped for battle. Nature had not given the horse feet designed for the traction required to pull a wagon when an inch of ice clung to the ground.

I do not buy the argument currently in vogue, that shoes on horses were a giant two-millennium mistake. Again, horses were naturally the creatures of the vast, grassy plains. (Donkeys are the equines that evolved on the flinty mountain passes, and their feet reflect that.) Man, in domesticating the horse, did two things. First, as we've said, he required all sorts of service from it—weight-carrying, pulling, and operating on hostile surfaces—that nature had not required. Second, he bred the animals through hundreds of generations for all sorts of qualities having nothing to do with the soundness of their feet. He bred horses for speed, agility, courage, weight-carrying ability, pulling ability, and gait characteristics. Remember, every horse on the face of the earth is a domestic animal. The horse as we know it is as different from what he would have been without man's domestication of him, as the Holstein cow is from the musk ox or the water buffalo.

Thus, the argument that simply letting a horse run in natural conditions will produce feet that will never need shoes is illogical. It assumes we can undo all these generations of selective breeding, and it implies that the horse's "natural" state includes the uses to which we're likely to put him. I'm not swayed in this by the fact that wild (properly feral) horses run barefoot. When a horse within a herd of mustangs comes up lame, it either starves or is pulled down by a mountain lion or another predator. Survival of the fittest is the rule of the day, and we do not usually see the animals that do not make it. And, of course, these horses do not carry the weight of a human on their backs.

Our 1,200 acres in Montana is about as natural an environment as you could imagine. A combination of soft, irrigated fields, rocky hills, cobblestone river bottoms, and pine-studded coulees, the terrain does indeed build tough muscles and feet. Our broodmares, pasture-breeding stallion, and young stock run without shoes. Seldom is trimming needed. We're proud to have maintained bloodlines with good hoof walls and feet of adequate size.

Fine, so far. But when we *use* these horses different rules apply. When Little Mack is asked to carry me while deftly cutting a cow and calf out from the rest of the herd during icy March, he needs the traction provided by shoes, and the shoes are for my benefit, my own safety, as well. When we pack up a camp and head for the high plateau during summer, crossing granite slides where the trail has been blasted out by dynamite, to take a horse barefoot would be, in my opinion, abusive. However, in areas of the country with abundant topsoil, where trails are dirt and the biggest traction problem is mud, it's just fine to ride your trail horse barefoot as long as his traction is adequate, his hooves are tough, and he stays sound.

*In some areas of the Rockies the trails have been blasted out of granite slides.*

Even in our rough country, I'm certainly not closed to alternatives. Many of us take Easyboots of several sizes along on pack trips for emergency use, and I know of a few riders who use them and similar products in place of iron shoes. New approaches to this old problem are continually introduced into the marketplace. Some are products that nail on like a regular shoe, but are made of a plastic or alternative material that is said to absorb some concussion and still wear well. Very possibly we'll eventually settle on products that do a better job than traditional shoes. Time will tell.

If, however, you're still using traditional shoeing as I am, let's make sure of a few extremely important things. First, shoeing with extra toe for improved gait (common with gaited horses, but also done for increased action in breeds that show at the trot) is an absolute "no-no" on the trail. As I mentioned back in the breed descriptions, even light-shod Walking Horses and American Saddlers often are shod with an inch or two of extra toe in front. On rough trails this sort of shoeing is abusive to the horse and dangerous for the rider. That extra toe extension *will* cause tripping in rough country, and I travel to places where tripping is extremely dangerous. An elderly friend of mine who has raised gaited horses and used them in rugged Wyoming most of his life believes that uphill use with extra toe also promotes the development of ringbone.

Equally verboten are what some call "trailers," the rear tips of the shoes extending past the back of the hoof, often for an inch or more. In this case the farrier uses a shoe a size or more too large for the horse, narrows it on his anvil, and nails it on. This is a foolish sort of shoeing for the trail. While going uphill, the long-striding horse is likely to clip that trailing portion of the shoe as its rear foot comes up toward its front, causing a loose shoe at best, an injury at worst. Even if that doesn't happen, a rocky trail is bound to contain a stone placed just right to lever off the shoe from behind.

Ask your farrier to shoe the trail horse at an angle that is natural for his pasterns and shoulders. And *don't* allow your farrier to trim out the whole frog. The tissue on the bottom of the center portion of the hoof, called the frog, is a natural shock absorber. Some farriers get rid of it. I suspect that custom has come from wet areas of the country where horses, particularly stall-bound ones, are more prone to thrush, an infection of the frog. But a healthy frog is a great help to the horse on stone-covered trails.

*Close shoeing with neither extra toe, nor shoe trailing behind the hoof, is best for the backcountry horse.*

The terrain will determine the nature of the shoe itself. On relatively smooth trails, with occasional rocks, rims will do just fine. Some swear by them even in extremely rough terrain, believing the ridge on the shoe offers nearly as much traction as caulks. But I still believe that caulks on both heels and toe of the shoes make for the greatest traction in the most demanding conditions. Since a horse carries most of its weight on the front, and since downhill riding is where I most desire traction, I sometimes specify caulked shoes on the front and rims on the back.

The downside to any shoe that affords great traction is that the shoe also puts more torque on the animal's pasterns and legs. Back when I played high school football, our shoes had giant cleats on them. If a player was tackled from the side, his shoes would stay planted, refusing to slide, and injuries were thus common. Football shoes have much milder cleats today. For the same reason I stick with regular rims on young horses.

In winter, of course, everything changes. People who ride on ice might look into borium, which your farrier can apply to the shoe with a torch. My farrier favors spots of weld, the very hard stuff known as "hard-surfacing," which he welds to each caulk to dig into the ice. (The

*Winter work in icy conditions—time to consider shoes with caulks of borium or hard-surface lugs welded on.*

shoe must be shaped first, because the heat of the welding tends to harden it.) Similar traction schemes have existed for years. Shoes for draft horses often had threaded holes into which sharp studs could be screwed for extra traction as needed. More modern versions of the same idea exist today for show jumpers and winter riders.

Beware of early spring, however. No shod horse or barefoot one is safe from slipping on an inch or two of mud lying on top of frozen ground. Shoes, even caulked ones, don't penetrate the mud down into the frost, and an unshod hoof has the same problem. The mud itself, however, slides on top of the frost as if greased. During this season, try to ride early in the morning while the top layer is still frozen.

Before we progress to other items of equipment for the horse, "Can we talk?" as Joan Rivers used to say. When Emily and I raised our first babies—human ones—we learned of a phenomenon involving the baby food we bought at supermarkets. We learned that the manufacturers tested it by having people taste it. Seems normal enough until you realize that babies did not taste it, *mothers* tasted it. The people who concocted the stuff were not concerned much about whether the babies would like it. They were extremely concerned that the adults who tasted it liked it, because they were sure these parents would approve if they, themselves, found the taste pleasant.

Today, much of the world of horse-related equipment is driven by two concerns, one legitimate, one warped for purposes of profit. The fact that more horsemen than ever are concerned with the welfare of the horse is laudable. We owe it to these wonderful animals to make their lives comfortable and to avoid their unnecessary suffering. However, I continually see products marketed with the word "humane" in front of them, with comparisons made to the product the new item replaces. In many cases the implication is: "You've been using an item of equipment that is cruel and inhumane, that's the bad news. The good news is that our product *is* humane. By buying and using it you can quit being an uncaring, cruel slob." The problem is that people actually believe this stuff, and some adopt a snobbish attitude toward those unregenerate souls who have not seen the light in the way they have.

Mark Twain said, "Nothing needs reforming so much as other peoples' habits." And so some people look down on anyone who uses a bit, or perhaps, any bit other than a snaffle. Some people claim that any shoeing method other than the "revolutionary" one they've adopted is cruel. Others carry this over to training methods, adopting one school of colt-starting and condemning all others.

What makes this thinking dicey is that there truly is, and always has been, much abuse in the horse world. But we have to do our best critical thinking when examining advertising that pushes us to buy a product or adopt a training regime for supposedly humane purposes. A trainer condemns curb bits as torture devices, and markets an expensive alternative, complete with training methods that match it. A saddle company explains in detail why the saddle tree it uses is easier on the horse's back than all others. Although we shouldn't dismiss such claims out of hand, we should look at them closely. How much of the appeal stands up in the light of day? How much is directed at making us somehow feel good, feel we've improved the lot of our horses and others? Are we buying the "baby food" because it's really better for the horse, or because it simply tastes good to us?

There *are* training devices and methods that are inherently cruel. No redeeming feature in my mind can be found for the torture involved in soring a gaited horse, creating constant pain that gives the horse a choice only between pain and extreme pain. Thankfully, such approaches to so-called training are illegal and, hopefully, on the wane.

For the most part, the element that separates your training devices and your equipment for riding and directing your horse from those of a rival school of thought is merely the degree of leverage. As we said in the training section of this book, there is little difference in terms of potential for abuse among a whip, a long lead rope, or a set of long driving reins. Similarly, a horse's head can be yanked cruelly when its headstall is only a halter with reins. Its mouth can be pinched wickedly with a snaffle. Its tongue can be cut nearly in half by a curb bit. But all any of these abuses really proves is that a dud of a horseman, a yank-and-tear hothead, is at the helm.

I go into some detail on this issue because there is now an unfortunate lack of "live and let live" in the horse world. Too many people have

*A well-equipped day rider. The relatively long-shanked curb bit is fine for this woman, who rides with an extremely light hand.*

an axe to grind, a principle to prove. A man I know was sitting on his stallion watching events in a practice arena when someone fully fifty feet away yelled out in coarse language that the curb strap on his bridle was too tight. The man invited the accuser to come over and check, and when the individual would not do so, dismounted and placed his entire hand between the horse's jaw and the curb strap, which, in fact, was quite loose. "See," he yelled back, "it's not tight at all." Instead of apologizing, the complainer turned in a huff and walked off.

Yes, Mark Twain was right. No matter what style of equipment one chooses today, someone may well take issue and decide your "bad habits" need reforming. If you ride in unknown company, you should be prepared for that. So when we discuss bridles and bits you won't see me pushing any agenda. Lots of things work well. I have a right to complain only if your horse is out of control. If your horse endangers my horse and me, that's certainly another story.

As I've said, I admire hackamore tradition, but did not grow up with it. I prefer the snaffle bit for early training, followed eventually by a mild curb. For me, moving to the curb is a move to fewer ounces of pressure on the reins. But let's back up a little for readers who need definitions.

A snaffle is a non-leverage bit, usually, but not always, with a broken (jointed) mouthpiece. A snaffle has no shanks, and no bit with shanks should be called a snaffle. Non-leverage simply means that pressure exerted on the rings where the reins attach is not compounded, as with a lever or pulley. A pound of pressure on the left rein translates into a pound of pull on the side of the horse's mouth; no more, no less. Pressure is transferred to the horse on the bars (toothless upper portions) of his lower jaw, but primarily via the ring on the opposite side, which pressures on the right side of the mouth when the left rein is pulled.

If you add shanks to the mouthpiece of that snaffle you have a curb bit, even though such are often miscalled shanked snaffles. As we've said, there is no such thing. A popular bit of this sort looks exactly like a ring snaffle, but has short shanks and a curb strap underneath the jaw. Often called a Tom Thumb, this can be a very useful bit for transition between the snaffle and curb. For me it has been a mixed bag. Some horses I start like the Tom Thumb while others are annoyed by it. Colts in the latter category often take more readily to a very mild curb.

All shanked bits have some leverage. Pressure is exerted on the bars of the mouth and also on the bottom of the jaw via the curb strap or chain, as well as on top of the poll behind the horse's ears, which is a sensitive nerve area. Pressure is exerted up there because as the shanks are pulled to the rear, they pull the headstall forward.

The ideal outlook on curb bits is the one I've mentioned, that they are finesse bits that solicit fingertip riding. Through history, though, they have also been used to exert more control of the animal's head. Current philosophy is that if a horse can't be controlled with the bit you have, you probably need to do some retraining.

There is much misunderstanding about measuring the relative leverage of curb bits. Some people look at shank length only, which can be deceiving. A proper evaluation is to compare the length of the shank below the bit with that above the bit. In other words, if the shank below the bit is 4 inches, but there are two inches of shank above the bit, between it and the attachment to the leather headstall, the bit has just a 2-to-1 advantage, which is quite mild. If, on the other hand, there are four inches of shank below and only one above the ratio is 4-to-1, which is quite severe. Many other factors determine severity. The tighter the curb strap or chain, the more severe. The mouthpiece usually has a port, a horseshoe shape that works on the horse's palate. That

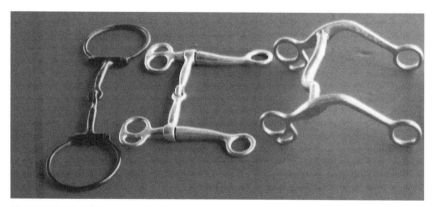

*Three useful bits, left to right, are the ring snaffle; the Tom Thumb (which should be properly considered a curb bit); and a grazing bit, a mild curb with swept-back shanks to facilitate grazing during rest stops.*

shape, along with the thickness of the metal itself, contributes to relative severity; thicker tends to be milder.

Bitting is an extremely complex subject. My advice for the novice regarding curb bits is to acquire a thorough understanding of how they work and how to adjust them. Don't, however, be afraid that you can never acquire the competence to use one.

If your type of horsemanship includes bits and headstalls, ride on the trail with a good halter kept underneath the headstall. For this purpose flat halters are more comfortable to the horse than the rope type. We carry halters because reins are for riding, not for tying. Yes, the trained

*Tie-type halter is strongest, having no metal parts to break, but may be less comfortable under bridle than a flat, nylon type. Remember, halters and lead ropes, not reins, are for tying.*

horse will normally stand tied by the reins, but if a major spook occurs, such as a low-flying helicopter or a bear in the brush, we want him tied with something stronger than reins, for if he breaks loose, he may well learn to pull back. A horse that has become convinced he can successfully pull back and get loose can be extremely hard, if not impossible, to retrain. Furthermore, if a horse pulls hard on the reins, the bit is likely to hurt its mouth.

Sometime before we purchased her, Rosie, my Thoroughbred/Quarter mare, had learned to pull back. Reins were like kite string to her. A strong lead rope simply resulted in her breaking either the halter or the post she was tied to. Since this mare was a dandy in every other respect, a good cow horse that could turn on a dime, and since she was my primary using horse, her inability to be tied was a major inconvenience.

Elmer studied out the situation, then went to town and bought a length of ¾-inch nylon rope. No horse alive can break ¾-inch nylon. In the corral was a snubbing post, a railroad tie set 40 inches into the ground, possibly the most solid post on the entire ranch. Elmer threaded the nylon rope through Rosie's halter ring, then around her neck, tying it off with a bowline. He led her over to the snubbing post and tied the rope to the post, also with a bowline, knowing that he'd never get any other knot he knew untied, once great pressure was applied. Then we both stood back.

Rosie gently tested the setup, and when she realized she was tied, hauled back. She snorted and struggled and squealed, and the dust flew. She had clearly met her match. Then Elmer, cowboy that he was, could not stand it. He shook his head and circled the rodeo gingerly. Pulling out his pocketknife, he waited for an instant between her heaving so that she would not flip over backwards, then sneaked in and cut the rope. He pushed his hat back on his head and said, "It's not worth it. She'd really hurt herself. She'd pull every muscle she had loose before she'd give up. You'll just have to put up with it, Dan."

And so I did. I carried a set of hobbles on my saddle and hobbled Rosie whenever I had to stop and work. She was enough of a chowhound that if the grass was good where I fixed fence or set irrigation water, she would obligingly drop her head and enjoy herself, not moving around too much, until it was time to head home.

Leave your halter in place under the headstall and carry a stout lead rope. I like lead ropes to be at least 9 feet long, but 10 is better. Around the arena you can tie to a ring or a slim post, but sometimes out on the trail you need extra length to go around something fatter. And let me ask you to take a page from Rosie's book and also carry a set of hobbles. They are light and easy to tie to saddle strings or insert into saddlebags. Why? To tie to trees is to risk damaging them. We do so, but only for extremely short times and when there is no other alternative. One way to minimize impact during your rest stop is to tie one horse, preferably a dominant one, and hobble the rest. When there is a choice, keep the hobbled horses farther up the trail than you are. In other words, stay between the hobbled horses and the trailhead while you eat your lunch, which will decrease chances they'll head home, hobbles and all. In any case, you have that dominant horse to round them up if that should happen.

Training your horse to hobbles is easy. If you've taught him to yield each foot, and to be led by each foot as I recommend, there is probably

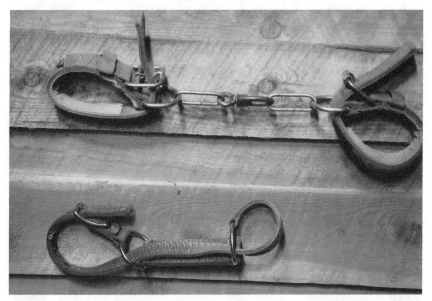

*Nylon hobbles below are light and inexpensive, but they may chafe a horse not used to them. Grazing hobbles above are padded and safer, but horses soon learn to travel rapidly while wearing them.*

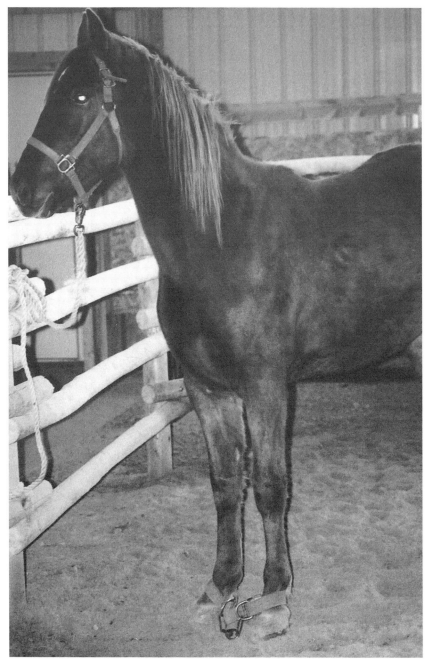

*This colt is wearing grazing hobbles briefly while tied, then will be allowed to get used to them in the safe, sandy arena.*

nothing to teach. With other horses there will be a bit of a protest, so stay out of the way. Soft arena sand, a garden with deep footing, or deep snow will tend to prevent injury. Choose gentle hobbles, preferably padded, or at least leather and not nylon for this first experience. Although some training books show hobbles on the cannon bones, I'm of the school that says that risks injury to the flat tendons on the forelegs. All packers and outfitters I know put hobbles where I do, down on the pasterns.

Hobble your horse in a safe, soft place, and then get out of the way. Confusion doesn't normally last too long. Some horses fight the hobbles, while others stand like rocks for a long time, believing they are unable to move. Soon they take baby steps, then hop with their front feet in synch. Many learn to move *too* well. We had a Walking Horse colt that could deftly jump a barbed wire fence while hobbled, and did so several times.

Saddles, like bits, tend to be chosen because of custom and culture, and your particular school of horsemanship. Except for the occasional use of my McClellan replica cavalry saddle and one ride in an English saddle I had been given, I had never ridden a saddle without a horn until Emily and I went to Spain. Our guide, a British native who had been raised in Spain, favored English cavalry saddles. With their iron and wood trees, these saddles were rugged and comfortable. We took to them quite readily.

With my limited knowledge of English saddles, I can merely recommend those with a deeper seat that are intended for three-day eventing's cross-country use. Ample cantle behind your rear furnishes support going up steep hills. If you show gaited horses, leave your show saddle behind when you ride the trails. Walking Horse show saddles place your weight to the rear on the animal. This frees his front end for action that will please judges, but it's poison on the animal's back. Your horse will suffer on a long trail ride with this sort of saddle, and placing your weight so far behind the horse's center of gravity is bad for his surefootedness. Another shortcoming of English saddles for trail purposes is their lack of saddle strings or D-rings to which you can tie your raincoat or water bottle.

Between English and Western saddles are several other types of interest to trail riders. The traditional plantation saddle built for using

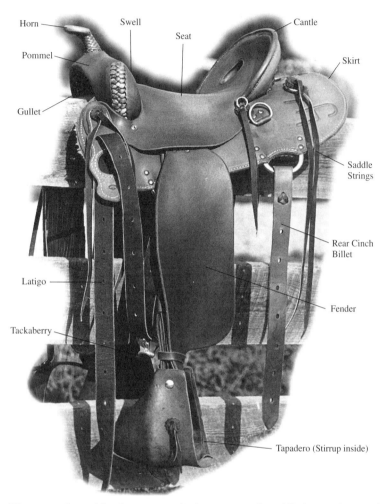

*The parts of a saddle shown on author's custom-made saddle by Erickson's of Ennis, Montana. Holes in cantle allow threading rope through to sling loads to the saddle should it need to double as a packsaddle.*

horses is often seen among hunting dog-field trial folks. One type called the "Trooper saddle" is more ruggedly built than most English saddles, and usually features plenty of D-rings, since a bird hunter must be able to tie on his shotgun scabbard and other equipment. Field trial folks ride long and hard on their gaited horses, covering many miles through brush and bramble, so both their horses and equipment are of interest to trail riders. One typical feature of field trial saddles is tapaderos, a safety and comfort feature desirable on the stirrups of any backcountry saddle.

Australian stock saddles came to America in force approximately twenty-five years ago. Some gaited horse owners took to them readily. They found them comfortable, and also found that the saddles, built for the somewhat narrower, higher-withered Australian horses, fit their gaited American ones. However, these saddles tended to be too narrow for some other modern American breeds. Thus the manufacturers widened the trees in many cases, good or bad depending what sort of horse you own. One importer offers several tree widths.

For this book I surveyed companies that offer trail rides in various areas of the country. From them and from the advertising one sees in magazines, it appears that the Western saddle has become the saddle of choice for trail riders even east of the Mississippi. Indeed, Western saddles have many advantages (and one big disadvantage) for much of the

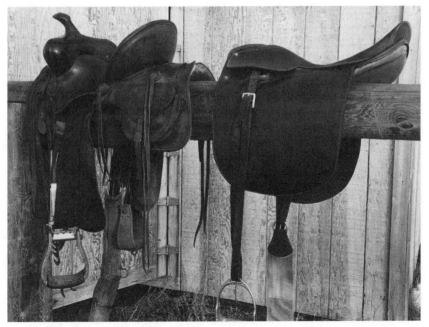

*A study in contrast—1919 Montana stock saddle on left, English flat saddle on right.*

backcountry riding we do. The disadvantage is weight. Most, if well built, are heavy.

Virtually all saddles are built over a frame called a tree. The tree normally features two bars of soft wood that can be easily shaped, each bar a flat piece of board fitting along the animal's back, one on each side of its spine. In Western saddles, traditional tree construction is rawhide over the wood tree, the rawhide applied when wet. As the rawhide dries it shrinks and binds the tree together with tremendous force. This rawhide and wood tree is still considered by many to be the ultimate saddle tree, though synthetic materials such as fiberglass have now been used to construct good serviceable saddles.

Western saddles are heavy because of their somewhat longer bars, which is good for weight distribution, and because the entire saddle— pommel, cantle, and all—is covered with leather. Underneath there is usually a layer of sheepskin (with wool) or a similar synthetic to protect the horse's back. The skirts of most Western saddles are also ample and add to the weight. Western saddles can be built relatively light, but leather thickness tends to be compromised, and such a saddle may not be rugged enough to stand up to the abuse dished out by working cowboys.

Old-fashioned Western saddles with deep seats seem to be coming back in vogue. Do not overlook your grandfather's saddle, which might be a treasure. However, be careful of fit if you intend to use a pre-WWII Western saddle on your modern Quarter Horse, Paint, or Appaloosa. The old cowboys rode a narrower sort of horse, which early saddles often reflect. Such a saddle may pinch the wider, stockier type of horse. Conversely, many of these saddles fit gaited horses and Arabians quite well.

Because deep seats and A-forks—Western saddles with no swells, the type used exclusively before 1900—are becoming so popular, many companies and individual saddle makers are duplicating these older styles, but often on somewhat wider trees. I find many of these efforts extremely attractive, comfortable, and tied into our history as a population on horseback.

Saddle fit is complicated and important. Some companies offer virtually unlimited opportunities to try their saddles for proper fit; I've known folks who have returned a dozen or more. This approach, unfortunately, would never suit me, because my saddle must work for a colt I'm training one morning, my working gelding that afternoon, and perhaps old Major, who is built considerably wider, the next day. What are you to do when you can afford only one good saddle but contemplate using it on many horses?

Like it or not, you must err on the large side. A saddle that's a bit too wide for the horse can usually be made to work with an extra pad. A saddle that's too narrow can never be made to work and will sore the animal, usually on each side just behind the withers. That sort of pinch is quite painful. Another pitfall is lack of clearance under the gullet for the high withers I advocate in trail horses. Do make sure, especially with a saddle that is on the wide side, that there is ample clearance (two fingers worth) between the top of the horse's withers and contact with the gullet.

A saddle that fits well feels good as you nestle it in place. The front of the tree should dovetail with the horse's body as it widens toward the shoulders. When you rock the saddle back and forth, it should resist your effort to roll it off the horse, even before cinching. Indeed, a saddle that truly fits can be difficult to remove from your horse. You can't simply roll it off; you must lift it nearly clear of the horse's back.

After a good, vigorous ride, remove your saddle and pad and look critically at the horse's sweaty back. Dry spots indicate pressure. A general rule is that large dry spots are okay, because the pressure has been distributed over a reasonable area. Small dry spots are bad. In some cases these pressure points can be prevented by additional padding, but some change must be made. The small dry spot will become a sore, the heat eventually destroying the pigment in the hair, with the end result the familiar white saddle mark.

A saddle that fits really well needs only a thin Navajo blanket underneath it. A saddle that fits less precisely must be a bit wide to work at all. An extra pad can more widely distribute the pressure that creates these small dry spots, and prevent them. I personally do not care for extremely thick saddle pads, which I would only use only with an ill-fitting saddle whose tree was far too wide. A thick pad tends to remove you from the horse, to lessen your contact with it. I've seen some pads so thick you feel top-heavy when mounted, pads that separate the saddle from the horse so much that it tends to rock side to side.

In the case of the Western saddle, a variety of riggings have been used over the years. The most popular today is the full-rigged saddle. These have two cinches, the front fairly far forward, the rear originally intended for preventing the saddle's back end from rising during roping. Earlier Western saddles had just one cinch, and one is certainly all that is needed for the trail saddle. Some full-rigged saddles have provision for moving the main cinch a bit to the rear, so that you can remove the rear cinch and have what is called a ¾-rigged saddle. For trail use none of this is very critical as long as the cinch does its job of securing the saddle without causing sores. Some cinch setups that crowd the horse just behind the front legs are prone to causing pinching and soring there.

In hilly country, especially with a trim horse lacking in belly, a breastcollar keeps the saddle from sliding back, and thus allows use of a looser cinch. I have used the type made of stranded cinch material, but found they were magnets for burrs. Ditto for those of nylon with padding underneath. I've settled on good-quality leather, a bit more expensive, but easiest on the horse. Talk to packers and you'll invariably find affection for natural materials—leather, cotton, and wool—as least likely to cause sores and abrasions.

I've mentioned the wisdom and safety of adding tapaderos to any sort of saddle you use out on the trails. They serve two important functions. Taps well secured to the stirrup prevent a foot from slipping through. They also protect the foot from brush and bramble, from splash in the creek, from creeping frost. Out west, where horsemen hunt the mountains during fall, taps allow an oversized stirrup to accommodate bulky hunting boots, footwear that would otherwise be dangerous for riding. Also, any child's saddle, in my mind, should have tapaderos for safety's sake.

Another add-on too rarely used in the US is the crupper. A leather strap that extends from the rear of the saddle around the base of the tail, the crupper also allows a looser, more comfortable cinch on long, downhill grades. A horse's tail has a large bone and considerable muscle. The animal soon learns to tuck its tail while going downhill, holding the saddle off its withers. Every saddle we saw in the mountains of Spain had a crupper.

*This man's saddle sports a crupper, an extremely useful (and too seldom seen) accessory to help the horse hold back the load while going downhill.*

## Gear for the Rider

Trail riding occurs over such a variety of climate and culture that it would be silly for me to comment on clothing for the rider, except at the body's extremes, the head and the feet. Helmets make sense, period.

*Helmets make sense, period.*

We all should wear them, and even we in the stubborn West, we who cling to our Western hats as if removing them would leave us naked, *should* wear them regardless of culture.*

Perhaps the Western hats I've seen advertised that contain a helmet underneath might be the answer to some folks' cultural sensibilities and commonsense need to protect the noggin. In choosing a helmet, make sure the thing is comfortable. Otherwise, you'll be too tempted to leave it behind. If you can't be persuaded to wear a helmet, at least choose a hat that protects you well from sun and sudden showers. Broad-brimmed hats should have a "stampede string," a thong under your chin that holds the hat in place when heading into strong winds. If the string annoys you, it can be tucked up into the hat out of the way when conditions don't require it. A thick felt hat has nowhere close to the protective properties of a helmet, of course, but it does tend to prevent scratches from branches and even provides a modicum of padding.

For footwear, I am very much a traditionalist. In other words, I advocate *boots*. The whole idea of riding boots wherever they are found, from Wyoming to Italy, rests in having a heel that discourages the foot's sliding on through the stirrup. Smooth leather soles tend not to catch during dismounting. You have probably seen a person get all the way off, then find his or her foot briefly stuck in the stirrup because of a shoe sole designed for traction. Even a split-second hang-up is frightening. Furthermore, a leather boot protects your ankles from abrasion and bruising where they come into contact with the upper portion of the stirrup and the fender.

Make sure your booted foot fits the stirrups you are using. Stirrups that are too large could allow your foot to go on through unless you're

---

*But culture is a strong thing. When Emily and I rode in the Alpujarra Mountains of southern Spain, we, along with our guide, wore Australian-style hats. The other couple with us wisely wore helmets. After several days of interaction with the mountain folks in that part of the world, of wonderful evening strolls through the villages, when Spaniards enjoy visiting with neighbors and sauntering along cobblestone streets, Emily and I were aglow with the friendliness of the people. However, the couple with helmets kept commenting that the people were cold toward them. We finally figured out that, in this former police state, helmets were associated with the past dictatorship and viewed with suspicion.

*While it would be insufferable in Florida, Emily's attire here is just right for Montana mountains in May. Fleece-lined hat is warm and protective, while tapaderos (always good for safety) help keep feet warm.*

using taps. Too small, and your foot could hang up should you fall or be bucked off. During the above-mentioned ride in Spain I foolishly climbed aboard Bruno the first morning, after only eye-balling the stirrups on the cavalry saddle and not testing them with my foot. Our guide knew that we were experienced horsemen, so she didn't mess around. We hit a dirt road at a trot, then heard her sing out, "Canter on," as she kicked her Andalusian/Thoroughbred cross into what I'd call a gallop, not a canter. Invigorated by the cool, breezy mountain morning, our horses dashed up the road for a quarter of a mile or so.

My enthusiasm was somewhat dampened by the realization that my right boot, size thirteen, was not free to move fore and aft in the stirrup. The stirrup was too small. I did my best to keep at bay the horseman's normal phobia of anything that glues him to the saddle. Luckily, at the first rest stop, I found that another rider's stirrups were too large. We switched, and all was well.

Whether you wear spurs on your boots is a matter of your training tradition and your competence as a rider. Do not be bluffed out of wearing them by anyone who claims they are inherently inhumane. I have seen folks who eschew spurs practically dislocate a horse's ribs by kicking extremely hard with their bare heels. I'd personally rather just touch the horse with a spur than bang it with a heel. Spurs, when properly used, are part of lightness, and they make it easier to isolate cues. However, for me they are more of a training aid than a necessity, nice to have when I'm working cattle and need my horse tuned to the top of his game. I've never trained a horse with spurs that then required them later on. During late fall and winter, our riding boots and spurs go into the closet and are replaced with insulated boots, oversized stirrups, and tapaderos. The horses, trained to be sensitive to leg cues, remain responsive.

For day rides on the trail, the rest of your riding outfit will be dictated by climate, condition, and the proximity of civilization and aid should there be an emergency. I write this portion of the book during late September, my favorite Montana time of year, with warm days and crisp nights, when rain in the valleys transforms to a light dusting of snow on the high peaks. Here, at this time of year, a long-sleeved shirt may be fine for daytime, but you'd better have some additional warmth rolled up and tied to the saddle strings behind you. Conditions can change very rapidly. Meanwhile, friends in Florida still trail ride at night after meeting together at a restaurant for a nice meal. If your comfort level and the climate allow, consider long sleeves on any shirt you wear unless the country is extremely open and free of brush and scratching branches.

Although I've seen people ride in shorts, I'd as soon walk barefoot over hot coals. On the opposite extreme, chaps (pronounced "shaps") can add warmth in cold weather, while providing great protection for your legs in brushy country. Although I've never used them, the riding pants with leather panels sewn in front should also prevent some scratches.

Even short trail rides require attention to safety. The tiniest first aid kit, one you can tuck into a pocket or a very small saddle or pommel bag, can be precious in case of a cut, a headache, or worse. The larger the trail ride, the more riders, and the more horses, the greater the odds that some sort of first aid will be needed. These large rides call for structured leadership with contingency plans for injuries and other eventualities involving both horses and riders. With the help of a veterinarian who is a member, our Back Country Horsemen chapter assembled an extensive equine first-aid kit, complete in custom saddlebags. The setup is available to members and others to check out for trail rides and carry on one of the horses.

## An Equine First-Aid Kit for Trail Riders

This kit was assembled for Beartooth Back Country Horsemen by Bill Routen, DVM and fits into one set of saddlebags. The (Rx) notation indicates a prescription product.

1. Bandage material: Sheet cotton, rolled gauze, Vetrap, duct tape, Telfa pads, gauze sponges.
2. Disinfectant (plastic bottle): Nolvasan or Betadine (to be mixed with water to make disinfecting solution.
3. Antibiotics: Tube of triple antibiotic ointment; Tube of Amoxi-Mast (good for puncture wounds); trimethoprim Sulfa tablets (Rx) with oral dose syringe. (Injectable penicillin can be carried along with disposable syringes, but the glass bottle and requirement for refrigeration are disadvantages.)
4. Anti-inflammation: Phenylbutazone ("bute") paste or pills (Rx); Banamine paste (Rx)
5. Miscellaneous: 1 pr. hemostats; tongue depressor; nitrofurazone topical wound dressing.

I always carry a combination tool on my belt. The knife blade could cut a horse loose in a tangled wreck, or free it from the saddle if unbuckling the cinch were impossible. With the tool's punch, I can add another hole in a latigo or other strap if necessary. A roll of duct tape (pick one half used, so that it will be less bulky) can be used to fix darn near anything.

An unanticipated result of America's rejection of tobacco smoking is that a group of assembled riders may not include one carrying matches or a lighter. Fire-making ability is still a basic necessity. Even in warmer climates, as night comes on you may need to start a fire to keep an injured person warm, or to use as a signal. Disposable butane lighters are best, but don't buy a childproof one. You want the adjustable sort that can really turn into a torch for igniting damp tinder. And, speaking of fire and light, don't forget to include a small flashlight in what the mountain men called your "possible sack."

## My Possible Sack

The mountain man's "possible sack" was usually a deerskin bag that contained a minimal assembly of survival items. During the first half of the nineteenth century, likely contents might have included flint and steel for fire starting (sulfur matches existed but were not reliable); jerky or pemmican (dried, pulverized meat and berries) as emergency food; extra flints for the lock of the all-important rifle; and, a few fishhooks.

Basic survival requirements have not changed all that much, but we have vastly superior equipment today for trips far less challenging than the live-off-the-land forays of the mountain men. My possible sack expands and contracts according to the task at hand, swelling for longer trips in more challenging terrain or during those seasons when rain below becomes snow higher up. Instead of housing these essential items in my saddlebags, I favor a hiker's fanny pack which I carry at the pommel of my saddle, its waistband threaded through the gullet of the saddle. I can retrieve items from the sack while mounted, and, should I tie my horse for a side trip on foot, quickly strap on the fanny pack. An equally practical container is a fisherman's vest with many pockets, available in net material for warmer weather.

Here are some items essential for me. Add and subtract as you wish.

*Land Navigation*—I always take my old orienteering compass, along with a topo map of the area. On longer trips I add my very tiny GPS unit. (These units, incidentally, are great fun even when they're not essential. Two heavy rubber bands hold mine to the saddle horn; at a touch I can tell how far I've gone, average speed, current speed, direction, etc.)

*Health*—A tiny, but very complete, first aid kit; aspirin; Imodium A-D; Ziploc bag with toothbrush, dental floss, and toothpaste; DEET-based insect repellent for me (a roll-on repellent for my horses rides in my saddlebags).

*Light and Fire*—I like the Mag-Lite type of penlight, along with an extra battery. I've added a couple of those tiny LED units that clip on anywhere. A stub of candle can help start a reluctant fire, as can an adjustable butane lighter. A 35mm film case makes a good waterproof match case for the shorter wooden strike-anywhere matches.

*Repair*—A deluxe combination tool on my belt replaces a host of tools in my possible sack: scissors, knife, pliers, saw, screwdriver, hoof pick, etc. The tiny sewing kits issued in the military are handy and available at surplus stores. Duct tape (a small or mostly-expended roll, for lightness) can fix almost anything.

*Sustenance*—A bit of jerky in one Ziploc bag and some gorp (trail mix) in another could get you through a cold night.

*Communication*—Much as I hate to impose technology on the back-country, I do now take my diminutive cell phone for emergencies only. (An excellent way to ruin a trip is to call in to the office to see how things are going and have the responsibility of some workplace crisis descend on your shoulders and perhaps prompt you to cut the trip short.)

Of course, what goes into your possible sack depends on the gear packed along in other places. On a full-fledged pack trip, the possible sack exists to keep a few important items at the ready, without having to unpack a manty or search in a pannier. On a very light, solo trip, the possible sack may have to be more complete.

We've been discussing extremely light contingency gear for day rides relatively close to civilization. When we get into real backcountry, we'll kick this up a notch. Unless the trail is truly groomed (more what some would call a bridle path than a trail) someone in the party should have a saw. Wind can blow down trees or branches between you and the trailhead. In addition, you'll probably want to contribute to the overall condition of the trail by taking a break, getting off your horse, and sawing away a branch that is likely to snag someone. Mentioned earlier in this book was the Oregon pruning saw (there are similar saws marketed under different names), a light, sharp, curved saw that cuts on the pull stroke. In its nylon case, such a saw ties to the saddle strings and adds little weight or bulk to your load.

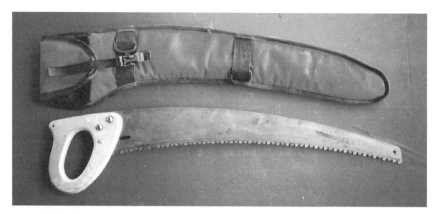

*The Oregon pruning saw cuts on the pull stroke and is safe and easy to use.*

Cell phones, though annoying to many of us, have become vital safety equipment even for short rides. I've heard rescue personnel talk of one negative side: People often call for help now who would formerly have worked the situation out on their own. A hiker deep into wilderness mildly sprains his ankle and expects a helicopter to pick him up. The crew of the rescue helicopter has true emergencies to attend, and is likely to be unsympathetic. At the very least, such a rescue will be extremely expensive.

Additionally, few of us want to hear the gurgle of a pretty creek drowned out by a discussion of business by someone who can't trust the office while he or she is away. If we want to hear such conversations, we'll eat at a restaurant rather than taking a trail ride! My suggestion is to make an ironclad agreement at the trailhead that all cell phones be turned off (there may be horses in the party not trained to ignore the ring of a phone) and used only in true emergency. Then, before counting on them, let's remember that cell phones do not always work in certain locations, particularly in deep canyons. (As technology improves and satellite phones become more commonplace, this will change.)

But calling for help in case you have a rider seriously ill or injured does very little good if you do not know where you are. The leader of the party should know the riders' exact location at all times. That is a requirement of leadership. If you are not the leader, you should still have an extremely good idea of where you are. Make it a point to be aware of the lay of the land, of approximately how far you've traveled from the trailhead, and whether the prevailing direction is north, south, east, or west.

As we get deeper into the backcountry and into true wilderness, land navigation skills become essential. Before going, brush up on basic map and compass skills. If you never learned them, now is the time. Technology in this case is both a blessing and a curse. GPS units in automobiles seem designed to contribute to the dumbing of Americans. The hype seems to say that you can spend even less time watching where you're traveling. Just follow the cursor on your screen, and the unit will get you there. Thus people become even less aware of their environment.

However, the tiny GPS units now available are truly wonderful. You can mark way points for easy return, tell direction of travel, speed of travel, and your precise location. You must learn how to use them, however, and their capabilities are best when they overlay a basic knowledge of map and compass navigation. Further, they are not likely to work should you drop them in the creek or run out of batteries.

Adopt a constant awareness of safety. I'm not encouraging excessive worry, but there truly is much potential for accident. The size of your party, the experience of its members, the sort of terrain are all related to potential for accidents. Be bold enough to choose not to ride with those who are reckless or who have no control of their horses.

# 13

## Techniques for the Trail

At its very simplest level, trail riding requires little in the way of skill or technique. Nearly anyone can sit on a rental horse that yawns along with its nose in the tail of the horse in front of it just as it did with yesterday's rider, sauntering along a groomed trail. There is nothing wrong with this. Tourists in many locations who crave just one experience of sitting on a horse and seeing the scenery enjoy scenarios of this sort.

But we made it clear from the beginning that this book was about something else entirely. This book is about the full spectrum of trail (and off-trail) riding, about negotiating a competent, well-trained horse over good trails and bad ones, through brush and bramble and across sagebrush flats.

Good riders in all equestrian disciplines have already acquired most of the skills needed for the trail. If you barrel race, you know how to stay on a horse. Ditto if you jump, race cross-country, or cut cattle. But the trail offers some situations you may not have learned in organized equine pursuits, particularly the arena-oriented ones.

Here is a quiz question. You are on a trail that is about 4 feet wide. The ground rises steeply to your left, while to your right is a drop-off. Your partner behind you hollers, "Judy, we took the wrong fork. See, we're headed out of this drainage, and we should be following the creek." You know from experience that your horse can turn around in this narrow space because you've seen him do it in the trailer. In which direction do you turn him?

The correct answer is that you turn him to the right (clockwise) so that he faces the drop-off. If the place on the trail is narrow enough to make this turn scary, get off. Keep the reins on your horse's right side as you slip back behind him, then turn him around, again facing the drop-off. The reason is that for all their wonderful senses, the horse really doesn't always know where his hind feet are stepping. Facing the drop-off, he'll keep his front feet on the trail. Turning the other way, the hinds might just slip off.

Another question: Everyone knows that you lean forward when you go up a steep hill. What do you do when you go *down* a steep hill? If you remember *The Man From Snowy River* you probably answered this *incorrectly*. I enjoyed that film as much as you did, but after it was released one of my mentors, Col. Clark Irving, whose service harkens back to the last days of the cavalry, commented, "Yes, the kid could ride, but he leaned the wrong way when he went down that bank."

Yes, the correct answer is that you should lean forward going down as well. Army cavalry manuals show a man going down a hill as steep as the one in the movie, but with the rider leaning forward, not back.

*This trail is intimidating (often more so to riders than to horses) because of the frothing and roaring river below. However, should these riders need to turn around, it would be safest to turn the horses toward the drop-off.*

How can this be? An excellent explanation can be found in Dr. Deb Bennett's first volume of *Principles of Conformation Analysis*, but to paraphrase her, the horse's center of gravity is usually just behind its foreleg and about a third of the way up its body, pretty much directly below the withers. For the horse to handle his weight and your own, particularly over rough terrain, your weight should be as centered as possible over the horse's own center of gravity. If you lean back while heading down a hill, you tend to throw your weight back on the animal's hocks, making it difficult for him to get his hind legs under his body and brake with them. Worse, if the animal's speed frightens you and you haul back on the reins, you make a bad situation worse. His back tends to hollow, his head comes up, and he is likely to fall.

Both going steeply uphill and steeply downhill require giving the horse plenty of rein. He must use his head to balance, and he needs freedom of movement to nod his head as he powers uphill with his hind legs. He needs similar freedom as he brakes with them going downhill. In each case, lean slightly forward to keep your weight as closely as possible over the animal's center of gravity. If your horse is still in the early training stages, practice going downhill slowly. Frequently stop your colt as he faces the slope. Train against any tendency to let gravity accelerate the two of you. You'll feel the horse develop his "brakes" as he hardens the required muscles.

Here's another one: You need to go either up or down a steep bank, perhaps a barrow pit or drainage ditch. It's only 10 feet or so to the bottom, and you're sure your horse can handle it, but the slope is fairly steep, perhaps 45 degrees. Dew glistens on the grass. Do you go straight down (or straight up) or do you slant down as if on the switchbacks of a trail?

By way of answer, let me tell you how I broke a couple of ribs two summers ago. Trying to retrieve a lost calf, I was alternating between a running walk and a lope on Little Mack, my gelding. We were cruising along on a reasonably steep sidehill, going along the slope, neither up nor down. The footing seemed safe enough to go this fast on a surefooted horse. However, there was an irrigation ditch up the slope above us, and we suddenly hit an area of nice grass greened by seepage from the ditch. The slope was as slick as grease. Before I could make any adjustment, Mack's four feet slid out from under him on the downslope side, his body and mine falling to the uphill side. What saved me from greater injury (and him from any at all) was that the slope in this spot was free of rocks, and the wet ground was soft. Although Mack was lying on my right leg, both of our bodies had taken the impact evenly all over, not in one concentrated spot. Thankfully, my feet were free of the stirrups. Mack got up, and then I did. I remounted, got the calf with help from my son, and didn't realize how hurt I was until an hour or so passed. The injury could have been far worse, but it was agony to sneeze or laugh for more than a month.

One of the most dangerous falls that a horse can take is on just such a sidehill, because his feet slide downhill, his body uphill, and your leg pins under him. So, go straight up or straight down that steep bank. The horse might scramble for traction going up, but he'll make it. If his feet slide out going down, he'll brace them, and on such a short slope, get you to the bottom. But slant down, and he just might fall and break your uphill leg.

We have discussed training the horse to cross water, but the rider, too, should approach all stream crossings with care. Mountain streams tend to run swiftly, often with water clear enough to allow seeing the bottom. Obviously, this helps gauge depth. A ford on a well-used trail, where points of entry and exit from the water are clearly visible, is *probably* safe, unless you are tackling the stream at flood stage. Emily remembers well the advice of her father to look at the far bank when crossing, not down at the water. Looking down did not make Emily dizzy, but it has that effect on some riders.

Do remember that "slow waters run deep." A riffle normally means shallow water, but possibly also a rockier bottom. (In the western mountains, virtually all stream bottoms are rocky, in themselves an excellent argument for shoeing.) On the plains or wherever the fall (slope) of the valleys is more gradual, streams will tend to be muddier, with trickier bottoms. As to the business of swimming a horse, I have little experience because the rivers in my home area are very swift; if you're in water so deep that the horse must swim, you'll likely climb out of the river somewhere in the next county. Horses are good swimmers, but not so good that they can swim with most of your body out of the water on top of them forcing them down. The positive buoyancy of flesh and blood is not that good, which is the reason you can't swim well if you insist on holding your entire head out of the water.

If my horse suddenly went into water so deep he had to swim, my canoeing instincts would kick in. I'd get clear of the horse on the up-stream side (we don't want to be pinned between the horse and a downstream obstruction such as a log), then grab his tail as he went by, letting the horse's power help pull me to the far shore.

When it comes to technique on large group rides, I must defer to those who organize them. Most will have rules of one sort or another. For those who like truly large-scale trail riding, a host of wonderful possibilities now exists. Facilities offer RV hookups, concessions, and sumptuous meals. Entertainment around the campfire, sometimes by well-known musicians, is common. Rides are labeled as to speed and difficulty. People who favor this approach make trail riding a very social affair. My advice is simply "When in Rome . . ."

One rule virtually universal in group trail rides is that banning dogs. We all love our own dogs, but, unfortunately, we expect others to love them equally well. The truth is, loose dogs are dangerous around horses, many of whom (unlike the horses of field trial competitors) are not used to strange animals suddenly darting under their bellies.

*The clear, cold rivers of the mountains normally allow you to see the bottom. Slower water tends to be deeper.*

When meeting hikers on the trail, sing out a friendly greeting. This both builds good relations and usually elicits an answer, necessary because a pack or bright, unusual clothing often changes the silhouette of a human and makes your horse question its identity as such. Do *not* expect the hiker to know the first thing about horses. I've seen them leave valuable fishing poles straddling the trail, apparently assuming my horse would step neatly over.

Most hikers these days have a dog with them, usually loose, and while many hikers have the common sense to get it off the trail and hold its collar, some do not. In a nice way, ask them to do so. Hikers in our western mountains are supposed to get off the trail on its lower side. Few, however, seem to know this rule. In fairness, some terrain does make it a bit scary, but it is still safer for the hiker than for the horses to be pressured toward the lower edge. Common courtesy and shared information will usually get us by.

Some trail riders gravitate toward smaller groups, a dozen riders at most. Many of the rides we take are within a wilderness area where fifteen horses in a single group are the maximum allowed. I ask people on rides I lead to keep approximately one horse length between themselves and the rider in front of them. This distance is adequate for safety, but you should always be a bit leery of the horse in front of you. A known kicker should wear a red ribbon in its tail. Even kinder horses, unfortunately, occasionally kick, particularly when tired. Sometimes they just get crabby, especially if a horse is crowding them from behind.

If your horse kicks at one behind it, reprimand sharply, but learn to watch for the behavior that leads up to this misbehavior. Usually the horse lays back its ears and adjusts its gait in order to get a good crack at its target. When this happens, spur hard and yell, "Quit!" or whatever you use when your horse is misbehaving. This dangerous behavior is as antisocial as your dog's biting a visitor. Besides endangering the other horse, your horse's kick could land squarely on the leg of the rider behind you. Provide your mount some sort of negative reinforcement, coinciding as quickly as possible with any tendency to kick.

An interval of more than a horse length causes problems as well, particularly when riders lag and then decide to catch up. If several riders lag and then simultaneously regain their positions, the whiplash effect means horses to the rear must suddenly kick into a lope to catch up.

*Horses, even well-conditioned ones, are not machines. They appreciate a nice rest as much as you do.*

*An interval between riders of one horse length is about right, but leave a little extra space when crossing bridges or obstacles.*

Should you be in the position of organizing and leading a ride, the more knowledge you have of the horses and riders the better. It is best if all are somewhat compatible. When the group consists of Walking Horse people, I don't close the ride to someone who wishes to come along on a nongaited horse, but I do warn them that they are likely to be trotting hard a good deal of the time. Usually they do not have the stomach for that and think better of the idea.

I've developed the habit of pausing for an instant just before departure and asking, "Does everyone have everything? Water? Lunch? Camera?" It's better to catch an omission before everyone is mounted.

*A typical posture for a ride leader, looking back to make sure all is well and everyone is ready.*

I also ask an experienced person to bring up the rear (often called "riding trail"). Although I'm not crazy about such an intrusion of technology, with a larger group I give the rider at the rear one of the tiny, high-quality two-way radios now available. In timbered country I can't see the entire group, and it's important that the person riding trail is able to tell me to hold up the group during the inevitable tack adjustment.

Leading a ride requires a steady pace. Any variation in speed is exaggerated toward the rear of the column because gaps between the riders increase and decrease with accumulating effect for riders at the tail end. As with leading a pack string, slow down when crossing a log or a creek, slackening your pace on the other side of the obstacle until all riders have crossed. As leader, pay twice as much attention to safety as you normally would. Be a bit of a pessimist, thinking constantly of worst-case scenarios. As they say, it's lonely at the top.

# 14

## Competition on the Trail

I raised one son who, from the very beginning, insisted on making everything into a competitive game. As a baby, after learning quickly to place different-sized rings on a cone in proper order, David would deliberately mess up the order, look away as if to clear his head, then rapidly rearrange the rings to fit the taper of the cone. A little later he structured all his games to keep score in some way. He was pleasant about this, even occasionally letting another child win. But the fun of the activity was directly connected to the existence of some sort of competition. Little wonder that he went on to be an excellent athlete.

For me, however, trail riding was always the antithesis of competitive activity. I grew up in the outdoors and always felt the same about hunting and fishing, having an innate distaste for making either into a "mine is bigger" sort of competitive sport. But I have come to increasingly understand this need in many folks to compete. Some riders, jaded by the dog-eat-dog level of competition on the horse show circuit, crave trail riding, but like the possibility of excelling, of bringing home a ribbon or prize. For them, several forms of competitive outdoor riding have arisen, each with one or more associations to establish uniform rules. Here are several approaches for those who would like to branch out from purely recreational outdoor riding.

## Competitive Trail Rides

Competitive trail riding has become an extremely popular sport, emphasizing proper handling and conditioning of the trail horse. Entrants in the rides are judged 40 percent on condition, 45 percent on soundness, and 15 percent on trail ability and manners. In addition, the riders

*Glimpses of the Absaroka ride, a judged trail ride held on the author's ranch: a) leaving the arena, contestant must open the gate on horseback; b) John—the deputy—directs contestant across highway; c) contestant is rated on how horse crosses stream, key words being "boldly and carefully;" d) Travis has his colt checked by Sarah, the vet; e) the grand finale required contestants to circle two penned llamas; f) and the next day, a mountain ride through golden aspens.*

compete for various horsemanship awards through a weekend ride, much emphasis being placed on safety.

Unlike endurance riding, competitive trail rides are not races. NATRC, the North American Trail Ride Conference, has created uniform judging criteria and sanctions rides. In their words:

> All horses are worked over the same course in the same amount of time giving a basis for fair comparison for determining the horse's soundness, condition, and manners. Timing and pacing are important; the winner is usually the one who rides a consistent pace rather than hurrying and waiting. No special breed of horse is necessary or favored. The most important requisite is a well-conditioned, well-mannered horse.

Competitive trail rides have several divisions determined by experience of the riders, age of the horses, and weight of the riders plus tack. Stallions are allowed, but only when handled by competent adults. Junior riders must wear helmets. The attitude toward dogs is even more extreme than for the typical trail ride. "Don't even think about showing up with one," a ride schedule reads.

### Judged Trail Rides (Also Known as Trail Trials)

The judged trail ride is a less-known format than the competitive trail ride, but I expect it to grow rapidly. Here the emphasis is on the competence of horse and rider at crossing various trail obstacles. Judging is also different, since a separate judge is found at each obstacle. Rules are less uniformly established from ride to ride (in some ways, not such a bad thing), but typically riders will encounter from eight to a dozen challenges, such as creek and bridge crossings, deadfalls, cattle on the trail, and penned llamas.

Emily and I have sponsored a judged trail ride for gaited horses here at the ranch, an event that kicks in a bit of the competitive trail ride philosophy, since horses are expected to move along briskly. Trail riders seem enthusiastic about the judged trail ride format because it so closely meshes with actual training experiences. These rides are wonderful tests for your horse's progress toward becoming a complete trail horse.

### Ride-and-Tie

Are you a runner? Ride-and-tie is a physically challenging event that involves a team of two riders and one horse. One person takes off on foot, the other on horseback. At a designated point the person on horseback dismounts, ties up the horse, and begins *his* two-legged run. The partner catches up to the horse, mounts, and heads down the trail, catching and passing his partner, and eventually again tying the horse.

Though ride-and-tie as a sport may be of recent invention, this mode of travel is actually extremely old. Folklorist Jan Brunvaand located references to it from many years back. It made sense when two people had only one horse between them. Each of the humans plus the horse got some rest time, yet distance was covered more rapidly than if both people had been on foot. In any case, there is renewed interest in ride-and-tie, and an internet search should yield plenty of information from like-minded enthusiasts.

## Mounted Orienteering

This one is on my things-to-do list. Orienteering was originated by the Scandinavian military and combines the physical challenge of cross-country running (or skiing) with the land navigation knowledge expected of any good soldier. With map and compass in hand, the runner takes off with a set of objectives marked on a map. Using his compass and the topography marked on his map, he decides the best course to each objective. Once the objective is reached, he records the number found on the marker (usually a sign of some sort) and heads for the next one. Upon his return, a judge looks at the scorecard and grades according to time of completion and correctness of the recorded numbers.*

The mounted version is very similar. I plan to join NACMO, the National Association of Competitive Mounted Orienteering, because it seems to me that the only way to improve on regular orienteering is to add a good horse. Only map and compass can be used (no GPS). Objective stations range over an area from 2 to 12 square miles, with

---

*This takes me back to some beautiful woodlands in Virginia, to a snowy day when the humid wind was unlike my accustomed Montana air, when there was more than just a rumor of war. Most of the graduating classes of Marine officers at this Quantico school were heading straight to Viet Nam. It was very fine, then, to be left alone out of the rigors of training to take the land navigation test, a hike alone through deer-filled woods to locate the correct markers. The test filled the day, a good day, and my 100 percent grade at the end of it was one of the very few perfect scores I earned during those trying months.

code numbers recorded on paper plates. The object is to find as many of these stations as possible, record them correctly, and get back in good time. NACMO's characterization of their activity as "the thinking horse sport" seems appropriate.

Like the judged trail ride, competitive mounted orienteering is a good test of the trail horse. You, as competitor, determine the best route to each station, but that is usually off-trail. Two difficulty levels are featured. The short, easier courses are aimed more toward those wanting to simply have fun or to train a young horse. A fine prospect indeed: a young horse, still a tad apprehensive, but honest and willing, a good day, some congenial people, and the chance to mildly challenge yourself, your training job, and your colt.

# PART V

## PACKING IN

# 15

## The Ultralight Approach

There will come a time (and it may have come already) when a day's ride on even your favorite trail will leave you vaguely unsatisfied. There will come a time when your good horse tugs at his mooring and looks at you as if to say, "This cove is fine all right, and the sail across the bay yesterday was good as well, but there is Cape Horn, you know, and if not that at least the Sea of Cortez or the Marquesas." And although the spirit of adventure may not prompt you to take a summer off, to ride the spine of either the Rocky Mountains or the Appalachians, it will eventually insist on your leaving the trailhead farther behind, on saying goodbye for a while to the office, the telephone, to pavement, superstores, and machines with motors. Good horses do that to you.

When we contemplate more extensive adventures on horseback, several things happen. Self-reliance and safety standards kick up a notch because we are likely to be riding far from assistance. We must carry our homes on our backs, home now being a careful selection of light gear that is still stout enough to be up to the required task. Our light-on-the-land mentality must also sharpen even further, because we'll now be truly living out there, even though for a relatively brief time. And we'll be living there without much infrastructure, without concrete to bear our weight or sewers to carry our waste or garbage services to remove our trash. And so we must learn to minimize any trash coming back out with us, our living and that of our horses structured for the least possible impact on the land.

In July 1990, *Equus* magazine published my article called "Going It Light and Alone." The subject was an extremely light form of horse packing in which all necessary gear fits on one's saddle horse. The framework of the article was a trip I took on my big gelding Rockytop Tennessee, whose handsome mug graced that issue's cover. There was nothing radical about this approach, but it was certainly ahead of the curve, as was the book with which I followed it, *Treading Lightly with Pack Animals: A Guide to Low-Impact Travel in the Backcountry* (Mountain Press, 1993).

Backcountry travel, particularly in wilderness areas that prohibit motorized vehicles, had tended to fall into two camps. On the one hand were backpackers, that activity peaking in the 1980s when chil-

*Rockytop, as featured in the* Equus *article, carried me and a modicum of gear including a tent fly for shelter, an ultralight sleeping bag, and a backpacking stove with food for a couple of meals—adequate equipment for a short trip in nice weather where horse feed was readily available. Roomier packs are available but encourage overloading the horse, particularly over the kidneys. (Do not tie a horse on such a steep slope for long.)*

dren of the '60s were still young. (Backpacking continues to be popular, of course, but during the '70s and '80s a generation took to the mountains in droves.) On the other hand were the horse packers, who tended to travel in luxury, with canvas wall tents, tables, stools, and assorted accoutrements. They were, perhaps, a bit more traditional in method than the backpackers, and in those days sometimes less sensitive to the low-impact credo.

The *Equus* article preached a lightweight approach that married the excellent light gear marketed to backpackers, with travel on horseback. The book took this a step further, delineating traditional packing methods, but featuring lighter gear. It also encouraged backpackers, especially those with small children (who tend to add more to the camp burden than they can safely carry themselves), to consider adding a pack animal. A large dog can carry at least his own food supply plus a poncho or two, while a burro, pony, or llama can lighten the packs of all concerned. The hope was that practical, low-impact travel could be preached, and that along the way the distinct contrast between the two groups—backpackers and horse packers—could be logically blurred, possibly lessening tensions between them.

Years have passed and equipment has been improved on both ends. The "heavy" group now has access to full-sized wall tents of synthetic materials that weigh little more than backpacking tents. Ultralight packers have an even greater array of quality lightweight gear available than they did twenty years ago. Various equipment companies offer streamlined packing systems made of innovative materials.

But some things do not change. Horses are still creatures of flesh and blood, and the wilderness is still unforgiving, beautiful when all goes well, but merciless when it doesn't. As time has passed I've become even more passionate about two imperatives: being prepared in the backcountry and visiting that backcountry leaving as little trace as possible.

It is definitely feasible to enjoy an overnight trip or even one of several days with all necessary gear packed on your saddle horse. But in order to do so, conditions and climate must be right. In fact, I'll go so far as to say that to pack safely without pack horses, you must be willing to travel *even lighter* than a strong backpacker does. How can this be, when you have the assistance of a big, stout horse? Because his presence in the backcountry requires a few pieces of gear that the backpacker need not carry.

Let's get to specifics. My oldest son runs many miles each day and stays in superb shape. Every year he meets a friend for a backpacking trip, the friend being just as robust. These two like challenges, often eschewing the trail and tackling the high plateaus. Through the years they've pored over their gear lists, meticulously rejecting anything not truly needed. However, they are also out to have fun, so they retain such things as light fishing gear. Further, since their treks are in true wilderness, they don't short themselves on vital safety and land navigation equipment. For all of their efforts at lightening their loads, when they depart the trailhead for a trip of three or four nights, they are carrying packs weighing from 45 to 50 pounds.

Let's do some math. It's my understanding that the average American adult now weighs around 180 pounds. Add a saddle

*David, right, and Justin, conditioned, experienced backpackers, tackle the wilderness for several days carrying the minimum necessary for safety and bare comfort, but still have packs weighing 45–50 pounds. Can you put the same gear on your saddle horse along with yourself and your saddle without exceeding the 25 percent limit, or placing undue weight on the horse's kidneys?*

of 20 (it's hard to find a rugged trail saddle that weighs less, and most weigh more) and the lower estimate, 45 pounds, of the backpacker's load. We're now up to 245 pounds, which our 1,000-pound horse can handle. But we aren't finished yet. We must allow a little extra packing weight for the hobbles that are essential equipment, and rope for a highline (so that we won't be tying to trees) and, perhaps, a picket line and picket pin. The weight is mounting, isn't it? We're still not finished. In many areas grazing is not available or allowed. For instance, the whole eastern half of the million-acre Absaroka/Beartooth Wilderness Area in Montana allows stock use but prohibits grazing. All feed must be packed in. We are now most definitely over the top in terms of allowable weight.

Even this computation is oversimplified. Let's say the area to which you are headed does indeed allow grazing, and you anticipate that the available feed will be adequate. Also, you weigh less than 180 pounds, so you feel you can carry the same gear as my son does in his backpack and be well under the total weight limit of 25 percent of your horse's own weight. Sorry, but you still have a problem. And to explain the problem, I must tell you about Tommy.

Tommy was big but not huge, a bay medley of Percheron, Saddlebred, and grade Western stock. He stood about 15.3, but because of the Percheron he was heavy for his height, perhaps 1,300 pounds. Although inclined to be lazy, Tommy was a good serviceable saddle horse, tremendously strong and steady. I rode him a great deal when Emily and I were first dating, our favorite date involving horses and saddles and rides to the hills on the east side of the valley to the scent of juniper and sage.

Emily's father Elmer always assigned us some minor duty to do on the way, something that would ease his workload for the following day. We always checked to see that the bulls were at home with their own cows; and occasionally Elmer would send a hundred pounds of stock salt up with Tommy and me. Yes, a hundred pounds! In football condition, I weighed about 190 pounds. The saddle I used belonged to my future mother-in-law Nora and weighed about 40 pounds. Add it up and Tommy was packing around 330 pounds! How could he get away with carrying such an immense load?

Well, there were several reasons. First, he was very strong. Second, he did not have to go very far, only about a mile and a half, although this involved a 350-foot climb. Last, and most important, he could carry this great weight for a short distance because of *where* on his back it was placed. Elmer readied us for the trip by putting each 50-pound salt block into a burlap bag. He gathered the extra burlap above each block and made it into a loop, secured at the bottom with a tight tie of baling twine. Thus each block was packaged in the bag with a burlap loop at the top. He then slipped each of these loops over the saddle horn. Tommy now had a 50-pound salt block hanging at the front of the saddle, one on each side. As I rode, they pressed into the fronts of my thighs, but for a short distance this was not too uncomfortable.

Earlier we discussed the importance of keeping weight over the animal's center of gravity, which normally is a little way behind the forelegs of the horse, about one-third of the way up its body and under or just behind the withers. The salt blocks Elmer loaded were probably just in front of Tommy's center of gravity. My weight in the saddle was probably just behind it. Average it all out, and Tommy's considerable load was smack where it belonged: right over his center of gravity.

Even half that weight, even in softer form, behind the saddle over Tommy's kidneys, would have been extremely hard on the animal. And therein lies the biggest problem with some of the systems I've seen for hauling your camp on your saddle horse. Most systems, because of the size of their packs, tempt you to put far too much weight back behind the saddle over the kidneys, shifting the center of gravity of the horse's load to a point far behind the animal's own center of gravity. Furthermore, even if loaded with light, bulky stuff, most such systems create a genuine hazard to all but the most nimble riders when they mount and dismount. One's leg must make a high arc over the load, and chances for a hang-up during an emergency dismount increase.

Am I discouraging you from the ultralight approach that involves only your saddle horse combined as mount and packhorse? No, not at all. It's inherently lighter on the land, because it involves fewer horses. But we must be extremely careful to see to it that while being lighter on the land, we're not extremely hard on our horses.

Here are some things that can help make packing in with your saddle horse alone more feasible. Sharing necessities with companions can lighten your load. Examine every ounce of equipment to make sure that there is no unnecessary duplication among members of the party. A couple need take only one very light tent and can share a single backpacking stove, pretty much a necessity in these days of tight fire restrictions. If you have past backpacking experience, as I do, you've already learned to eliminate all but freeze-dried or dehydrated foods. Soft drinks, beer, or anything else canned is out of the question for single-horse packing. So is very much water. You'll be relying on another essential these days, the water filter, but your group can share just one.

As with all sorts of packing, pay attention to the surfaces that lie against the horse. Anything hard or sharp should be padded underneath by clothing or your sleeping pad. But most important of all, remember Tommy's load. Choose a packing system that provides generous storage up front, and try to put half the total weight up at the pommel of the saddle. The front is the place for water bottles, your backpacking stove and its fuel, binoculars, the bag of tent stakes–anything dense and heavy.

Most of us can stand to prepare in another way (as I recently felt compelled to do) by dropping a few pounds during the weeks we're preparing for this trip. Your horse will be thankful. I've noticed that even a minor weight loss can make mounting that tall horse ever so much more pleasant.

*Quality time with a friend in camp. Note man's use of hard pannier as stool, and also the lightweight backpacking tent.*

When you've gone over your list and are certain you've covered basic necessities and comforts, spread everything out on the livingroom floor and weigh it all. Everything, full water bottles and the clothes and boots you'll wear, saddle, bridle, breastcollar and pad. Then weigh yourself. Total the weight. Unless you plan an extremely short trip, limit everything, including you, to one-quarter of your horse's weight. On a short trip over easy terrain a well-conditioned horse can certainly carry more, but stay as close to the limit as possible. Get rid of anything in the load that you can do without, but don't compromise safety. The compass (and perhaps GPS), the first-aid kit—such things must stay.

Just as tachometers are "redlined" for maximum RPM, here are some possible "redlines" for the ultralight, one-horse-per-person approach:

1. *Your physical condition and age.* A young, hardy person may be able to get along without a sleeping pad. Others, however, may hurt their backs if they try. Similarly, that same gung-ho individual might not mind slathering himself with DEET and sleeping under the stars or with the aid only of an ultralight nylon tarp arranged as shelter. What is your own required comfort level?

2. *Climate and altitude.* Quality rain protection in the forms of clothing and a good tent is far more important in Minnesota than in Arizona. Similarly, high altitude converts mild climates into four-season ones. I've withstood snowstorms and freezing weather in mid-July in the mountains of Montana, then faced shirt-sleeve heat two hours later when I dropped into a valley. A wide range of clothing adds weight. Some of us relish fall in the mountains, when the weather alternates between autumn at best and winter at worst. Not only does the possibility of true cold create greater clothing needs, but it causes greater reliance on a quality backpacking stove to heat the liquids needed to keep the body warm and hydrated. More use means more fuel and again, a better tent and warmer (translate heavier) sleeping bag. An insulated pad underneath that bag becomes a necessity. Finally, the shorter days of winter mean a greater requirement for light. When the sun sets just after supper, your need for candles (if you use a candle lantern) or a larger lantern with fuel increases. People also require more food during colder weather, the

requirement for fats increasing. This means more fuel for the back-packing stove.

3. *The need to pack feed.* I'm afraid that the one-person, one-horse approach is pretty much out when feed must be packed in. I simply see no way it can be done. Such a feed prohibition can come from government antigrazing regulations or from the environment and the time of year. In some places, at some times, there is simply no grazing available.

4. *Missions other than recreation.* If you are on a hunting or photography trip or a scientific expedition, extra equipment must be taken along and may prevent your saddle horse from being able to do it all.

All the "redlines" call for a somewhat heavier outfit, the addition of a pack animal, and some expansion of our trail horse repertoire, both for us and for our horses. We'll dedicate ourselves to minimizing the greater impact of additional animals by first limiting the total number of horses just as strictly as we can, and then by following every possible precaution against damage to the environment.

## A Low-Impact Checklist

1. Travel as lightly as possible, at your minimal comfort requirement, but within limits of safety for both humans and horses. For short trips in favorite climates, where feed need not be packed in, go without pack animals if you can limit your saddle horse's load to 25 percent of its body weight distributed so that the loin area is not stressed. On better-equipped trips, limit two riders to one pack animal (three to one, or five to two, is an even better ratio). To accomplish this, assemble your camp equipment with lightness and compactness constantly in mind. Substitute backpacking equipment and the new synthetic horse packing gear for heavy, traditional items. Less weight and fewer animals mean slighter impact.

2. In assembling your gear, check regulations for the land on which you plan to travel.

3. Pack out all garbage (and anything else that you pack in and which is not consumed). Do not bury trash. Where legal, burn truly

combustible items (such as paper plates), but keep foil wrappers and other fire-resistant items out of the firepit. Pick up trash left by others as well. End your stay with a thorough on-line policing of the area.

4. Avoid reliance on campfires by using a backpacking stove for cooking. If fires are legal, burn only dead, downed wood, keep them small, and build according to the recommendations of whoever administers the land. Doctrine in some areas has changed. In regions where few travel, the desired method may still be to remove sod from a small circle, put it aside intact, build the fire, then, when done, drown and scatter the ashes and replace the sod, watering it to help the grass grow again. (Do *not* ring the circle with rocks.) In some jurisdictions, permanent firepits exist at campsites—use them instead. Other low-impact techniques include building the campfire on a fireproof fire blanket of the type used by firefighters as lifesaving equipment. Unserviceable, used fire blankets are often available from Forest Service administrators, and a commercial version just for campfires is now available. Be extremely careful with fire. Today, your bank account as well as your conscience is likely to hurt should you cause a wildfire: You may be billed for the astronomical cost of fighting the fire you caused.

5. Do not cut any living trees or shrubs. Sleep on a pad or self-inflating air mattress. (The days of the pine-bough bed are long gone.)

6. Bury human waste in single holes one shovel blade deep; replace the sod to make the area look as it did when you found it. Select sites for this purpose on high ground at least 200 feet from streams or lakes and away from areas that drain toward them. Use only white, unscented toilet paper, and bury that with the waste. (Large parties in stationary situations should follow whatever waste procedures the jurisdiction requires. For larger groups, a latrine is normally prescribed.)

7. Bypass any camping sites better suited to backpackers. When you choose your campsite, keep livestock out of the camp area itself.

8. Avoid travel during rainy seasons, particularly in regions with heavy topsoil. Animal feet (and those of humans) do more damage when the ground is wet. Leaving muddy bogs laden with the tracks of your horses scars the countryside, causes erosion, and sullies us further in the eyes of those who oppose livestock in the backcountry.

9. Keep all livestock at least 200 feet from streams and lakes (or far-ther if regulations require). Take your horses to water in a rocky place twice each day rather than leaving them to water themselves. Packing water to them with a folding bucket is better yet. Hobble stock, rather than picketing, when possible (assuming that grazing is legal). Tie to trees only when there is no other option and then only to large ones for very brief duration. For longer-term tying rig a highline using tree savers, wide straps, or cinches around trees to protect the bark. Locate the highline over high, rocky ground. If you do picket stock (with a hobble half by one front foot) move the line frequently to avoid grazed circles. The lowest-impact method for holding stock (where grazing is legal) is a portable electric corral, extremely compact and easy to relocate, consisting of a small charger, electric fence tape, and plastic posts. But you'll still probably need a highline during the night—a deer or moose can destroy an electric fence, releasing your stock.

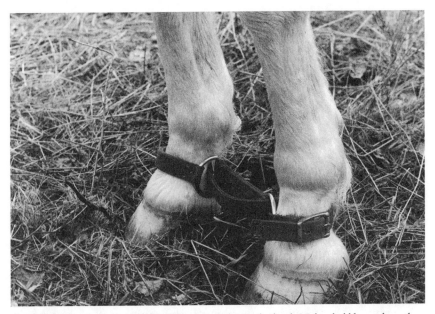

*Where grazing is allowed, hobbling horses is light on the land. Nylon hobbles such as these are light and inexpensive, but may chafe if used on horses that resist them. Reserve such hobbles for experienced animals.*

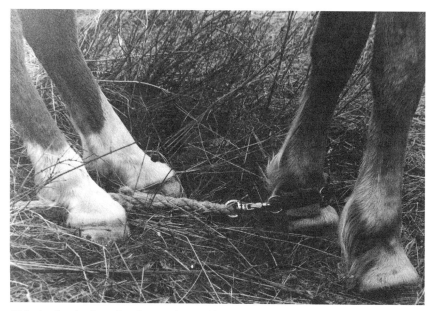

*Picketing by the front foot, here with a padded hobble half with a swivel on the snap, is a good way of restraining stock where grazing is allowed. Do move the animal frequently to prevent grazed rings.*

10.   Consider leaving your dog at home. (I write this a few days past witnessing a close call on a treacherous trail; a large dog burst up to the trail from out of brush—his master was below fishing a stream—under a spirited mare, causing her to jump off the trail. Fine horsemanship by the woman on the mare saved the day.) Should you insist on bringing your dog, keep it under your control at all times (tough to do from the back of a horse) and realize that you could be liable should the animal cause an accident. Also, consider packing the animal so that it shares in the work. Dogs are extremely efficient pack animals, able to carry one-third their weight, learn to do so easily, seem to take pride in it, and adopt the purposeful attitude typical of working dogs. Treat dog waste the same as human waste.

11.   In camp, do not drive nails into trees, and do not trench your tent.

12.   When traveling, stay on the trail. Don't shortcut switchbacks. Trail crews often attempt to steer your path around eroded stretches by placing obstacles over or in front of them. Respect their efforts.

13. When breaking camp, leave nothing behind. Police the entire area. Scatter horse droppings so that they fertilize rather than degrade the area. Pay particular attention to the area under the highline, smoothing any damage with your camp shovel.

14. Fewer people smoke these days, but if you're one of the diehards, never leave a cigarette butt behind. The filter is not quickly biodegradable. Follow the military example of completely extinguishing the cigarette, then putting it into your pocket, burning it later, or packing it out.

15. Do not overgraze fragile areas such as alpine meadows. Unless you're certain there will be abundant natural (and legal) feed for your livestock, pack plenty in. Certified weed-free hay is best (bales are easy to manty), but weed-free pellets or hay cubes are also available. The US is currently plagued by exotic, nonnative noxious weeds such as leafy spurge and spotted knapweed. Keep these out of the backcountry. Use mesh feed (nose) bags for grain and other supplements, rather than feeding it on the ground. Equally important in the battle against weeds is cleaning your horses' coats and hooves thoroughly before the trip. Look especially to their manes and tails for burrs (which are seeds). Starting your animals on weed-free feed several days before the trip helps assure that unwanted seeds are not transplanted in their manure. (This procedure is also a health preventative: it's risky to change feeds just as you stress animals by long trailer rides and new surroundings.)

16. Pay particular attention to storage in camp for your own food and that of your horses. Many areas now require either bear-resistant storage boxes or hanging food high and out of reach.

17. Use biodegradable soap to clean your body and your dishes.

18. Treat the outdoors as if it were your livingroom. You may not like picking up after others, but if boorish guests visited your house, you'd clean up after they left. Similarly, pick up and pack out trash left by others. If we all pitch in, the backcountry is likely to stay both more enjoyable to visit and accessible to our horses and us.

# 16

## A Packing Primer

Few feelings rival that of assembling a pack outfit at the trailhead, checking to see that all loads are balanced, snug, and properly secured, then picking up the lead rope of the front packhorse and hitting the trail. About the only thing comparable for me was loading my young family along with carefully selected gear into a canoe on the Missouri River and launching downstream. Both imply adventure, but adventure for which one is truly prepared. Both involve, too, an interaction with nature free from most accoutrements of civilization.

The first mile or so in either case is touched by anticipation colored by a dash of apprehension. Did we remember everything? And for the pack trip the horses, of course, are charged, their restlessness in the trailer finally finding release, their noses to the wind, reliant on their people to take them through a strange new landscape. A pack trip into the backcountry is today the closest we can get to Lewis and Clark, to Jim Bridger, to Daniel Boone. There is potential for surprise even in country we know, whether a moose on the trail, or a frightening storm brewed up by nature. Nature, we know, just might test us in these or other ways. "Bring it on," we tell ourselves, not with arrogance but with confidence. We have prepared, our horses are trained, and we are ready.

Packing is both art and science. As with horsemanship in general, we continue to learn indefinitely, to look back later on ourselves as having been rank amateurs just a few years before. But although packing is best learned by hands-on instruction (many, including myself, offer clinics for this purpose), don't be intimidated. You can quickly learn enough to get by, to get your load to camp without hurting yourself or your horses. We will not attempt to tell you here how to do it, but rather how it is done. Other books and, hopefully, teachers can take you from there.

We have already dealt in the training section of this book with getting horses accustomed to packsaddles. Before packing in, review these lessons with your horse. Do not show up at the trailhead intending to pack a horse that has never had a breeching under its tail nor a pannier rub against a tree. Train your horses at home, including trial runs.

The first principle is balance. The packs on each side of the horse must be close to equal in weight, though this can be mitigated with the Decker/manty method. Second, weight must be controlled, because packs do not help the horse with movement and balance as any decent rider does. Thus, a total pack weight of 150 pounds is considered plenty by many packers for a full-sized horse or mule. Third, we must keep the packs from pressuring either forward or back, again more difficult when the load is dead weight. Fourth, we must keep the load from galling or otherwise injuring the horse. And, if all that is not enough to think about, we must pack in such a way that our eggs stay unbroken. (Yes, the addition of pack animals means *real* eggs are now possible.)

A very minimal setup for a single packhorse is a set of saddle packs that drape over a conventional riding saddle. Usually consisting of two nylon or canvas bags called panniers (often corrupted to "panyards") connected by a cloth panel with cutouts for the cantle and pommel of a riding saddle, these packs are often used by hunters. They can be carried on the hunter's saddle horse rolled up behind the saddle. Should the hunter need to pack out elk quarters, he places the pack in place over the saddle, puts one of the quarters in each pannier, and hikes out leading the horse, then returns later for the second pair of quarters.

For only very occasional packing where you wish to minimize cost, but you have an extra riding saddle, saddle packs may get you by. Packing with them is simple enough. Put an oversized pack pad under the saddle. Then keep the weight even on each side, and put a layer of soft stuff—sleeping bags, extra clothing—next to the horse. Many of these saddle packs are open-topped, so you'll want to put your cargo in duf-

*Saddle panniers; okay for occasional trips as long as saddle has breastcollar and crupper, or breeching.*

fel bags or, in a pinch, in heavy plastic trash bags for rain protection. A belly strap normally goes under the horse and connects the two panniers to keep them from flopping around. Pull it snug.

There is one limitation. Your saddle probably has a breastcollar that it will need for packing, but it's likely to lack a crupper or a breeching (often pronounced "britchin"). One or the other is needed. Remember, the pack is dead weight. A crupper will do for light loads and will double for use on your riding saddle. A breeching is better for packing, since on downgrades it distributes the load over the horse's entire hindquarters. If you don't want to invest in a new one, look for horse harness in secondhand stores or farm auctions. The breeching section off a buggy harness can be adapted to your saddle for packing purposes with a leather punch and a little ingenuity. Adjust the breeching on the horse so that the main strap is parallel to the ground, with most of the slack taken out, but loose enough that you can easily slide your hand under it. The breeching exists to hold the load back on descents, and should not kick into play until needed.

I suspect that once you experience packing it is likely to hook you. If so, you'll want to consider purchasing first-rate equipment designed for the job. In the United States there are two basic types of packsaddle, the sawbuck (also called crossbuck) and the Decker. The sawbuck tends to be slightly less expensive (though with equal quality rigging, that may not be so). Named for the stand used to hold wood that is being sawed, the sawbuck saddle consists of a wooden tree having two bars connected by wood pieces that rise from the bars and cross, fastened in an X shape. Sawbuck saddles are usually double rigged with two cinches and have a simple breast strap in front and a breeching behind. Padding, such as sheepskin, on the undersides of the bars should be supplemented by a good thick pad underneath the saddle.

Sawbucks are best used with panniers, either the soft sort or hard-sided ones. Soft panniers are similar to saddle packs, but those used with sawbuck saddles are separate and not connected to each other. Their material is normally nylon or canvas. Often each has a dowel or aluminum pipe sewn into the material along the top inside edge to better hold the shape of the load. Each pannier has two short adjustable straps

*A sawbuck packsaddle. Note double rigging (two cinches).*

at the top, buckled into loops. To load them onto the packhorse, you simply slip each loop over the top of the sawbucks. In practice it's best to have a helper. The stronger person holds the loaded pannier in place, while the helper, on the other side of the horse, reaches up and slips the loops into place.

Hard panniers are usually made of plastic, aluminum, fiberglass, or plywood. Normally the inside is curved to better conform to the side of the horse. Very sophisticated (and expensive) bear-resistant models are made for those areas where bearproof camping is required by the government and by common sense. An advantage of hard panniers is the protection they offer to sensitive cargo. A disadvantage is that they can't expand to carry that last bit of additional stuff, and, since they are inflexible against the horse, more attention is required to padding between the pannier and the horse's side. An extra-large pack pad provides this protection. Another disadvantage of hard panniers is that in case of a wreck in which a horse falls onto its side, injury might be more likely.

Packing with panniers and a sawbuck is relatively simple. Adjust the strap loops so that the tops of the packs ride evenly with each other.

*Horses with hard fiberglass panniers; left, on a Decker, right one on sawbuck.*

Keep weight as identical as possible. If you do not carry a scale, and there are exceedingly compact ones available, try picking each pannier up from the ground and flexing your forearms in a full curl. Your muscle memory, if you handle each pannier in identical fashion, will normally tell you which is heavier. Shift gear from one to the other as needed for balance. On the trail, your partner should watch the sawbucks, not the packs, to determine whether all is riding well. Should one pack sink lower, don't hesitate to add a rock to the lighter one. Better a bit of extra weight than a sore-backed horse.

The sawbuck/pannier method also lends itself to a top pack, should you need more capacity. Normally tied with one of the many versions of the diamond hitch, the top pack is a bit more technical, better taught by showing than by writing. However, no-knot approaches to top packs, bags that make clever use of buckles and Velcro, are now available from some packing suppliers.

The Decker packsaddle was developed in the mining areas of northern Idaho. Looking like a square of cloth with two steel D-rings protruding from the top, when stripped down, the Decker is not all that

*Packers in the process of tying top pack with diamond hitch on mule.*

different from the sawbuck. Again we have two connected wooden bars, but now the connectors are two steel loops. This construction is considerably stronger than the wooden crossbucks that connect the bars of the sawbuck saddle. The steel rings also make the Decker somewhat adjustable, though a torch is required to heat the steel. At a certain point the steel can be bent to narrow or widen the saddle for a particular animal. Professional packers often custom-fit their saddles for each animal in the string and label them with the name of the horse or mule.

Over the top of the Decker tree comes the square of canvas (or nylon) called the half-breed, the D-rings protruding through slots in the top. The half-breed is built like an envelope, two layers of material with space in between into which horsehair can be stuffed for padding. Some commercial versions now also contain foam padding. Equally important is a light wooden board that fits horizontally toward the bottom of the half-breed, one on each side, held by pockets on the ends. This thing called the half-breed, with padding and boards to distribute the weight, is the secret of the Decker. Positioned above the saddle tree but under whatever load is packed, this innovation allows packing awkward loads, such as bundles of tools for trail maintenance, onto the Decker without injuring the horse.

The Decker can be used with panniers, just like the sawbuck. Hooks are available to install on the pannier straps so that unbuckling them is not required for attachment. You just hook each pannier onto the D-rings, and hit the trail.

However, there is another method, a bit more complicated, but easy to learn and having far more versatility than packing with panniers. This is the "manty" method (after the Spanish word *manta* for blanket or traveling rug). Manty refers to the canvas tarp used (usually about 7 by 8 feet in size), to the completed bundle, and to the method itself. The beauty of mantying is its adaptability to loads of various sizes. You can manty a bale of hay, a bundle of sleeping bags, or cardboard boxes full of food.

To manty a load requires nothing more than the tarp and a ⅜-inch manty rope, usually of manila, about 30 feet long, with an eye splice (loop) in one end. The tarp is laid out and cargo is arranged on it diagonally. (We want a finished bundle that is more vertical than horizontal in shape.) I like the center of gravity to be slightly below the middle of

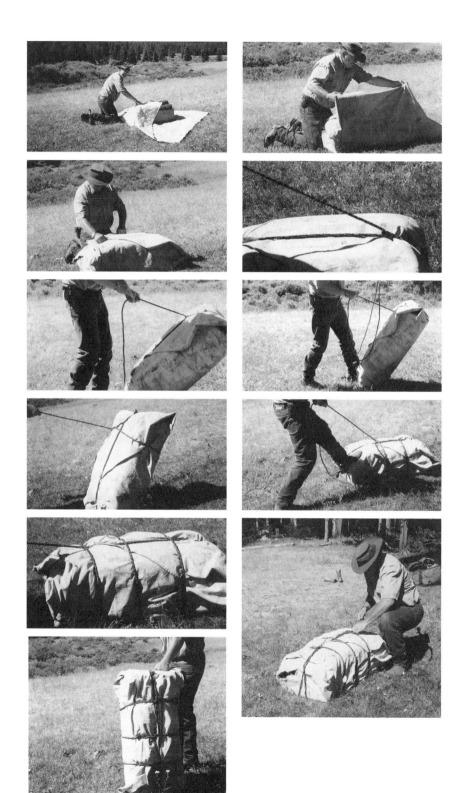

*The steps in mantying.*

the manty, so items are arranged with this in mind, and with attention as well to the vulnerability of the cargo.

I have long used a set of open-topped plywood boxes for mantying the bulk of our pack load when we head into the backcountry. Although these boxes add weight, they organize and protect the load. In camp, one becomes the food storage box, while the other, inverted with detachable wooden legs attached, becomes our camp table, thus eliminating the rather heavy portable one we used to pack along.

As you can see from the photo sequence, the load (in this case the optional pack box) has been laid on the manty tarp diagonally. First the bottom of the tarp is folded up, then each side, and finally the top comes down over the other folds to act as a rain flap. The manty rope has been arranged so that the eye-splice end comes lengthwise underneath the pack, over the top, the splice itself lying at the top front of the pack. The other end of the rope comes up and through the eye splice. Now, having a 2-to-1 mechanical advantage (the loop acts as a pulley), I pull up the top of the load and bounce it several times, holding the manty rope to cinch it tightly.

Then I flop the rope in a loop which, when inverted and passed over the top of the load, becomes a half hitch around the bundle, a simple

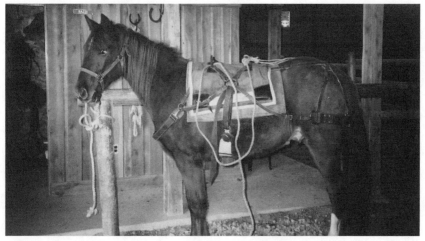

*A Decker packsaddle. Note single cinch and D-rings on top. The sling rope is rigged for the basket hitch. Loop will go over manty horizontally, while dangling end will be brought up under the load and secured to middle of loop.*

process but far easier to show than to tell. I usually use three of these half hitches, but two will do for short loads. For awkward loads, you might want to alternate the half hitches so that they oppose each other. Throughout the process I keep the manty rope extremely tight. After the last (bottom) half hitch I pass the rope around the bundle vertically again, and tie it off at the top half hitch. Several knots work for that purpose, but I usually use two half hitches, the second of them with a quick-release loop.

It's important to remember that the manty rope has nothing to do with holding the load onto the horse. The rope exists only to contain the manty itself. For attaching it to the horse we use a stronger rope (normally ⅝-inch manila) to form a very simple sling called the basket hitch.

The basket hitch, as shown in the photos, is readied so that you can, without assistance, lift the manty in place against the horse, pass the big loop of the hitch in front of your belly and around the manty, then pull with both arms underneath the load, cinching it tight. (We joke that a little "packer's shelf," just enough potbelly to hold the manty while working the rope with your hands, is an essential tool for the process.) Then it's just a matter of bringing the loose end up and tying it to the horizontal rope. Two half hitches work, but a quick-release knot is better.

It's hard for a buddy to help you, but I do ask Emily to hold up on the first manty with just a little pressure while I go around and do the one on the other side. No need to fully lift it. Just a bit of pressure is usually enough to keep the saddle from listing too much toward the loaded side. When both are in place, we lead the horse around for a bit (also a good idea when the animal is loaded with a sawbuck and panniers) to see that the loads ride well. I am of the school that believes in leaving the manties free-swinging, not tied to each other either below or above the horse's barrel. That way after they hit a tree or other obstacle they just swing back and return to position.

Still another advantage to manties is that they need not be exactly the same weight. If one is a tad heavier, you can hitch it just a little higher than the other one. When the manty rides higher it is also in closer to the center of gravity, and thus pulls down with less leverage. Beware of slinging manties so high that they are top-heavy on the horse, but also of slinging them so low that the weight on the ribcage makes it tougher for the horse to breathe.

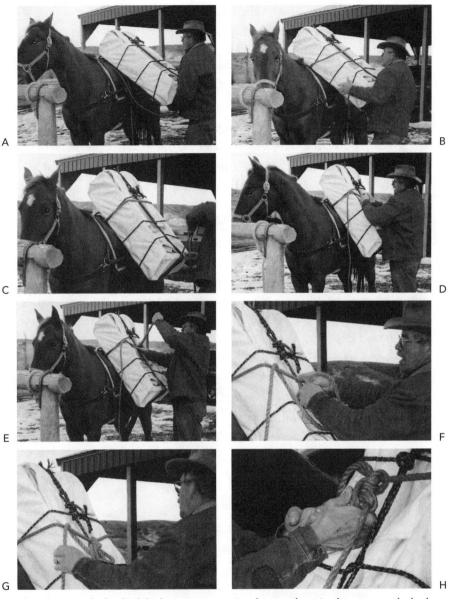

*a) Author starts basket hitch by laying manty against horse and passing loop up over the load; b) while balancing the manty on his "packer's shelf" he grasps trailing end of rope under pack and pulls hard, tightening the loop over the pack; c) rope from underneath comes up, forming bottom of hitch; d) is slipped under horizontal loop; e), f), and g) and secured first with quick-release half hitch, then, for security; h) the loop end tied in a second half hitch. Some packers prefer various quick-release hitches, but this knot has worked well for the author.*

Since the above is at best a thumbnail sketch, I'd recommend for further reading my own *Treading Lightly with Pack Animals* (out of print, but available used); Smoke Elser and Bob Brown's *Packin' In on Mules and Horses*, a staple of the art and particularly strong on the Decker/manty method; and Francis Davis's *Horse Packing in Pictures*, back in print and living up to its title, with extraordinarily clear illustrations. Although its text rather delightfully harkens back to an earlier day, Joe Back's *Horses, Hitches, and Rocky Trails* is a perennial favorite. Both its text and its sketches are true homespun art. Don't look for political correctness, but instead enjoy this book's humor, anecdotes, and beautiful illustrations.

To become a packer, follow up on your reading by attending packing clinics such as those offered by chapters of Back Country Horsemen of America. If you can afford it, go on a full-fledged trip with a professional packer. While on the trip offer to help whenever you can, and don't be shy about asking questions. Master the simple knots: quick-release, sling, and tie-up knots, the essential bowline, the clove hitch. (Davis's book is outstanding in this regard.) Learn to make eye splices and back splices in three-strand rope. All these things take a little time, so put aside that destructive American tendency to demand instant gratification. With just a little preparation you can be headed down the trail next summer with a neat, properly loaded packhorse at the end of your lead rope. And with that, whole new horizons will open to you.

# 17

## On the Trail with Pack Animals

It is true that a pack animal cramps your riding style just a little bit. Like a motorcyclist who adds a trailer, your outfit is just a bit more complicated now. Adding one or more pack animals requires some riding technique and even greater attention to safety, for there is now more to go wrong.

Emily and I try very hard to limit ourselves to one packhorse. That's a good rule of thumb: one pack animal for every two riders. Don't overload animals, but do pack them to capacity. The fewer you take along, the lower the impact. We do, however, commonly take a second packhorse when feed must be packed. Two bales of weed-free hay (required by law to prevent the spread of noxious weeds) or two bags of weed-free pellets or hay cubes pretty much load that additional horse. During fall elk hunts, survival needs also require more capacity. Tent stoves, for instance, become requirements when the temperature drops to zero or below on November nights at high altitude.

If you're traveling with another couple or are a family with children, chances are good you'll be leading more than one packhorse. The day has pretty much passed of letting packhorses follow behind loose with a member of your party riding trail and herding them along as necessary. That used to be commonplace, but today there is too much potential trouble with hikers and other packers. Loose horses are also hard on the trail, shortcutting switchbacks and detouring occasionally for a bite of good grass.

The rear of your packsaddle tree, whether Decker or sawbuck, should contain a loop of strong rope, often nylon, called a pigtail. This provides a place to tie the lead rope of the second packhorse in line. However, few packers tie lead ropes directly to the pigtail unless they're riding in extremely flat, safe conditions. The last thing you want is for one packhorse to slip off the trail and pull the others with him. Also, if an inexperienced horse cuts off the trail on the wrong side of a tree, we don't want him jerked mercilessly. It's better something should break him free.

I like a short piece of quarter-inch manila rope, tied into a loop with a square knot, between the pigtail and the rear horse's lead rope. This breakaway loop will give way before damage is done. I've used a doubled length of baling twine in a pinch, but we don't want the breakaway link to be too weak. If it is, we'll soon tire of reattaching the packhorse that hesitates slightly at every creek or bridge crossing. It's better that his more experienced leader be able to give him a bit of a nudge.

I have led long strings of packhorses by myself, but it is not a task to be taken lightly. Such a job leaves you with a crook in your neck, for you must constantly crane around to eyeball the packs. Even when

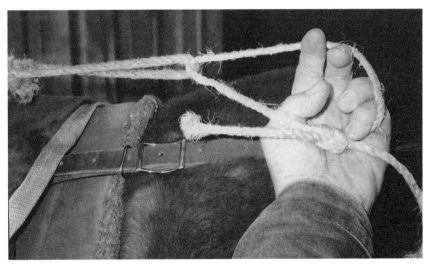

*The stronger rope, left, is the pigtail, while the one being held is the breakaway loop, in this case ¼ inch manila tied in a loop with a square knot.*

leading just one horse, frequent rearward glances are required, and that is why a good partner is such a help. Your buddy rides behind the pack-horses with them constantly in view, studying them and watching for the slightest irregularity. Most-watched must be the D-rings on top of Deckers and the crossbucks on top of the sawbuck saddles, for these must ride centered in the horse's back. How the packs themselves ride is not that critical, but at the first sign of D-rings or crossbucks edging to one side, you should stop and tie up. With panniers, shift a little weight or add a rock to the light side. With manties, raise the heavier one a tad.

"A stitch in time saves nine," says the proverb, and it aptly applies to slight pack adjustments that prevent big wrecks. We packers like to brag about taking several pack animals from trailhead to camp without having to adjust even a hair, but don't let such pride keep you from stopping and improving your chances. Better to fix a small problem on an easy stretch of level trail than to cope with a big wreck on the ledge trail far-

*Ready to go, two saddle horses and two packhorses, the right one loaded with a Decker and manties, the left with panniers and a top pack. Tying to the downed aspen tree is ecologically sound, but you wouldn't leave horses tied so low without supervision—tie high and short, with no more than 1½ to 2 feet of slack.*

ther up the drainage. Incidentally, more of these incidents occur when loaded lightly going downgrade than when loaded heavily going up. I've observed also that if you're going to have trouble with a pack, you usually have trouble within a mile or so. After that, problems are rare.

When you lead packhorses, think of yourself as being the head of a snake. You pick your way along, always with a sense of what must follow. You *must* slow down not only when crossing even minor obstacles, but after you cross them as well. Slow down, cross, then proceed at a snail's pace until the last packhorse has also crossed. Then resume speed, but don't acclerate quickly. Think of that last animal. We don't want to be jerking him around. Remember the "snake dance" back at your high school homecoming, how impossible it was to stay on your feet very long if you were at the tail end? Let's not do that to a packhorse.

Don't even think about tying the lead rope of your packhorse to your saddle horn, even if you use a quick-release knot. Many quick-release knots are not all that quick or easy to release if they've been jerked really hard, and when things go to pot in a pack string they go to pot *fast*. When crossing a stream or a treacherous area, just hold the lead

*Leaving camp in the morning, author's hand circles the coil of lead rope. Do not wrap the packhorse's lead rope around your hand, and never tie it to the horn.*

rope doubled in your hand, but never wrapped around it. On easy ground I'll sometimes rest my hand by passing the lead rope once over the horn and down toward the ground, holding it under my knee. At the slightest slip of the rope, I'm alerted to pick it up again.

The horse with which you lead these others must be experienced and steady, not ruffled by a lead rope up under his tail. Obviously, he does not belong doing this job unless he effortlessly neck reins. He should also understand pulling from the horn. Although we don't want to be dragging reluctant packhorses across streams or other obstacles, an indecisive animal can favorably change his mind when he feels a strong tug from the horse in front of him. To apply this force, the saddle horse can't be unnerved by the feel of rearward pressure on the saddle horn.

Probably the easiest way to characterize the horse we entrust with this job is to label him with the theme of this book, "the complete trail horse." He neck reins, stays at whatever pace we put him, tolerates ropes and straps in strange places on his body, and has a trail savvy that lets him pick the best place to walk when the trail offers options. Little Mack, one of my geldings, is a hard-charging handful when we work cattle. But on the trail with packhorses behind us, he throttles back to the perfect pace, needs little guidance, and seems constantly aware of his job and of the horses behind him. That's what we're after.

# PART VI

# A WILDERNESS CAMP

# 18

## Filling the Niche

"Moose," I heard behind me, in that loud-but-shushed whisper you use when trying to stay quiet while still projecting your voice. Then, louder, "Moose, Dan, can't you see it?" I couldn't. Strain as I might, Little Mack now frozen as I wished, the moose had eluded me in the heavy timber, the sound of its easy trot audible, its big body invisible. "A bull," Emily said, "with great big horns."

I have seen moose before, and did not greatly regret missing this one. It was enough to know that the animal was there, to hear its presence and to hear my wife and long-time trail partner exude this enthusiasm. Seeing such a creature of the wild is a thrill and a privilege.

For many years, now, Emily and I have insisted on one good pack trip each summer. On rare occasions we have missed one, and it seems that afterwards we have suffered the whole following winter. When we do not get to go, there is a vacant spot where the pack trip should have been, and we are nearly desperate to fill that niche the following summer.

We have been doing this a long time. Three boys, trained to the mountains first as backpackers, grew up mounted on a big old mare named Mona, who took care of each in turn up the rugged trails of the Beartooth Mountain Range. When the packs stay tight, when the horses settle down into a steady pace, there is much time to think on a pack trip. I suspect that like me, Emily is touched by nostalgia. Most of the drainages we ride contain camps we once occupied with noisy, chattering boys, boys who whittled and boasted and stoked the camp-fire and threw Frisbees.

But in spite of nostalgia, in spite of the intense summer work de-mands of a ranch and guest business, summer jobs that make Emily's "vacation" from the teaching year into an ironic joke, we still must go. Some years ago I wrote about a summer that we missed:

> And so, at the end of this very busy summer . . . I regret a certain void—our family was unable to take its usual pack trip in the Beartooth Mountains. Since Emily and I were able to go to Spain in June, we cannot cry too loudly. But I do fear some repercussions. Our summer pack trip is like compressed, solid fuel, stored to slowly burn later, warming us on those snowbound days of winter when the sun disappears at four in the af-ternoon. Melville's Ishmael, whenever it was "a damp, drizzly November" in his soul, when the blues were upon him, when thoughts of death preoc-cupied him, when surliness toward others surfaced, looked to the sea. I look to the mountains.

And so, Emily and I were on a pack trip we probably should not have taken, not if such things as responsibility are considered. Crippled by its fifth year of drought, our ranch had struggled through part of a tough summer dominated by attempts to get irrigating water to all sorts of places it did not want to run, the ground underneath sucking it like a sponge. But we were determined. We had drawn big X's on the calendar over several days early enough in July that we would likely dodge the campfire ban, an every-summer occurrence since the beginning of the drought. We had steered everyone we knew away from those days, close friends and relatives, travelers to our guest house, because these few days were ours. We had appropriated them, and that was that.

Where we went on the trip was less important than *whether* we went. We chose one of our favorite drainages with the vague intent to camp again in a big park (as large clearings in the timber are known in Montana) where we had last camped ten years earlier with all three of our boys. There would be adequate grass there for the horses, but we really wanted to continue the next day to the high plateau, the beauti-ful plateau of many lakes with crystal water and willing trout.

Up there the alpine meadows would still be green, but we could not expect much feed for the horses, so we decided to pack pellets with us.

This put us over our one-packhorse threshold. We would take a second packhorse, my big black colt Skywalker, only three but very seasoned and experienced for that age. Still, big as he was, he was not mature, so he would get the light load, packed on a sawbuck. Our old reliable Major, veteran of just about everything that can be thrown at a trail horse, would sit this trip out for the first time. Emily's young gelding Redstar would carry the Decker with mantied pack boxes. Emily would ride Doll, her snazzy, spirited, silk-gaited mare, and I would return to Little Mack. He is now eleven, though I still think of him as my "young" horse. I'm working on Skywalker and a two year old named Jed as eventual replacements. They'll have big shoes to fill.

After the usual bustle of preparations, the first day began with a late arrival at the trailhead but still with daylight enough to reach the park in question. There were beautiful smaller campsites along the way, pristine clearings near the river. But for years I backpacked. Like any good horse campers, we are dedicated to passing by any campsite that looks just perfect for backpackers, leaving those little ones to them and keeping the areas near them untouched by horse droppings and hoofprints.

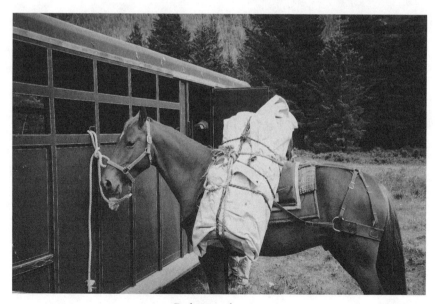

*Redstar, ready to go.*

Our good old campsite was there in the near end of the park, unoc-cupied. (We had launched our journey on a Monday, and that paid off. We saw not another individual until we reached the high plateau, and then only at great distance.) Things looked subtly different than they had ten years earlier—perhaps it is mainly one's memory of them that changes. A large slanting tree on which we had rigged a tarp to shield us from sudden rain on that earlier trip had fallen. There was now a permanent fire pit, a reflection of change in Forest Service policy. A decade ago we'd all been encouraged to dig shallow, low-impact fire pits, removing the sod for replacement later, the ashes eventually scattered, little trace remaining afterwards. But only so many of those can be dug at a much-used campsite. Also since it was discovered that replaced sod on top of ash-laden ground rarely lived, the Forest Service in our area now prefers one permanent fire pit at such sites, the overall impact being less.

But very tired from ranch work and preparations, more than from the ride, we passed on the fire that evening. It was quite dry, even at this higher elevation. We decided instead to enjoy a fire the next evening up

*The permanent camp in the big "park" featured a pole for saddle storage. The saddles were covered by a tarp at night.*

*A highline with cinch used as a tree-saver.*

on the high plateau. Besides, we were busy. There is much work to do when arriving at camp with horses.

We always keep the horses out of the living area of the camp, at most walking each packhorse over very briefly, dropping his pack, and taking him back to horse country. Right after dropping the loads I fish out my highline, a poly rope that I have spliced together in sections with eye splices. The loops of these splices are made large enough to accommodate the horse's lead rope so that a picket-line hitch, a non-sliding knot often used, is unnecessary. I look for two trees in a high rocky area for building the highline. Instead of carrying commercial tree savers, I steal two cinches from the pack saddles and circle the trees with them to protect the bark, then stretch the line tightly between. It's important, in using the cinches, to remove any bits of bark from them when you put them back on the saddles for the good of the horse.

Grazing was allowed, so we hobbled two horses and tied the other two to the highline. Every hour or so we switched them. At bedtime all were tied, though I picketed the youngest, Skywalker, by the front foot so that he could graze through the night. We firmly believe in the old proverb, "Better to count ribs than tracks." In other words, better that your horse drop a few pounds during the night than leave only tracks for you to follow in the morning. Besides, we would supplement with the pellets.

We always take along a tiny, strongly built cooler packed with frozen meat, cheese, and butter. As long as the cooler is kept in the shade or under a sleeping bag in camp, these items will last for several days, often still frosty in the middle at the end of trip. Our traditional first-night steaks were frozen solid, but they quickly thawed as they bubbled in the pan, sending their scent into the night air. We ate them with bread and macaroni and cheese, washed down with the beer that had been chilling in the creek.

It was the next day, after the good night's sleep and the big breakfast and the work to break camp and pack up, that Emily saw the moose. We had settled into a nice, easy, but ground-covering walk. Mack seemed to know that there would be a long, tough climb to the plateau. Although he had been his usual spirited self during saddling, there was something steady and conservative about him on the trail today. He was pacing himself and the others. We would climb to 9,500 feet, then descend to about 9,100, this from a valley floor three thousand feet lower.

It is amazing what a good trail horse knows. In drainages where he has camped before, Mack will turn into campsites he has not seen for years if you let him. In drainages where he has never been, late in the day when we are all tired, he will scope out possible campsites alongside the trail, and when he spots one, attempt to convince me by subtle nudges in that direction that we should turn in there.

As we climbed, we stopped relatively often to let the horses blow. Steep grades in the timber are always deceiving. Out in the open, they look steep. In deep timber you often do not know how sharply you have climbed until you return and look down. This particular trail continues to follow the drainage as long as it can, crisscrossing the creek, breaking out occasionally into pretty clearings spiced by flowers.

After the moose encounter and after a brief rest stop in one of those clearings, we broke out of the timber and looked above us. In alpine tundra, on a hillside kept green by springs, the trail wound up, zigzagging on tight switchbacks. We have been on scarier trails, but this one was sufficient to make me look very critically at the packs before the

*A mountain meadow just after the moose, but before the steepest climb.*

*Emily has become expert at detecting a slipping or off-balance pack.*

final ascent. Switchbacks on nearly vertical slopes are no place for a loose cinch or a slipping manty. All looked good, and up we went. At times like this, with good trail horses, you wonder who is leading whom. The horses did all this with serene confidence. Their example inspired us, not the other way around.

But that is not so unusual. Wordsworth said, "The child is the father of the man." Horses are not children, but they are, in their way, subordinates to the adults who claim to be their leaders, and leaders are often inspired by the quiet courage of those they lead.

When we broke over the top, the scene flooded back to me. This one had changed only because the snowbank we passed was much smaller than it had been ten years earlier at this same time of year. There was an indigo sky and a tiny, crystal lake, too shallow for fish, since winter would bring freezing straight to the bottom. It was a good place to pause so that the horses could breathe deeply of the high-altitude air. Then there was the descent to "our" lake and a campsite on the far side in a clearing up in the timber, well away from the water, not a secret campsite, but one still known by few.

It appeared that the campsite had been used lightly if at all this summer, a rare treat in today's populated world. We strung our highline on the rockiest ground. But once the horses were secured we did little, unpacking only to find our camp stools, a light luxury we bring. We sat in the shade and let our bodies catch up, drinking deeply from our water bottles to hydrate. Acute mountain sickness is primarily a matter of dehydration, and it's equally threatening in winter and summer. We drained our water bottles, went to the lake to filter more, and drained them again. Slowly our strength returned.

We set up our tent, a modern version of the old range tent, high at the peak so an adult can stand up to pull on pants in the morning. Though quite large, our tent is not heavy. Made with a synthetic called Relite, it weighs scarcely more than a backpacking tent but is luxurious by comparison. Each corner requires just one short pole, and the center pole is jointed for easy breakdown to packable length.

Gradually, our camp became our home. And truly, there is not too much more to tell. We did sample the hungry rainbow trout that surface-fed in swarms that evening, fresh in the pan, perfect protein. We

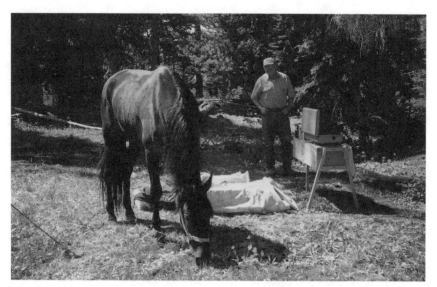

*Skywalker, hobbled, continually tried to join us in the living room.*

took just two, though there were enough to feed an army probably without denting the population. We relaxed, read, and enjoyed each other's company. We came to know sides of Skywalker's personality. I had considered him aloof, but not so—he was the hobbled one that would come to the campfire and would have, if we'd let him, come into the tent with us.

The stressful summer did not go away, because I awoke many times hoping that Steve, our youngest son, holding down the fort, was not having too many problems with the irrigating and the cows. But worries did not destroy the respite.

Here is Emily's version from her journal:

> We're late, as usual. The horses are loaded, and the cows have just broken the fence into the alfalfa. Dan hurries to get Steve, who has company, and neither is happy when they return, task completed, fence fixed.
>
> We're on the road headed toward the mountains and relief for a couple of days. Is my blood-pressure medication along? It's hot.
>
> At the trailhead finally. We saddle and load the horses and 2 hours later are at our first destination. It's still hot at the park where we camp. We unload the horses, make camp, eat something, and fall into bed too tired for a campfire.

After a sleep-in, Dan till almost 6:00 A.M. and myself till almost 8:00, we have breakfast and load up again. "Moose—moose on the trail!" Dan doesn't ever see the huge beast with wide, beautiful horns, just keeping ahead of us in the timber. The horses are mildly curious.

The trail is spectacular with switchbacks and incredible views. Little Mack is an old hand, and Redstar and Doll have been on these trips, but Skywalker is only 3, and this is his first one. He's doing great.

Three hours up we reach the plateau and go a bit more till we reach our favorite lake. It's as remembered. Last time we were here we had young sons Jon and Steve along—ten years ago. It's where our mare Rodeo—now one of our sweetest broodmares—earned her nickname. Memories fly through my mind. It's so beautiful here.

We're glad to unload and make camp again. Horses are two hobbled and two on the highline—will switch after a while.

We're tired. Dan says the solar shower is ready. Standing on one of the manty tarps with the shower hanging on a tree above us, we help each other direct the cool spray and then, slightly shivering, we grab our towels and run naked, laughing, into the tent.

Supper is good. On my way to the "fridge." I am suddenly *this* close to a woodpecker! He scoots around the tree and certainly can see more to eat there than I can.

"Fish are jumping! Hurry!" Dan rigs his pole and before I can follow him to the water, he is bringing in his second rainbow. He quickly cleans them and they are in the pan, even though we have already eaten, dessert by the fire. Nothing has ever tasted so good! We sit by the fire sipping bourbon and coke from blue, specked, tin cups. "What are you looking for?"

"Bugs."

"Don't. It will only depress you." I go on sipping.

"DEET! DEET, you little unmentionables! Here—have my hand— here's my nose—my chin—go ahead, if you dare!" The thick mosquitoes almost land and then take off again as if chased by a tiger. "It works!" Always their high, whining, shrill buzz is near my ears. But no bites!

The ground shakes as Redstar lands with hobbled front feet just inches from my head in the tent. Munch, chew, munch, chew. I scratch on the tent wall and he changes direction. Time to get up. Dan has been up for hours. We've decided to cut our trip short by one day and go out the entire 18 miles today. Worries of the cows and the ranch in general.

Before leaving we hike to the end of the lake—find a great camping spot with a spectacular view for next time.

Regretfully we pack up camp again. It's a long 18 miles down. I'm glad I'm riding smooth little Doll.

"It's shifting to the right!" Before the words are out of my mouth the packs on Redstar have slid and are hanging under his belly. We've never really had a wreck in all these years, and we don't now. Redstar stands patiently, perfectly still, as I'm holding him and Doll while Dan gets him out of his predicament. Dan had asked me very quietly and politely if I would please get down off my beautiful little horse and perhaps be of some use. Not! At times I worry that he'll have a heart attack. Packing in can be incredibly physical. It's OK now, and we have no more trouble for the gorgeous and still just as scenic ride out.

As we reach the trailhead, we are greeted by hordes of campers and little kids scampering in every direction with their loose dogs which cause some consternation on the horses' part. At that point I am not very polite as I yell at the dogs, and mean the kids, too. Who, me?

In spite of it all, we manage to unload the horses and put everything in the trailer and pickup, grateful that there was no vandalism.

I'm so glad I rode Doll—I can still actually walk after 18 miles! But Redstar has almost made me feel guilty with those looks he's been giving me the whole time as if to ask why I didn't choose to ride him. Sorry, but she's smoother, and she wouldn't do as well with the packs—not as much experience.

We are on the most-horrible-gravel-road-in-the-entire-world out. When we finally hit the pavement, it feels so good!

Try with the cell phone to reach Steve at the ranch and fail. Hopefully all hell has not broken loose while we were gone . . . . Great trip. . . . Next time. . . .

When we packed up to go, we did what we always do: we went over the ground with a fine-toothed comb. Our trash was crushed and readied for transport out, but we took, in addition, several rusty flattened cans, remnants of a less-conscientious era. With our shovel we scattered horse droppings, for so scattered they are fine fertilizer. We had taken care of our own waste in the best low-impact tradition, on high places well away from any water, with a shovel-depth of dirt removed and then the sod replaced.

I will not claim that it would have been impossible the next day to detect that we had been there, but I know as well that we did not damage the place. It looked terrific when we left; the most fastidious party arriving after us would have been happy to camp there.

The long ride out, eighteen miles of the downhill sort, harder on horses and people than uphill, cramped my legs enough that I'd pile off every hour or so and lead Mack down the trail a while. That is good policy anyway, easier on your horse and on your own body.

In the clearing where we had camped the first night there was now a big string of pack stock, mostly mules, some packed and some loose. One has to be cautious in those situations, but we soon saw that there was no worry. Dominant animals were picketed, and the rest stared at us but did not come to the trail. And when we passed the camp to which these equines belonged, a smiling familiar face sang out "Hey, there," the voice of a good friend and outfitter, entertaining his fly-fishing dudes.

Yes, it was hard work to sandwich this trip into a hectic summer. But it was tonic, too. It will last us through the winter.

# Epilogue

I am finishing this book in late September. Our Montana air has turned crisp, the days warm but with a slight bite around the edges, most mornings already frosty. We never did get decent moisture, but there has been a little rain higher up and a dusting of snow on the mountaintops.

There will be time for one or two more. There will be time for rides up dryland hillsides, drab and brown but weeks ago, now lit up with buck brush turned scarlet and willow leaves yellow. There will be time yet for a mountain ride or two, time before freeze-up to go through groves of quaking aspen brilliant against the deep green pine.

Skywalker is finishing out beautifully, so gentle at three that I have put several dudes on him with confidence. He will become, I suspect, one of "mine." Emily and I each have several. She has Sugar, Redstar, and Doll. I have Major, Little Mack, and the stallion Pride. But I can't stop there. In addition to Skywalker, there is the two-year-old sorrel Jed, named after Jedidiah Smith, a very brave and enlightened mountain man who quoted to his companions passages from Shakespeare and the Bible. Smith died young, sacrificing himself by yet again fighting a rear-guard action to allow his companions to escape. His memory is marked by competence and quiet confidence. If one could choose from history a human companion for the backcountry, faithful through thick and thin, it would be hard to go wrong with Jedediah Smith.

Jed and Skywalker and Little Mack and Major, complete trail horses and works in progress, are companions I have chosen (and, perhaps, who have chosen me). I gave Jed his name because I fully expect to spend with him much time in the mountains. Maybe I will see you there.

# Appendix: A Suggested Gear List for Pack Trips

This is an updated version of my evolving list, much of which was first published in *Treading Lightly with Pack Animals*. You are not likely to need everything mentioned, and in ultralight one-horse-per-person packing you will have to delete many items. Gear for the full-fledged pack trip is included from which you can select as needed.

## Shelter and Sleeping

1. One good sleeping bag per person.
2. One insulating sleeping pad or air mattress per person.
3. Tent rated for one more person than is actually along (i.e. a four-man tent for three people)
4. Ground cloth if your tent has no floor. Manty tarp can be used.
5. Light plastic tarps for covering saddles and rigging shelter over cook area. Manty tarps can serve double duty.
6. Nylon cord and shock (bungee) cord for camp organization. Manty ropes can be used.

## For Equines

1. Packsaddle or riding saddle and pad for each horse or mule.
2. One halter and one lead rope per animal.
3. For each pack animal, a set of panniers or manty tarps and manty ropes plus sling ropes.
4. One bridle for each saddle animal.
5. One restraint system per animal. Total number of hobbles and picket-rope/hobble half combinations should equal number of animals, even if you plan a highline. (You might camp where there are no trees.) Tree-savers for highline. Optional electric fence.
6. Hoof pick.
7. Curry comb.
8. Shoeing kit—fence pliers, horseshoe nails, other items suggested by far-rier.
9. One or more pre-fitted Easyboots (or similar products) for emergency shoe replacement.
10. Equine first-aid kit.
11. Leather repair kit—punch and lacing material.
12. Fly spray or equine roll-on.

13. Feed based on regulations and environment; certified weed-free hay, hay cubes, or pellets as needed. With feed, mesh nosebags for feeding.
14. Documentation: any required brand inspections, health certificates, and proof of ownership.

## Camp Equipment

This is an extremely subjective category. Adjust according to lightness, size of party and ages of party members, length of stay, remoteness of country traveled, climate, etc.

1. Ax (a real one; hatchets are dangerous knee-splitters because of the short arc of swing.) Consider any ax as dangerous as a firearm, and keep it off limits to the untrained.
2. Trail saw for clearing trail and for firewood. Oregon pruning saw recommended.
3. Shovel.
4. Folding bucket. (Shovel, ax, and bucket are often required by US Forest Service for travel within national forest boundaries.)
5. Firearms—personal choice adjusted for legality; do consider the possible need to humanely put down a fatally injured horse when no vet assistance is possible. As with the ax, training is a must for safety.
6. Folding table, or material to rig a cooking service. This can range from the backpacker's slab of nearly weightless balsa wood, to removable legs on a pack box, to a full-fledged table for large parties.
7. Cookstove—backpacker type for ultralight travel ranging to propane-powered cook top for large groups.
8. Lantern (candle, liquid fuel, or propane). Least needed during long days of summer.
9. Cookware—On solo trips I get along with a Sierra cup, a two-pound coffee can that doubles as stove container, and a small frying pan with folding handle. For large outings we use a medium saucepan, large frying pan with folding handle, coffee pot, and coffee can for heating water.
10. Silverware—Military surplus sets of fork, knife, and spoon, which clip together work well.
11. Dishes—Particularly where fires to dispose of them are allowed, paper plates, cups, and bowls cut down on dishwashing.
12. Paper towels.
13. Plastic trash bags.
14. Toilet paper—rolls can be flattened and kept dry in resealable plastic bags.

15. Matches in waterproof containers.
16. Propane cigarette lighters.
17. Fire-starting paste.
18. Fire blanket.
19. Can opener.
20. Extra generator for any Coleman appliance; small wrench to repair.
21. Fuel for lanterns and stoves.
22. Sewing kit.
23. Biodegradable liquid soap.
24. Small whetstone.

## Food

Suggestions to modify for dietary or cultural considerations. Write out meal plans and take them along. Pack at least an extra day's food.

1. Freeze-dried foods—Outstanding for ultralight trips, but quite expensive for longer trips with larger parties. Dehydrated foods such as Lipton dinners, soups, noodles, hot chocolate, and hot cereal are excellent, and much cheaper than freeze-dried.
2. Frozen meat—A tiny cooler packed with frozen foods in leak-proof bags will last surprisingly long when covered with a sleeping bag or other insulation in camp.
3. Canned goods—Heavy because they contain water, a few might be permissible on a trip with pack animals. Foods "canned" in plastic, such as puddings, are lighter.
4. Bread—Difficult to pack into camp intact, but still useable if smashed. Consider learning to bake pan breads in camp.
5. Eggs—These keep surprisingly well. Forget the plastic containers sold in sporting goods stores. You'll break fewer by using the foam cartons in which eggs are sold, cut down to size for the number of eggs you take. Pad the eggs top and bottom with paper towels and tape the carton securely.
6. Margarine in squeeze bottles works as butter and replaces cooking oil.
7. Cheese spreads in squeeze bottles.
8. Beverages—Presweetened powders such as Tang work well. With pack animals, a few cans of beer or soda may be possible. (Flatten cans and pack them out.)
9. Water purifiers—Filters are best, removing even *Giardia;* tablets (or iodine drops) work well but taint. Boiling is the next best alternative.
10. Condiments—Salt, pepper, catsup, mustard, etc.

## Personal Items

1. Rain gear.
2. Clothing a bit warmer than you think you'll need. Wool is still hard to beat in cooler situations. Stuffable down or synthetic vests are nice when the sun goes down in mountain country.
3. Adequate (but not excessive) changes of clothing, socks, and underwear.
4. Hat with enough brim to protect from sun and rain.
5. Footwear—Broken-in cowboy or packer boots for riding; sneakers for camp or short hikes; slippers (if possible) for tent.
6. Medication—Whatever you need. Bring several extra days' supply.
7. Any required fishing or hunting licenses; fishing gear.
8. Camera and film with extra batteries. For digital, extra memory capacity.
9. Insect repellent.
10. Flashlights and extra batteries.
11. Pocketknife.
12. Binoculars.
13. Sunglasses.
14. Toilet kit.
15. Leather gloves.
16. Daypack or fanny pack for day hikes away from livestock.

## Entertainment

We like small paperbacks, particularly short-story collections or poetry. A recorder or harmonica is great if someone can play it. Toys such as Frisbees or Nerf balls add little weight to a manty or pannier. Playing cards help if you're rain- or snowbound in the tent. If you consume alcohol, choose types that don't require a mix and transport in metal or plastic containers.

## Safety

1. Map of the area.
2. Orienteering compass (and the knowledge to use it).
3. GPS.
4. Cell phone.
5. First-aid kit (check for completeness).
6. First-aid book.

# Bibliography

Below are works I've directly cited in this book, along with a few others. The field of equine literature is a very fertile one, containing myriad useful works, particularly on training horses. My advice is to read widely and to look with a skeptical eye at training approaches that claim to be revolutionary, that deny the validity of methods other than the one touted, and that work too exclusively to sell you on specific equipment and techniques.

Aadland, Dan. *Horseback Adventures*. New York: Howell Book House, 1995.

Aadland, Dan. *Treading Lightly with Pack Animals: A Guide to Low-Impact Travel in the Backcountry*. Missoula, MT: Mountain Press Publishing, 1993.

Back, Joe. *Horses, Hitches, and Rocky Trails*. Boulder, CO: Johnson Publishing Company, 1985. [First published in 1959; classic text and sketches.]

Bennett, Deb. *Principles of Conformation Analysis, Vol I-III*. Gaithersburg, MD: Fleet Street Publishing Corporation, 1989. [Recently reprinted.]

Davis, Francis W. *Horse Packing in Pictures*. New York: Charles Scribner's Sons, 1975. [Recently reissued.]

Edwards, Hartley Elwyn. *The New Encyclopedia of the Horse*. London: Dorling Kindersley, 1994.

Elser, Smoke and Bill Brown. *Packin' In on Mules and Horses*. Missoula, MT: Mountain Press Publishing, 1980. [Has been through many printings; excellent on manty method.]

Lyons, John and Sinclair Browning. *Lyons on Horses*. New York: Doubleday, 1991. [Eclectic.]

Price, Steven D., ed. *The Quotable Horse Lover*. Guilford, CT: The Lyons Press, 1999.

Russell, George B. *Hoofprints in Time.* New York: A. S. Barnes and Company, 1966. [Excellent foundation histories of major horse breeds.]

West, Don. *Have Saddle Will Travel.* North Adams, MA: Storey Books, 2001. [Color photos and narratives of one-person, one-horse packing in the sunny Southwest.]

Xenophon and M. H. Morgan, trans. *The Art of Horsemanship.* London: J. A. Allen, 2001. [This edition was first published in 1894. Written 2,300 years ago, this is the grandfather of all horse training treatises and puts to rest any belief that gentle horse training methods began with *The Horse Whisperer.*]

## About the Author

Author Dan Aadland ranches, writes, and trains horses in south-central Montana, where he and his wife Emily have raised three sons and many of the ground-covering backcountry horses that are their family legacy. Aadland holds a PhD in American Studies and has been a Marine officer and teacher. His many equine articles have appeared in magazines such as *Western Horseman, Equus,* and *Horse and Rider. The Complete Trail Horse* is his fifth book.

# Index

**A**
Aadland, Emily, 181,
    267–286
    photograph, 209, 273
Absaroka/Beartooth
    Wilderness Area,
    9, 237
Absaroka ride
    photograph, 226
Absolutes, 111
Abuse excuse, 138
Addams, Andy, 57
Advanced trail training,
    169–178
Age, 19–20
Air mattress, 242
Allan, 65
Alpujarra mountains, 129
Altitude
    ultralight packing,
    240–241
Amble, 55
American Morgan Horse
    Association, 46
American Paint horse, 49
American Quarter Horse,
    47–49. *See also*
    Quarter Horses
American Quarter Horse
    Association, 47
American Saddlebred, 43,
    46, 53, 55, 56,
    63–64
    bloodlines, 45
American Saddlers
    shoes, 189
American South, 56, 59
American West, 56
Antibiotics, 211
Anti-inflammation, 211
Antisocial behavior
    nipping in bud, 106
Antisocial horses, 12
Appaloosa, 50–52
Appaloosa Horse Club, 52
Appendages, 42
Arabian horses, 49–50
    bones, 23
    chest, 50
    disposition, 50

endurance, 50
    photograph, 51
*Art of Horsemanship*, 99
Attention span, 109
Australian stock saddles,
    203
Autry, Gene, 58

**B**
Back, Joe, 258
Back Country Horsemen
    of America, 152,
    183, 184
Backcountry horses
    shoeing
    photograph, 190
Backpackers
    camping sites, 242
    photograph, 236
Backpacking stove, 242
Backyard foals
    training nightmares,
    105–106
Bad habits, 177
Bald Stockings, 65
Bandages, 211
Barb horses, 54
Basket hitch, 256
    photograph, 257
Beartooth/Absaroka
    Wilderness Area,
    9, 237
Beartooth Mountains, 62,
    267
Beartooth Pass, 6
9Belgian-cross
    gelding, 116
Belgian-cross gelding, 116
Belly in the reins, 85
Bennett, Deb, 23, 43, 44,
    219
Big horse, little feet
    syndrome, 15, 22
Big lick training, 67
Biodegradable soap, 245
Birth, 100–101
Bits, 116, 124, 197
Bitting, 197
Blaze, 104
Boarding

spook prevention, 161
Bob Marshall Wilderness, 9
Bog
    fear, 150
Bones
    Arabian horses, 23
    cannon, 48
    measuring
    photograph, 24
Boot camp, 118
Boots, 78
Bosals, 116
Box canyons, 112
Breakaway loop, 260
Breaking camp, 245
Breastcollar, 176, 206, 249
Breeching, 249
Breed registries, 42, 43, 44
Bridges, 142, 148
Brio, 70
British Isles, 54
British ponies, 55
Broken pace, 55
Brown, Bob, 258
Brownie, 63, 64, 96
Bruno, 209
Buggies
    comfort, 56
Bulldog type, 48
Butane lighters, 211

**C**
Camp
    breaking, 245
    equipment, 282–283
Campfires, 242
Camping sites
    backpackers, 242
Canadian Pacer, 55, 63, 65
Cannon, 23
Cannon bones, 48
Canvas tarp, 253
Cape Horn, 233
Carriage/harness horses, 43
Cattle driving
    photograph, 134
Cell phones, 213, 214
Center-fire rigs, 28
Champion, 58
Chaps, 210

Chargers, 162–163,
    162–168
    prevention, 167
Chest, 30
    Arabian horses, 50
Chickasaw, 47
Chief Joseph, 52
Cigarette butts, 245
Cinch, 81
Cinching
    safety, 89
Cinch ring
    tying reins from snaffle
    to, 166
Climate
    ultralight packing, 240
Clothing
    safety, 89
Cloth panniers, 158
Color breed, 49
Combination tool, 211
Comfortable traveling, 56
Communication
    possible sack, 213
Complete trail horses,
    11–39
Confederate forces, 56
Conformation for trail,
    21–33, 34
    photograph, 27
Connemara Pony, 54
Coolers, 211
Cooper, James Fenimore,
    63
Copperbottoms, 65
Corrals, 112
Cowboys
    Montana, 55
Creeks, 148
Criollo, 69
Crises
    passing, 162
Crossbuck packsaddle,
    126, 250
Cruise control, 167
Crupper, 206, 249
    photograph, 207
Cues
    chargers, 164
Curb bit, 195

Curb bit *(continued)*
    leverage, 196
Custer National Forest, 184
Custom-made saddle
    parts
        photograph, 202

**D**
Davis, Francis, 258
Day rider
    curb bit
        photograph, 194
Decker packsaddle, 250,
    252
    panniers, 253
    photograph, 251, 255
Decker tree, 253
Deerskin bag, 212
Desensitizing, 100–101,
    102, 156
Desert environment, 50
Desirable habits, 98
    extinguishing, 98
Direct pull, 130
Direct rein, 130
Discipline, 118
Disinfectants, 211
Disposition
    Arabian horses, 50
Ditches, 152
Dogs, 221, 222, 244
Doll, 269
Dorrance, Tom, 93
Draft horses, 23, 43
Dragging, 176
Dressing
    safety, 89
D-rings, 261

**E**
Early
    107–108, training
Early training, 107–108
Earnheart Brooks, 65
Easyboots, 189
Elser, Smoke, 258
Endurance, 31
    Arabian horses, 50
        photograph, 51
England, 56
English flat saddle
    photograph, 203
English riding trails,
    129–130
English Thoroughbreds, 47
Entertainment
    list, 284
Equine generalist, 8
Equines
    gear list, 281–282

Equipment, 187–215
    camp, 282–283
Excessive spookiness, 155
Expectations, 79
Experienced horse
    training companion
        photograph, 146

**F**
Fake-spook, 155
Falls
    dangerous, 220
    fear of, 148, 160
Fanny pack, 212
Fast-walking horses, 175
Faulkner, William, 65
Fearless Fran, 171
Feed
    ultralight packing, 241
Feet, 15, 21, 22, 48
Fiberglass panniers
    photograph, 251
Field-trail enthusiasts, 68
Field trail saddles, 203
Figure, 44
Fire
    possible sack, 212–213
Fire pits, 270
First aid kits, 210, 211
Flashlights, 211
Flat saddle
    English
        photograph, 203
Flee
    impulse, 159
Fleece-lined hat
    photograph, 209
Foals
    backyard
        training nightmares,
            105–106
    pampered, 37
    photograph
        cradling, 102
        soft cotton rump
            rope leading, 104
        stroking ears, 103
    weaning, 106
Food
    camp storage, 245
    list, 282–283
Footing
    muddy bottoms, 149
    unaccustomed
        photograph, 149
Footwear, 208
Fort Worth, Texas, 47
Foundation registries, 42
Four-beat gait, 18, 68
Fox hunting, 56

Fox trot gait, 68, 69
Fright, 154
Frogs
    trimming, 190
Front, 30
Front feet
    weapons, 74
Full-rigged saddle, 206
Future trail horses
    photograph, 38

**G**
Gaited breeds, 53–70
    popularity resurgence,
        58
Gaited horses, 56, 58, 63
    myths, 58–62
    nongaited horse
        compatibility, 59
    for old and infirm,
        61–62
    running, 60–61
    smooth speed
        photograph, 61
    surefootedness, 58–59
    trot, 174
Gaited Morgans, 46
Gaits
    four-beat, 18, 68
    fox trot, 68, 69
    natural, 54
Galloway, 54
Garbage, 241–242
Garcia, Andrew, 57
Gear list, 281–284
Gelding *vs.* mare, 16–17
Genetic background, 41
Goldfields, 57
Government line
    Morgans, 46
GPS units, 215
Grazing, 245, 271–272
Grazing bit
    photograph, 196
Grazing hobbles
    photograph, 199, 200
Groom tails
    photograph, 77
Ground driving
    guidance, 121
    photograph, 121
Group trail rides, 221
Growth
    stallions, 107

**H**
Habits
    bad, 177
    desirable, 98
    intermittent

reinforcement, 98
Hackamore tradition, 124
Half-breed, 253
Hals, 65
Halter driving, 122, 199
Halter training, 106–107,
    115
Hard panniers
    photograph, 239
Hard pathology, 251
Hay
    pitching over corral
        fence, 155
Headstalls, 197
Health
    possible sack, 212
Heart, 35
Height, 17–19
Helmets
    photograph, 207
    selection, 208
Herd instincts, 117
Highline, 271
    cinch
        photograph, 271
Hikers, 222
Hills
    going down steep, 218,
        219
    going up steep, 219
Hind feet
    weapons, 74
Hind legs
    hock angle, 30
Hindquarters, 33
    photograph, 33
HIOs (horse industry
    organization), 67
Hobbles, 198–201
    nylon
        photograph, 199, 243
    padded
        photograph, 244
Hobby, 54
Hocks
    photograph, 33
Hollywood, 58
Homesteads, 57
Hoof, 23
Hoof wall, 22
Horse breeds, 41–52
Horse-clinic junkies, 94
Horsemanship as art, 100
Horsemen. See also Riders
    messy, 182
*Horse Packing in Pictures,*
    258
Horses. See also Arabian
    horses
    antisocial, 12

approaching, 74
    safety, 88
backcountry
    photograph, 190
Barb, 54
carriage/harness, 43
draft, 23
experienced
    photograph, 146
fast-walking, 175
going over backward, 36
hyper, 12
pacey, 67
points
    photograph, 22
with poor walks, 12–13
racing, 43
rest
    photograph, 223
single-footing, 57
small, 63
spotted, 49
stall-bred, 100
sweaty backs
    saddle fit, 205
tied low
    photograph, 261
traveling, 44
unsound, 15–16
unsuitable, 11–12
using, 35, 96
weapons, 74
well-trained
    reliability, 98
Western
    tacking up, 79
Horses, Hitches, and Rocky
    Trails, 258
Horseshoe Lake, 6
Horse shows, 57
Horse training
    beginnings, 100–110
    life long, 97
    saddles, 111–128
    yielding right and left, 84
Horse Whisperer, 94
Horse whisperers, 94
Huffman, L.A., 57
Human waste, 242
Hyper horses, 12

**I**
Iceland, 58–59
Icelandic Ponies, 70
Ill-tempered, 37
Implosive therapy, 156
    dangers, 157
Imprinting, 100–101, 102
    photograph, 102
Improper spooking, 154

Impulsion, 113
    on command
    photograph, 115
Incremental training,
    108–109
Indian ponies, 55
    slaughter, 50
Indian shuffle, 52, 55
Iron shoes, 187–190
Irving, Clark, 218

**J**
Jed, 269
    photograph, 127
Jennet, 54, 55
John Gray, 65
Johnson, Elmer, 16, 31, 63,
    64, 95, 96, 198
    photograph, 60–61
Judged trail ride, 227

**K**
Kentucky region, 63
Kentucky Whip, 63, 96
King Ranch, 47
Knowledge
    self-acquired, 145

**L**
Ladd, Alan, 58
Laggards, 162–168
    prevention, 167
Land, 182
Land navigation
    possible sack, 212
Land regulations, 241
Last of the Mohicans, 63
Lateral movement,
    171–172
Latigo
    length, 77–78
Leading
    by each foot
    photograph, 120
Leading packhorses,
    262–263
Lead ropes, 116
    hand circling
    photograph, 262
    holding, 262–263
Leather soles, 208
Lee, Robert E., 65
Left rein
    shortening
    photograph, 127
Lefty, 116
Leg cues, 171
    and side-passing, 171
Light
    possible sack, 212

Lighters
    butane, 211
Light horse breeds, 41
Light rein, 85
Lightweight packing, 235
Little Mack, 34, 141, 219,
    263, 269, 272
Livestock
    streams and lakes, 243
Log of a Cowboy, 57
Logs
    leading over, 152
    stepping over
    photograph, 151
    straddling trail, 151
Lonesome Dove, 58
Long lead ropes, 115
Loops
    safety, 89
Loose rein, 85
Low-impact checklist,
    241–242
Lyons, John, 145

**M**
Main cinch
    photograph, 80
Major, 7, 135, 269
    packing culverts
    photograph, 184
Man from Snowy River, 218
Manila rope, 260
Manty method, 253–255
    advantages, 256–258
    steps
    photograph, 254
Manty rope, 256
Marauder, 150
Mares
    advantages, 16–17
    experienced
    photograph, 20
    vs. geldings, 16–17
    work
        crossed with Morgan
        horses, 46
Massive muscles, 26
McMeen's Traveler, 65
Merry Go Boy, 67
Messy horsemen, 182
Midnight Sun, 67
Miller, Robert, 100–101
Missions
    ultralight packing, 241
Missouri Fox Trotter, 56,
    68–69
Montana, 45
Montana cowboys, 55
Montana stock saddle
    1919

photograph, 203
Monty
    packing tools
    photograph, 184
Moose, 272
Morgan, Justin, 44
Morgans, 44–46
    crossed with
        Percherons, 45–46
    gaited, 46
    government line, 46
    origin of, 44–45
    photograph, 45
    single-footing, 55
Morgan Single-Footing
    Horse Association,
    46
Mountain hunting, 57
Mountain meadow
    photograph, 273
Mountain Slashers, 65
Mounted orienteering,
    228–229
Mounting, 81–83
    photograph, 82, 83, 84
    preparation for, 86
    safety, 89
Mouthpiece, 196
Moving
    refusal, 128
Mr. Ed, 58
Murphy, Audie, 21
Myths
    gaited horses, 58–62

**N**
Narragansett, 63
Narragansett origins, 65
National Association of
    Competitive
    Mounted
    Orienteering
    (NACMO),
    228–229
Natural gaits, 54
Natural restraints, 112
Navajo blanket, 205
Neck reining, 129–135
    advantages, 130
    improving, 170
    teaching, 130
Nez Percé tribe, 50
Nip, 116, 117
Nongaited animal
    walking, 174
Non-leverage
    defined, 195
North American Trail
    Ride Conference
    (NATRC), 227

Nylon hobbles
    photograph, 199, 243
Nylon rope, 198, 260

**O**
Obstacles, 142, 147, 152
    stand-and-relax method
        photograph, 147
Oil of mustard
    pasterns, 67
Old West, 57
One hand reins, 129
One-rein stop
    safety, 89
Open
    raised in, 100–101
Open registration, 43
Ordinary people
    training, 95
Oregon pruning saw, 213
    photograph, 214
Outdoors
    care, 245
Ozarks, 68

**P**
Pace, 54
Pacey horses, 67
Pack
    diamond hitch
        photograph, 252
Pack animals, 259–263
Packhorses, 7
    leading, 262–263
    panniers and top pack
        photograph, 261
Packing. *See also* Ultralight
        packing
    balance, 248
    lightweight, 235
    photograph, 125
    primer, 247–263
    safety, 158
    surfaces lying against
        horse, 239
*Packin' In on Mules and
        Horses,* 258
Packs
    building trail reliability,
        157
    weight, 237–240
Packsaddles. *See also*
        Sawbuck
        packsaddles
    Decker, 250, 252
    panniers, 253
    photograph, 251, 255
    types, 250
    Padded hobble
        photograph, 244

Pampered foal, 37
Panniers, 248
    cloth, 158
    fiberglass
        photograph, 251
    hard
        photograph, 239
Parking lots
    photograph, 151
Parkman, Francis, 57
Paso breeds, 55
Paso Fino, 69
Perception, 141
Percheron
    crossed with Morgan
        horses, 46
ersistence
    laggards, 164
Personal items
    list, 284
Peru, 58–59
Peruvian Paso, 69–70
Physical environment, 39
Pigtail, 260
    photograph, 260
Pinto Horse, 49
Pintos, 49
Plains Indians, 112
Plantation saddles,
        201–202
Plow-reining, 171
Ponies
    British, 55
    Spanish, 55, 65
    Welsh, 18
Ponying, 158
Possible sack, 212
Posting, 56
Practice, 175
Prepotency, 45
Pressure and release, 99,
        119
    photograph, 120
Prey animals, 74
Pride, 14, 27, 29, 62
    chest, 30
        photograph, 32
    development
        photograph, 108
    direct-rein riding
        photograph, 132
    side-pass
        photograph, 173
*Principles of Conformation
        Analysis,* 219
Professional trainers, 95
Proper spooking, 154
Pruning saws, 152
    Oregon, 213
        photograph, 214

Public service, 185
Puerto Rico, 69
Punishment, 118

**Q**
Quarter Horses, 18, 42, 43
    bloodlines, 45
    charging
        correcting, 166
    muscles, 25
    Thoroughbred type
        photograph, 48
    types, 47–48
Quick release, 119
Quick-twitch muscles, 25
Quirt
    laggards, 164

**R**
Racing horses, 43
Rain, 242
Ranch-built training bit
    photograph, 123
Ranchers, 48
Redstar, 269
    crossing water
        photograph, 148
    photograph, 269
Regular walk, 53–54
Reinforcement
    chargers, 164
Reining. *See Neck* reining
Reins
    belly in the, 85
    safety, 89
    slack, 167
    tying off to one side, 167
Relite, 274
Repair
    possible sack, 213
Rhode Island, 63
Ride-and-tie, 227–228
Ride leaders, 224
    photograph, 224
Riders
    being dragged, 78
    glued to horses
        safety, 88
    inadvertently tied to
        misbehaving
        horse, 78–79
    physical conditioning
        safety, 89
    young
        photograph, 20
Riders age
    ultralight packing, 240
Riders gear, 207–215
Riders physical condition
    ultralight packing, 240

Riding boots, 208
Riding downhill
    safety, 89
Riding horses, 43, 96
Riding trail, 224
Riding uphill
    safety, 89
Riffle, 220
Ring snaffle
    photograph, 196
Rivers
    mountains
        photograph, 221
    photograph, 218
Roads, 56
Roan Allen F-38, 65
Rocky Mountain Horse,
        70
Rocky Mountains
    trails
        photograph, 189
Rockytop
    photograph, 234
Rockytop Tennessee, 79,
        124
Rogers, Roy, 58
Romans, 54
Rope reins, 124
Ropes. *See also* Lead ropes
    manila, 260
    manty, 256
    nylon, 198, 260
    photograph, 78
    rump, 104
Rosie, 30, 31
    pulling back, 198–200
Round pens, 112, 118
    round pens, 115
Rump rope, 104
Running, 31
Running W, 159–160

**S**
Sacking out, 156
Saddle horses, 8, 16, 63
    Decker and manties
        photograph, 261
    maintaining speed, 162
    moving forward
        training to, 114
    packing in with alone,
        238–240
    stopping
        training to, 114
Saddle loops, 77
Saddle packs, 248
Saddle panniers
    photograph, 249
Saddles
    custom-made

photograph, 202
English flat
    photograph, 203
field trail, 203
fit, 204–205
full-rigged, 206
noisy objects hanging
    from, 157
plantation, 201–202
sawbuck, 158
stock
    Australian, 203
    photograph, 203
    Trooper, 202
Western
    rigging, 206
    saddle tree, 204
    without horn, 201
Saddle storage
pole
    photograph, 270
Saddle training
timing, 108
Saddle tree, 193, 204
Saddle type, 44
Saddling
implosive approach, 157
    photograph, 80
    safety, 89
Safety, 81, 215
    checklist, 88–89
    clothing, 89
    list, 284
    packing, 241
Sage flats, 134
Sawbuck packsaddles, 126,
    250
    double rigging
    photograph, 250
    panniers, 250, 252
    photograph, 125
Sawbuck saddles, 158
Sea of Cortez, 233
Shane, 58
Shanked bits
    leverage, 196
Shanks, 195
Shelter
    gear list, 281
Shetlands, 18
Shirts, 210
Shoes
    rear tips, 190
Short whips
    laggards, 164
Shoulders
    leading from, 75
    photograph, 75
    safety, 88
    safe zone, 75

Shrubs
    cutting, 242
Side-pass, 172
    photograph, 173
Siler, Becky
    photograph, 45
Silver
    photograph, 60–61
Single-footing horses, 57
Single-footing Morgan, 55
Size, 17–19
Skirts
    saddles, 204
Skywalker, 143–145, 269,
    271
hobbled
    photograph, 275
Sleeping
    gear list, 281
Slopes
    safety, 89
Slough Creek valley, 5
Slow-twitch muscles, 25
Small horses, 63
Snaffle, 122
    defined, 195
Snaffle bit
    early training, 195
    photograph, 132
Sneakers, 78
Snubbing post, 198
Soap
    biodegradable, 245
Soring, 67
South America, 55, 56
Spain, 54, 129, 201, 206,
    209
Spanish ponies, 55, 65
Split reins
    in one hand
    photograph, 133
Spookiness, 35
    excessive, 155
Spooking
    improper, 154
    proper, 154
Spooks
    overcoming, 159
    prevention, 161
    on trail, 153–162
Spotted horses, 49
Spotted Saddle Horse, 70
Spurs, 116, 209, 210
    laggards, 164
Stall-bred horses, 100
Stallions, 13–14
    castrating, 107
    photograph, 14
Stampede string, 208
Stepping pace, 55

Stirrups, 78
Stock horse, 49
Stock saddles
    Australian, 203
    Montana
    photograph, 203
Stone-covered trails
    frogs, 190
Stove
    backpacking, 242
Streams, 152
Sugar, 7
Summer camp trips,
    267–286
Sustenance
    possible sack, 213
Swimming
    horses, 220
Switchbacks, 244, 274

T
Tackaberry
    photograph, 80
Tapaderos, 78, 203, 206
    photograph, 209
    safety, 89
Tarp
    canvas, 253
Teeth
    weapons, 74
Tennessee Walker
    flat walk, 66
    hoofprints, 66
Tennessee Walking
    Horses, 7, 41–42,
    55, 56, 58, 64–68
    bloodlines, 45
Tennessee Walking Horses
    Breeder's and
    Exhibitor's
    Association, 42
Tent
    photograph, 239
Termino, 70
Testosterone
    growth, 107
Thoroughbred, 47
    racing, 56
Tie-type halter
    photograph, 197
Toe
    extra extension,
    189–190
Tölt, 18
Tommy, 63, 64
Tom Thumb, 195
    photograph, 196
Torso, 31
Tough Trip Through Paradise,
    57

Trail
    obstacles, 141–412
Trail bridge
    photograph, 140
Trail closures, 183
Trail competition, 225–229
Trail deficient, 138
Trailering, 86–90
    backing out, 88
    photograph, 87
    safety, 89
Trailers, 190
Trailhead, 57
Trail horses, 8
    disposition, 34–39
    future
    photograph, 38
Trail performance, 43
Trail-ride leaders, 162
Trail rides
    lengths between horses,
    222–223
    photograph, 223
Trail riding, 58
    defined, 8–9
Trails
    stone-covered
    frogs, 190
Trail techniques, 217–224
Trail training
    advanced, 169–178
Trail trials, 227
Trainers
    professional, 95
    secret approaches, 94
Training. See also Horse
    training
    vs. education, 97
    incremental, 108–109
    time, 95
    on trail, 137–168
Training areas, 93
Training clinics, 95
Training formulas, 113
Training videotapes, 95
Transitions, 85
    from trainer to new
    rider, 86
Trash, 277
Traveler, 65
Traveling
    comfortable, 56
Traveling horses, 44
Treading Lightly with Pack
    Animals, 234, 258
Trees
    cutting, 242
Tree trunks
    straddling trail, 151
Trigger, Jr., 58

Trooper saddles, 202
Trot, 174
*Tumbleweed,* 21
Turning around, 217–218
  on narrow trail
    safety, 89
Turns
  signaling, 131
Twain, Mark, 35, 193
Two-handed riding, 130
  reverting to, 132
  side-pass, 174

**U**
Ultralight packing,
    233–258
  altitude, 240–241
  climate, 240
  feed, 241
  maximizing, 240–241
Unaccustomed footing
  photograph, 149
Unloading
  large trailer, 86
Unsound horses, 15–16
Unsuitable horses, 11–12

US Army Remount
    Service
  saddle horse tests, 17
  weight carried, 18–19
US Forest Service
  packing timbers
    seminar
    photograph, 185
Using horses, 35, 96

**V**
Videotapes
  training, 95

**W**
Walking, 174
  behind horse, 76
    photograph, 76
  regular, 53–54
Walking Horses
  shoes, 189
Walking Horse show
    saddles, 201
Waste
  human, 242
Water, 142

Weekend recreation, 95
Weight, 18, 26
  packing
    calculating, 240
  training to carry
    photograph, 125
Well-trained old horses
  reliability, 98
Well-trained young horses
  reliability, 98
Welsh ponies, 18
Western build, 15
Western country, 8
*Western Horseman*
    magazine
  annual all-breed issue, 42
Western horses
  tacking up, 79
Western saddles
  rigging, 206
  saddle tree, 204
Whips, 116
  short
    laggards, 164
Whip trainers, 115
Whitney

photograph, 75
Wide-open country
  photograph, 8
Wimpy, 47
Winter, 191–192
  icy conditions
    photograph, 191
Withers, 28
Working
  on same side of horse
    safety, 88
Work mares
  crossed with Morgan
    horses, 46
World Grand
    Championship, 67

**X**
Xenophon, 29, 93, 99

**Y**
Yellowstone Park, 5, 6, 9
Yellowstone River,
    113–114
Young riders
  photograph, 20